Light and the Flowering Process

Academic Press Rapid Manuscript Reproduction

Proceedings of the 3rd International Symposium
of the British Photobiology Society held at
Glasshouse Crops Research Institute, Littlehampton, England
September 7–9, 1983

Light and the Flowering Process

Edited by

Daphne Vince-Prue
Bryan Thomas
K. E. Cockshull

Glasshouse Crops Research Institute,
Littlehampton, England

1984

ACADEMIC PRESS
(Harcourt Brace Jovanovich, Publishers)
London Orlando San Diego New York
Toronto Montreal Sydney Tokyo

ACADEMIC PRESS, INC. (LONDON) LTD.
24-28 Oval Road,
London NW1 7DX

United States Edition published by
ACADEMIC PRESS, INC.
Orlando, Florida 32887

British Library Cataloguing in Publication Data

Light and the flowering process.
    1. Plants, Flowering of   2. Plants,
Effect of light on
I. Vince-Prue, D.   II. Thomas, B.
III. Cockshull, K.E.
581.13'0431   QK830

ISBN 0-12-721960-9
LCCCN 84-45572

Library of Congress Cataloging in Publication Data

Main entry under title:

Light and the flowering process.

    Proceedings of the 3rd International Symposium of the
British Photobiology Society, held at the Glasshouse
Crops Research Institute, Littlehampton, England, Sept.
7-9, 1983.
    Includes index.
    1. Plants, Flowering of--Congresses. I. Vince-Prue,
Daphne.   II. Cockshull, K.E.   III. Thomas, B. (Bryan)
IV. British Photobiology Society. International
Symposium (3rd : 1983 : Glasshouse Crops Research Insti-
tute)
QK830.L54   1984   582.13'0416   84-45572
ISBN 0-12-721960-9 (alk. paper)

CONTRIBUTORS

G. BERNIER, *University of Liege, Departement de Botanique, Bat B22, Sart Tilman, B-4000 Liege, Belgium.*

M. BODSON, *University of Liege, Departement de Botanique, Bat B22, Sart Tilman, B-4000 Liege, Belgium.*

C. F. CLELAND, *Smithsonian Environmental Research Center, 12441 Parklawn Drive, Rockville, Maryland, 20852, U.S.A.*

K. E. COCKSHULL, *Glasshouse Crops Research Institute, Worthing Road, Littlehampton, West Sussex, BN16 3PU, U.K.*

G. F. DEITZER, *Smithsonian Environmental Research Center, 12441 Parklawn Drive, Rockville, Maryland, 20852, U.S.A.*

D. FRANCIS, *University College, Dept. of Plant Science, P.O. Box 78, Cardiff, CF1 1XL, U.K.*

D. J. C. FRIEND, *University of Hawaii, Dept. of Botany, 3190 Maile Way, Honolulu, Hawaii, 96822, U.S.A.*

A. H. HALEVY, *The Hebrew University of Jerusalem, Dept. of Ornamental Horticulture, PO Box 12, Rehovot, 76-100, Israel.*

S. KAIHARA, *Kyoto University, Laboratory of Applied Botany, Kyoto 606, Japan.*

J-M. KINET, *University of Liege, Departement de Botanique, Bat B22, Sart Tilman, B-4000 Liege, Belgium.*

R. W. KING, *C.S.I.R.O., Division of Plant Industry, PO Box 1600, Canberra City, ACT 2601, Australia.*

C. N. LAW, *Plant Breeding Institute, Maris Lane, Trumpington, Cambridge, CB2 2LQ, U.K.*

P. J. LUMSDEN, *Glasshouse Crops Research Institute, Worthing Road, Littlehampton, West Sussex, BN16 3PU, U.K.*

R. F. LYNDON, *University of Edinburgh, Dept. of Botany, Mayfield Road, Edinburgh, EH9 3JH, Scotland.*

D. G. MORGAN, *University of Cambridge, Dept. of Applied Biology, Pembroke Street, Cambridge, CB2 3DX, U.K.*

C. B. MORGAN, *University of Cambridge, Dept. of Applied Biology, Pembroke Street, Cambridge, CB2 3DX, U.K.*

E. MOSINGER, *University of Freiburg, Institut fur Biologie II, Schänzlestrasse 1, D-7800 Freiburg, W. Germany.*

K. NAPP-ZINN, *University of Cologne, Botanisches Institut, Gyrhofstrasse 15, D-5000 Köln 41, W. Germany.*

V. OTTO, *University of Freiburg, Institut fur Biologie II, Schänzlestrasse 1, D-7800 Freiburg, W. Germany.*

R. M. SACHS, *University of California, Dept. of Environmental Horticulture, Davis, California, 95616, U.S.A.*

R. SCARTH, *Plant Breeding Institute, Trumpington, Cambridge, CB2 2LQ, U.K.*

E. SCHAFER, *University of Freiburg, Institute fur Biologie II, Schänzlestrasse 1, D-7800 Freiburg, W. Germany.*

W. W. SCHWABE, *University of London, Dept. of Horticulture, Wye College, Wye, Nr. Ashford, Kent, TN25 5AH, U.K.*

A. TAKIMOTO, *Kyoto University, Laboratory of Applied Botany, Kyoto 606, Japan.*

B. THOMAS, *Glasshouse Crops Research Institute, Worthing Road, Littlehampton, West Sussex, BN16 3PU, U.K.*

D. VINCE-PRUE, *Glasshouse Crops Research Institute, Worthing Road, Littlehampton, West Sussex, BN16 3PU, U.K.*

J. A. D. ZEEVAART, *Michigan State University, MSU-DOE Plant Research Laboratory, East Lansing, Michigan, 48824, U.S.A.*

PARTICIPANTS

A. M. H. ABDELAZIZ, C/o M.C.R., Wye College, Wye, Nr. Ashford, Kent, TN25 5AH, U.K.

S. ABOU-HAIDAR, Laboratoire du Phytotron, C.N.R.S., 91190 Gif-sur-Yvette, France.

R. DEGLI AGOSTI, Laboratoire de Physiologie Vegetale, 3 Place de l'Universite, 1211 Geneve 4, Switzerland.

H. EL ALAOUI, University of Liege, Departement de Botanique, Bat B22, Sart Tilman, B-4000 Liege, Belgium.

J. G. ATHERTON, University of Nottingham School of Agriculture, Sutton Bonington, Loughborough, LE12 5RD, U.K.

C. BAGNARD, University of Dijon, Laboratoire de Physiologie Vegetale, BP 138, 21004 Dijon Cedex, France.

A. J. BAKER, Glasshouse Crops Research Institute, Worthing Road, Littlehampton, West Sussex, BN16 3PU, U.K.

E. A. BASHER, University of Nottingham School of Agriculture, Sutton Bonington, Loughborough, LE12 5RD, U.K.

N. H. BATTEY, University of Edinburgh, Dept. of Botany, The King's Buildings, Mayfield Road, Edinburgh, EH9 3JH, U.K.

G. BERNIER, University of Liege, Departement de Botanique, Bat B22, Sart Tilman, B-4000 Liege, Belgium.

C. BESNARD-WIBAUT, Universite Pierre et Marie Curie, Laboratoire de Cytologie et Morphogenese Vegetales, 4 place Jussieu, 75230 Paris Cedex 05, France.

M. BODSON, University of Liege, Departement de Botanique, Bat B22, Sart Tilman, B-4000 Liege, Belgium.

M. BONZON, *University of Geneva, Plant Physiology Dept., 3 Place de l'Universite, 1211 Geneve 4, Switzerland.*

A. BRACKPOOL, *Wye College, Dept. of Horticulture, Wye, Nr. Ashford, Kent, TN25 5AH, U.K.*

J. L. BREWSTER, *National Vegetable Research Station, Wellesbourne, Warwickshire, CV35 9EF, U.K.*

A. C. BUNT, *Glasshouse Crops Research Institute, Worthing Road, Littlehampton, West Sussex, BN16 3PU, U.K.*

R. E. Butters, *ADAS, Glasshouse Crops Research Institute, Worthing Road, Littlehampton, West Sussex, BN16 3PU, U.K.*

W. S. CHOW, *Glasshouse Crops Research Institute, Worthing Road, Littlehampton, West Sussex, BN16 3PU, U.K.*

C. F. CLELAND, *Smithsonian Environmental Research Center, 12441 Parklawn Drive, Rockville, Maryland, 20852, U.S.A.*

K. E. COCKSHULL, *Glasshouse Crops Research Institute, Worthing Road, Littlehampton, West Sussex, BN16 3PU, U.K.*

R. P. COX, *Glasshouse Crops Research Institute, Worthing Road, Littlehampton, West Sussex, BN16 3PU, U.K.*

B. CUMMING, *University of New Brunswick, Dept. of Biology, PO Box 4400, Fredericton, New Brunswick, E3B 5A3, Canada.*

L. G. DAVIES, *Trent Polytechnic, Dept. of Life Sciences, Burton Street, Nottingham, NG1 4BU, U.K.*

G. F. DEITZER, *Smithsonian Environmental Research Center, 12441 Parklawn Drive, Rockville, Maryland, 20852, U.S.A.*

D. ELPHINSTONE, *Glasshouse Crops Research Institute, Worthing Road, Littlehampton, West Sussex, BN16 3PU, U.K.*

D. FRANCIS, *University College, Dept. of Plant Science, P.O. Box 78, Cardiff, CF1 1XL, U.K.*

D. J. C. FRIEND, *University of Hawaii, Dept. of Botany, 3190 Maile Way, Honolulu, Hawaii, 96822, U.S.A.*

M. FURUYA, *University of Tokyo, Dept. of Botany, Faculty of Science, Hongo, Tokyo, 113, Japan.*

U. GERTSSON, *The Swedish University of Agricultural Sciences,Dept. of Horticulture, Box 55, S-230 53 Alnarp, Sweden.*

R. GONTHIER, *University of Liege, Departement de Botanique, Bat B22, Sart Tilman, B-4000 Liege, Belgium.*

N. R. GORE, *May and Baker Ltd., Ongar Research Station, Fyfield Road, Ongar, Essex, U.K.*

R. GOREN, *The Hebrew University of Jerusalem, Faculty of Agriculture, PO Box 12, Rehovot, 76-100, Israel.*

R. I. GRANGE, *Glasshouse Crops Research Institute, Worthing Road, Littlehampton, West Sussex, BN16 3PU, U.K.*

C. J. GRAVES, *Glasshouse Crops Research Institute, Worthing Road, Littlehampton, West Sussex, BN16 3PU, U.K.*

J. H. GRIFFITHS, *Glasshouse Crops Research Institute, Worthing Road, Littlehampton, West Sussex, BN16 3PU, U.K.*

P. E. GRIMBLY, *Glasshouse Crops Research Institute, Worthing Road, Littlehampton, West Sussex, BN16 3PU, U.K.*

A. H. HALEVY, *The Hebrew University of Jerusalem, Faculty of Agriculture, PO Box 12, Rehovot, 76-100, Israel.*

D. W. HAND, *Glasshouse Crops Research Institute, Worthing Road, Littlehampton, West Sussex, BN16 3PU, U.K.*

G. HANKS, *Glasshouse Crops Research Institute, Worthing Road, Littlehampton, West Sussex, BN16 3PU, U.K.*

P. L. HEDGE, *41 Windmill Avenue, Hassocks, West Sussex, BN6 8LJ, U.K.*

L. C. HO, *Glasshouse Crops Research Institute, Worthing Road, Littlehampton, West Sussex, BN16 3PU, U.K.*

G. E. HOBSON, *Glasshouse Crops Research Institute, Worthing Road, Littlehampton, West Sussex, BN16 3PU, U.K.*

J. S. HORRIDGE, *Glasshouse Crops Research Institute, Worthing Road, Littlehampton, West Sussex, BN16 3PU, U.K.*

R. G. HURD, *Glasshouse Crops Research Institute, Worthing Road, Littlehampton, West Sussex, BN16 3PU, U.K.*

T. J. INGRAM, *University of Bristol, Dept. of Organic Chemistry, Cantock's Close, Bristol, BS8 1TS, U.K.*

R. JINKS, *Glasshouse Crops Research Institute, Worthing Road, Littlehampton, West Sussex, BN16 3PU, U.K.*

H. G. JONES, *East Malling Research Station, East Malling, Maidstone, Kent, ME19 6BJ, U.K.*

B. R. JORDAN, *Glasshouse Crops Research Institute, Worthing Road, Littlehampton, West Sussex, BN16 3PU, U.K.*

A. KADMAN-ZAHAVI, *ARO, The Volcani Center, Bet-Dagan 50-250, Israel.*

S. KAIHARA, *Kyoto University, Laboratory of Applied Botany, Sakyo-Ku, Kyoto 606, Japan.*

A. KANAKIS, *8 Duke Street, Bath, Avon, BA2 4AG, U.K.*

R. KANDELER, *Botanisches Institut, Universitat fur Bodenkultur, Gregor Mendelstrasse 33, A-1180 Vienna, Austria.*

J.-M. KINET, *University of Liege, Departement de Botanique, Bat B22, Sart Tilman, B-4000 Liege, Belgium.*

R. W. KING, *C.S.I.R.O., Division of Plant Industry, PO Box 1600, Canberra City, ACT 2601, Australia.*

A. M. KOFRANEK, *University of California, Dept. of Environmental Horticulture, Davis, California, 95616, U.S.A.*

F. A. LANGTON, *Glasshouse Crops Research Institute, Worthing Road, Littlehampton, West Sussex, BN16 3PU, U.K.*

R. LARSEN, *The Swedish University of Agricultural Sciences, Dept. of Horticultural Science, S-222 53, Alnarp, Sweden.*

C. N. LAW, *Plant Breeding Institute, Trumpington, Cambridge, CB2 2LQ, U.K.*

H. S. J. LEE, *University of Newcastle-Upon-Tyne, Dept. of Plant Biology, Ridley Building, The University, Newcastle, NE1 7RU, U.K.*

D. V. LOUIS, *Trent Polytechnic, Dept. of Life Sciences, Nottingham, NG1 4BU, U.K.*

P. J. LUMSDEN, *Glasshouse Crops Research Institute, Worthing Road, Littlehampton, West Sussex, BN16 3PU, U.K.*

R. F. LYNDON, *University of Edinburgh, Dept. of Botany, Mayfield Road, Edinburgh, EH9 3JH, U.K.*

D. M. MASSEY, *Glasshouse Crops Research Institute, Worthing Road, Littlehampton, West Sussex, BN16 3PU, U.K.*

R. MENHENETT, *Glasshouse Crops Research Institute, Worthing Road, Littlehampton, West Sussex, BN16 3PU, U.K.*

D. G. MORGAN, *Dept. of Applied Biology, University of Cambridge, Pembroke Street, Cambridge, CB2 3DX, U.K.*

K. NAPP-ZINN, *Botanisches Institut, Universitat Köln, Gyrhofstrasse 15, D-5000 Cologne 41, Köln, W. Germany.*

R. NICHOLS, *Glasshouse Crops Research Institute, Worthing Road, Littlehampton, West Sussex, BN16 3PU, U.K.*

M. NOIN, *Universite Pierre et Marie Curie, Laboratoire de Cytologie et Morphogenese Vegetales, 4 place Jussieu, 75230 Paris Cedex 05, France.*

J. ORMROD, *University College, Dept. of Plant Science, PO Box 78, Cardiff, CF1 1XL, U.K.*

M. D. PARTIS, *Glasshouse Crops Research Institute, Worthing Road, Littlehampton, West Sussex, BN16 3PU, U.K.*

C. PENEL, *University of Geneva, Laboratoire de Physiologie Vegetale, 3 Place de l'Universite. 1211 Geneve 4, Switzerland.*

S. E. PENN, *Glasshouse Crops Research Institute, Worthing Road, Littlehampton, West Sussex, BN16 3PU, U.K.*

A. J. PICKEN, *Glasshouse Crops Research Institute, Worthing Road, Littlehampton, West Sussex, BN16 3PU, U.K.*

M. C. POWELL, *Glasshouse Crops Research Institute, Worthing Road, Littlehampton, West Sussex, BN16 3PU, U.K.*

D. PRICE, *Glasshouse Crops Research Institute, Worthing Road, Littlehampton, West Sussex, BN16 3PU, U.K.*

J. G. PURSE, *Shell Research Ltd., Sittingbourne Research Centre, Sittingbourne, Kent, ME9 8AG, U.K.*

A. R. REES, *Glasshouse Crops Research Institute, Worthing Road, Littlehampton, West Sussex, BN16 3PU, U.K.*

E. H. ROBERTS, *University of Reading, Plant Environment Laboratory, Shinfield Grange, Cutbush Lane, Shinfield, Reading, Berkshire, RG2 9AD, U.K.*

J. ROMBACH, *Laboratory of Plant Physiological Research, Generaal Foulkesweg 72, 6703 Wageningen, The Netherlands.*

R. M. SACHS, *University of California, Dept. of Environmental Horticulture, Davis, California, 95616, U.S.A.*

H. SAJI, *National Institute for Basic Biology, Okazaki 444, Japan.*

S. SAWHNEY, *Guru Nanak Dev University, Dept. of Biology, Amritsar 143005, India.*

E. SCHAFER, *University of Freiburg, Biologisches Institute II, Schanzlestrasse 1, 7800 Freiburg, W. Germany.*

W. W. SCHWABE, *Wye College, Dept. of Horticulture, Wye, Nr. Ashford, Kent, TN25 5AH, U.K.*

A. F. SHAW, *Glasshouse Crops Research Institute, Worthing Road, Littlehampton, West Sussex, BN16 3PU, U.K.*

J. W. MAXON SMITH, *Glasshouse Crops Research Institute, Worthing Road, Littlehampton, West Sussex, BN16 3PU, U.K.*

A. GRAHAM SPARKES, *Perifleur Limited, Hangleton Lane, Ferring, Worthing, West Sussex, BN12 6PP, U.K.*

R. J. SUMMERFIELD, *University of Reading, Plant Environment Laboratory, Shinfield Grange, Cutbush Lane, Shinfield, Reading, Berkshire, RG2 9AD, U.K.*

A. TAKIMOTO, *Kyoto University, Laboratory of Applied Botany, Kyoto 606, Japan.*

B. THOMAS, *Glasshouse Crops Research Institute, Worthing Road, Littlehampton, West Sussex, BN16 3PU, U.K.*

D. VINCE-PRUE, *Glasshouse Crops Research Institute, Worthing Road, Littlehampton, West Sussex, BN16 3PU, U.K.*

W. WAGNER, *University of Freiburg, Biologisches Institute II, Schanzlestrasse 9/11, 7800 Freiburg, W. Germany.*

J. A. C. WEIR, *The Electricity Council, National Agricultural Centre, Stoneleigh, Kenilworth, Warwickshire, CV8 2LS, U.K.*

T. WELANDER, *The Swedish University of Agricultural Sciences, Dept. of Horticulture, Box 55, S-230 53 Alnarp, Sweden.*

J. A. D. ZEEVAART, *Michigan State University, MSU-DOE Plant Research Laboratory, East Lansing, Michigan, 48824, U.S.A.*

LIST OF SUPPORTING BODIES

The British Photobiology Society wishes to acknowledge the generous support given towards the expenses of the Symposium by:-

The Royal Society

Glasshouse Crops Research Institute

The Underwood Fund

Academic Press Inc.

A. R. Bales Ltd.

Bentham Instruments

C.U.E.L.

Delta-T Devices

Glen Creston Instruments Ltd.

Macam Photometrics

Martinus Nijhoff/Dr. W. Junk

Springer-Verlag Ltd.

PREFACE

This volume represents the Proceedings of the Third International Symposium of the British Photobiology Society held at
the Glasshouse Crops Research Institute, Littlehampton, from
7-9 September 1983. The purpose of the meeting was to bring
together workers studying all aspects of the way light influences the induction, initiation and development of flowers.
The control of flowering is still poorly understood despite
its importance both as a physiological problem and as a major
regulator of flower, fruit, and seed yield in agriculture and
horticulture. Among environmental influences, light is one of
the most important factors determining the time and magnitude
of flowering as well as the rate and direction of flower
development. The light climate itself is very complex, fluc-
tuating as it does diurnally and/or seasonally in intensity,
quality and duration. The spectral quality aspect of daylight
was the topic of the Society's first Symposium, Plants and the
Daylight Spectrum, and so this has not been emphasised here,
except for spectral studies to identify photoperceptive pigments. This Symposium focusses firstly on the informational
role of light in photoperiodically sensitive plants, including
the perception of daylength by long-day and short-day plants
and the subsequent steps leading to flower formation.
Secondly, the nutritional role of light acting through photosynthesis, either directly or through assimilate partitioning,
is discussed in relation to the regulation of flowering in
both photoperiodic and non-photoperiodic plants. Tradition-
ally, the photoperiodic and photosynthetic effects of light
have been considered separately and it was the objective of
this Symposium, in bringing these two aspects together, to
engender a greater appreciation of the interactive nature of
the two processes. For the organizers certainly and, we hope,
also for the participants, the venture was worthwhile and the
breadth of the approach has resulted in new insights into a
fascinating but complex problem.
Unfortunately, despite their intrinsic importance,
flowering studies are not one of today's major growth areas in
plant science, perhaps because answers to fundamental questions are hard to come by and because the experiments are

often long term and require rather specialized growing
facilities. If this volume succeeds in directing more
attention to this relatively neglected area of plant physiology, the organizers will be well satisfied.

The Symposium and the resulting publication would not have
been possible without the help and support of many people and
organizations. First we must thank the Divisional Secretary
in the Physiology and Chemistry Division of the Glasshouse
Crops Research Institute, Miss Anne Malcolm-Bentzon, who
single-handedly produced the necessary organizational paper-
work for the meeting and, with the exception of the artwork,
all of the camera ready copy for this Volume. We are also
grateful to the members of the Liaison and the Photography and
Visual Aids sections of GCRI without whose help in organising
receptions, lunches, poster displays, projection, and artwork,
neither conference nor book would have materialised. Finally,
of course, we thank the contributors who came from all parts
of the world to present and discuss their ideas and the participants who took part in the lively discussion sessions. We
would also like to acknowledge the generous contributions from
public bodies and private companies which partially defrayed
the travel and accommodation costs of the speakers, and the
generosity of the Director and Governing Body of the GCRI for
making available the conference facilities of the Institute.

DAPHNE VINCE-PRUE
KENNETH COCKSHULL
BRIAN THOMAS

Littlehampton, February 1984

CONTENTS

ABBREVIATIONS

ABA	abscisic acid
ADP	adenosine diphosphate
AMP	adenosine monophosphate
ATP	adenosine triphosphate
B	blue light
BA	6-benzyladenine
BAP	blue-absorbing photoreceptor
CAM	Crassulacean acid metabolism
CL	continuous light
DNA	deoxyribonucleic acid
DPM	disintegrations per minute
EDTA	ethylenediaminetetracetic acid
ER	endoplasmic reticulum
FR	far-red light
GA	gibberellin
GLC	gas-liquid chromatography
HIR	high-irradiance reaction
HPLC	high-performance liquid chromatography
IAA	3-indolylacetic acid
LD	long day
LDP	long-day plant
LSD	least significant difference
LSDP	long-short-day plant
NAA	1-naphthaleneacetic acid
NB	night break
ORD	optical rotatory dispersion
PEP	phosphoenolpyruvate
Pfr	far-red absorbing form of phytochrome
Pr	red-absorbing form of phytochrome
PS I	photosystem I
PS II	photosystem II
Ptot	total phytochrome
R	red light
RNA	ribonucleic acid
mRNA	messenger RNA
rRNA	ribosomal RNA
sRNA	soluble RNA
SD	short day

ABBREVIATIONS

S.D.	standard deviation
SDP	short-day plant
SLDP	short-long-day plant
TIBA	tri-iodobenzoic acid
TLC	thin-layer chromatography
USDA	United States Department of Agriculture
UV	ultra-violet light

LIGHT AND THE FLOWERING PROCESS

Chapter 1

LIGHT AND THE FLOWERING PROCESS — SETTING THE SCENE

DAPHNE VINCE-PRUE

Glasshouse Crops Research Institute, Worthing Road,
Littlehampton, West Sussex, BN16 3PU, U.K.

My task in this introductory chapter is merely to provide a
background for the main part of the book and to set the scene
for what comes later. I shall first briefly review the
characteristics of the natural light environment as they
affect flowering. This is followed by a consideration of the
importance of light in relation to flowering in agriculture.
Finally, as a prelude to the detailed discussions of the
photoperiodic mechanism in Chapters 3, 4, 7 and 8, I shall
conclude with some background remarks on the role of light in
photoperiodism.

THE NATURAL LIGHT ENVIRONMENT

Daylength and Irradiance

Daylength and irradiance change dramatically with season and
latitude. At high latitudes such as those of the United
Kingdom, daylength and irradiance change in parallel and so
long days coincide with high light integrals in summer and
also with the highest temperatures of the year. In the
tropics, the seasonal daylength change is, of course, much
less and longer days do not necessarily coincide with higher
temperatures and light (Vince-Prue and Cockshull, 1981).
Differences such as these might be expected to lead to a
variety of interactions between daylength, irradiance and
temperature in natural populations of different origins and it

is important to bear this in mind when considering the mechanisms through which light affects flowering. The complexity of these interactions are particularly well illustrated in relation to light and vernalization (see Chapter 6). Such considerations should also warn us that more than one mechanism may have evolved in the control of photoperiodism as well as in the contribution of photosynthesis, both to photoperiodism and to the regulation of flowering more generally.

Light Quality

Changes in the spectral quality of daylight have only been studied in detail within the past few years as the instrumentation for making detailed measurements has been developed. The most dramatic changes in spectral quality are those which occur as a consequence of the absorption of light by plant canopies. Because of the absorption characteristics of leaves, light under a plant canopy is enriched in FR relative to R and B (Smith, 1982). The low R:FR ratio will affect the phytochrome photoequilibrium and the ratio of Pfr:Ptot established will be substantially lower than in sunlight. The Pfr:Ptot ratio at photoequilibrium in sunlight is estimated to be approximately 0.55 (Smith, 1982) but it is not known how this ratio relates to that established in green leaves because of internal screening by chlorophyll. In this context, the precise location of photoperiodic perception is relevant. Some studies have suggested that the perception of photoperiodic signals may occur in the epidermis (Schwabe, 1968) where screening would be minimal. On the other hand, the marked shift in the action spectrum of about 50 nm towards shorter wavelengths in green as compared with etiolated plants (Ohtani and Kumagai, 1980) indicates a strong degree of chlorophyll screening. Under canopy shade, the Pfr:Ptot ratio may be as low as 0.15, depending on the density of the canopy (Smith, 1982). The importance of these changes for flowering have been relatively little studied but have been considered in an earlier review (Vince-Prue, 1981), in which it was suggested that in very dense canopy shade the low R/FR ratio might be limiting for flowering, at least in SDP. Changes in the R:FR ratio will also affect photosynthesis through StateI State II transitions (Barber, 1983). The strong reduction of B under a canopy must also affect the operation of the blue-absorbing photoreceptor but this is not generally thought to be of importance in photoperiodic perception in higher plants (Vince-Prue, 1979).

The other factor that influences light quality under natural conditions is solar angle and, during evening twilight, the R:FR ratio decreases from the daylight value of about 1.1 down to a value of about 0.7. Inverse changes occur at dawn (Smith, 1982). There has been much debate as to whether these light quality changes at dusk and dawn are important as natural end-of-day signals (Shropshire, 1973; Vince-Prue, 1981, 1983a; Salisbury, 1981; Smith, 1982). However, the quality changes during twilight are relatively small, whereas changes in irradiance during twilight are large and may be very rapid so that they could equally well be the end-of-day signal for photoperiodic timing (Salisbury, 1981). Most of the available experimental evidence indicates that the end of day is signalled and photoperiodic dark time measurement begins when the irradiance falls below a critical threshold (Takimoto, 1967; Lumsden and Vince-Prue, 1984) and the presence or absence of Pfr at this time does not appear to affect photoperiodic timing (see Chapter 8 in this volume).

Surprisingly few experiments have attempted to determine the threshold for the suppression of dark time measurement under natural conditions and for different plants, but there is some evidence that this threshold varies with plant species and with time of day. For example, *Pharbitis nil* was two orders of magnitude *less* sensitive than *Xanthium strumarium* at dusk, but at least 10 times *more* sensitive at dawn (Takimoto and Ikeda, 1961). More recently, Salisbury (1981) has shown that under natural conditions, the falling irradiance at dusk could give an end-of-day signal accurate to within 5 to 11 minutes for *Xanthium*.

LIGHT AND FLOWERING IN AGRICULTURE

Most major agricultural crops are seeds or fruits and in only relatively few, such as potato, are vegetative parts consumed. Even here, conventional breeding programmes and, in some cases, also seed production depend on flowering. The flowering process is, therefore, of the greatest importance for agriculture and limitations to the initiation and further development of flowers often adversely affect yield.

Table 1 summarizes some of the ways in which flowering can be manipulated and which offer actual or potential advantages for agriculture.

Direct Manipulation of the Light Environment

Perhaps the best known and most widely used application of the direct manipulation of light is the use of photoperiod control usually under glass. A good example is the production of chrysanthemums all the year round (Vince-Prue and Cockshull, 1981). Cultivars for controlled year-round cropping have been

TABLE 1   *Light and flowering in agriculture*

---

1. Direct Manipulation of Light Environment

    i. photoperiod
   ii. irradiance

2. Chemical Manipulation of Response

    i. growth regulators
   ii. photomimetic chemicals

3. Genetic Manipulation of Response to Light

---

selected from the autumn flowering types which show a marked
response to SD. Chrysanthemums are propagated from cuttings
and are maintained in the vegetative state during the rooting
period by keeping them in LD. Following the propagation
period, plants may be placed in SD immediately as when producing flowering pot plants. Alternatively, plants first
receive a period of long days before flowering is induced in
SD, in order to produce a long leafy stem for cut flowers. S
are obtained by covering plants with a black cloth while LD
are usually achieved with incandescent lamps, light being
given for several hours as a night-break. Although a SDP,
chrysanthemums appear to be rather insensitive to night-break
lighting for the initiation of flowers (Vince-Prue, 1983b;
Vince-Prue and Canham, 1983, and see Chapter 3 in this
volume). This has led to many experiments designed to
optimize the lighting treatments with respect to cost effectiveness and flower quality (Vince-Prue and Canham, 1983) and
such approaches are extremely important for the glasshouse
industry. Control of the photoperiod does not entirely
eliminate seasonal influence on flowering in chrysanthemum,
however, for in northern Europe the low light integral of
winter adversely affects initiation even though daylength is
not limiting. Particularly during the first two weeks of SD,
a low irradiance markedly delays initiation (Cockshull and
Hughes, 1972). This does not seem to be simply an assimilate
limitation since it cannot be overcome by growing plants in
high irradiance conditions prior to SD induction (Vince,
1960). Commercial manipulation of irradiance to improve
flowering is too expensive to be widely used, despite the
undoubted importance of light quantity in the control of
initiation and development of flowers and for flower quality
However, in chrysanthemum at least, crop quality can also be

improved in winter by manipulation of the daylength. The
slower rate of leaf initiation in low light conditions can be
compensated for by growing plants for a longer period in LD:
this delays initiation to give the same stem length as in
summer (Vince-Prue and Cockshull, 1981).

Chemical Manipulation of the Response

Chemical manipulation of flowering is largely outside the
scope of this symposium. Plant growth regulators are known to
have a great variety of effects on flowering and some of these
are exploited in agriculture (Weaver, 1972). Probably the
best known example is the use of auxins or ethylene-releasing
compounds to induce flowering in pineapple. Less well-known
is the fact that the ethylene-releasing compound, ethephon,
markedly delays flower initiation in chrysanthemum, offering a
possible means of chemical regulation of flowering, particularly for the control of premature bud formation (Cockshull *et
al.*, 1979).

Photomimetic chemicals, i.e., those which specifically
mimic the action of light in the leaves have not yet been considered to any extent and this type of approach awaits a
better understanding of the action of light to bring about
induction in the leaf and of those chemicals which might
replace or prevent that action (see Chapter 9 in this volume).

For many growth regulator effects it is not known whether
the action occurs in the leaf or at the apex: GA, for example,
may have effects at both locations (see Chapter 10 in this
volume).

Genetic Manipulation of the Response to Light

The genetic manipulation of the flowering responses to light
has, of course, been widely exploited through conventional
plant breeding. Most examples come from photoperiodic
responses but selection for chrysanthemum cultivars that
produce acceptably good quality flowers under low light
integrals has been attempted and this approach may have considerable potential. Chrysanthemum is also an example of a
crop where selection for a strong photoperiod response has
taken place in order to use photoperiod manipulation to
control flowering. Chrysanthemum cultivars are facultative
SDP and will eventually initiate flowers in LD, although they
require SD for their further development into open flowers.
Cultivars which show a long delay in initiation in LD are
better suited to photoperiod control because they are less
likely to produce buds prematurely during the period of growth
in LD (Cockshull, 1976; Langton and Cockshull, 1978). Another

crop which seems to have been selected for strong photoperiod
control is soya bean (*Glycine max*). The effect of photoperiod
on flowering in soya bean is so marked in North American
cultivars that most are restricted to within about 4 degrees
of latitude (480 km) of their adapted area: outside this
range, plants mature too early in the south and consequently
have low yields, or fail to mature before the frosts in the
north (Summerfield and Wien, 1979).

In contrast to the examples given above, the Mexican wheats
of the green revolution owe their success at lower latitudes
largely to the loss of photoperiod sensitivity, unlike the
traditional high latitude wheats which are quantitative LDP
(see Chapter 14 in this volume).

The photoperiodic control of flower initiation and development clearly offers alternative strategies for the plant
breeder. One strategy is to breed for responses that are
tailored to make the best use of particular seasonal conditions; for example, flowering early in the life of the plant
is usually associated with a low yield (Vince-Prue and
Cockshull, 1981) so that photoperiod responses that delay
flowering may be advantageous. The alternative strategy is to
remove control by daylength (and/or temperature) so that autonomous induction occurs and flowering is no longer under
strict control of the environment, being largely dependent on
growth rate, size and age. The possibilities that are opening
up with the development of genetic engineering techniques (see
Chapter 14 in this volume) mean that these choices may become
available in a wider range of crop plants. It is, therefore,
of the greatest importance to understand the genetic control
of the various components of the flowering process and the
consequences, for crop production of manipulating these.

LIGHT AND PHOTOPERIODISM

Whether by direct or chemical means, or through breeding techniques, the effective manipulation of flowering requires an
understanding of the basic process and how it is controlled
within the plant. It is also necessary to recognize and
understand the differences between plants that may be
important in manipulating them to agricultural advantage.
However, although the diversity of responses to daylength and
their ecological and agricultural importance are well established, the mechanisms through which these responses are
effected remain poorly understood.

In photoperiodism, plants respond to the duration and
timing of light and dark periods in the daily cycle. Any
mechanism must, therefore, involve at least two basic components: a photoreceptor that discriminates between light and

darkness and a system that measures time. Under natural 24 h
cycles, SD are associated with long nights, and vice versa. A
basic question for photoperiodism is, therefore, whether time
is measured in light or darkness, or in both. The now
classical findings that interrupting darkness with a night-
break prevented its effect, allowing LDP to flower while
preventing flowering in SDP, and that this night-break effect
depended on the time when it was given, have generally
focussed attention on time-measurement in darkness. Experiments with non-24 h cycles, in which very long dark periods
were interrupted at different times, showed that time measurement, as determined by the time of maximum sensitivity to a
night break (NBmax), was coupled to the light-dark transition
with NBmax occurring at a constant time from light off irrespective of the duration of the photoperiod once this has
exceeded a certain length (Papenfuss and Salisbury, 1967;
Lumsden *et al.*, 1982). Many other experiments have yielded
similar results and have emphasized the role of the photoperiod in poising or setting the timer. Thus, from this kind
of approach has developed the general concept that light has
at least two functions in photoperiodism: the photoperiod sets
the timer in some way, while a night break interacts with the
timer to induce (LDP) or prevent (SDP) flowering at certain
times (Lumsden *et al.*, 1982). If, as now seems evident for
many plants, the timer is an endogenous circadian rhythm, this
concept comes close to Bunning's original hypothesis (see
Bunning, 1973). An external coincidence model (Pittendrigh,
1972) of this kind, is consistent with many of the experimental results obtained with SDP (Vince-Prue, 1983c) but other
types of interaction of light with the timer cannot be
excluded (Saunders, 1982, and see Chapter 7 in this volume).

If we turn now to studies of the photoreceptor, it has long
been established that the Pfr form of phytochrome appears to
be required during the photoperiod (Nakayama and Borthwick,
1960). This is particularly evident when short photoperiods
are used since their effect can often be completely prevented
by removing Pfr at the end of the photoperiod with an exposure
to FR; this FR inhibition of flowering is reversed by R.
However, the *first* evidence for the involvement of phytochrome
with photoperiodism came from the classical night break reversibility experiments carried out by Borthwick and his
colleagues working at USDA (Borthwick *et al.*, 1952). The fact
that Pfr appears to be required in the main photoperiod but
inhibits flowering in SDP at the time of the night break,
together with the spectrophotometric studies of phytochrome
properties in etiolated seedlings, led to general models for
photoreceptor behaviour in photoperiodism of the kind shown
schematically in Fig. 1. A high level of Pfr is established

in the photoperiod and is required for flowering. Following transfer to darkness, Pfr is lost and restoring it with a night break at a particular time prevents flowering in SDP, or promotes flowering in LDP. Implicit in this model is the

PHYTOCHROME

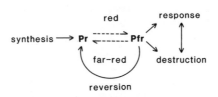

MODELS FOR PHOTOPERIODISM

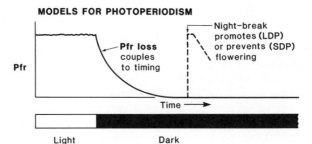

Fig. 1. Schematic showing the reactions of phytochrome in etiolated seedlings and a derived model for Pfr involvement in photoperiodism.

assumption that a reduction in Pfr through dark reactions is required for the perception of the light-dark transition so that the beginning of dark time measurement is coupled to the attainment of a threshold level of Pfr. However, there is now good evidence that phytochrome in light-grown plants behaves differently from that in etiolated seedlings and that Pfr is stable for many hours in darkness (see Chapter 2 in this volume). Consequently, the widely accepted models of this kind must be re-evaluated in the light of this new information. A special, rapidly-decaying pool of Pfr may be involved, or other types of phytochrome reaction such as cycling between the two forms, or the formation of 'new' Pfr, may be important for the coupling of the photoreceptor with the timer (Vince-Prue, 1983a; Lumsden and Vince-Prue, 1984, and see Chapter 8 in this volume).

The traditional view of the photoperiodic mechanism in LDP
was that it is simply the mirror image of that in SDP, the
only difference between the two groups of response being that,
at the time of night break sensitivity, light was required for
induction in LDP instead of preventing it, as in SDP. However, it has now been recognized for some time that the
photoperiodic control of flowering in many LDP appears to
operate through a somewhat different mechanism, often
requiring long daily exposures to light and being relatively
insensitive to a night-break treatment (Vince-Prue, 1975).
Another common feature is their relative insensitivity to day
extensions with R light, optimum flowering being achieved with
mixtures of R and FR. In contrast, when given as an extension
before a main photoperiod in daylight, R light often induces a
high degree of flowering (Vince-Prue, 1975, 1976). Character-
istically, therefore, flowering in many LDP is strongly promoted by FR particularly at certain times in the photoperiod.
A circadian periodicity in the timing of this promotion of
flowering has been demonstrated in at least two species,
Lolium temulentum (Vince-Prue, 1975) and *Hordeum vulgare*
(Deitzer *et al.*, 1979, and see Chapter 4 in this volume).
It is interesting and noteworthy that not all LDP show
these characteristics. There are some that show maximum
promotion of flowering in R light, for example, *Calamintha
officinalis* (Tcha *et al.*, 1976) and *Fuchsia hybrida* (Vince-
Prue, 1976): in the latter, flowering has also been shown to
be maximally inhibited by only a brief R night-break. Thus,
Fuchsia shows none of the characteristics normally associated
with LDP and does seem to behave like the mirror image of a
SDP. There are also some SDP (e.g., strawberry) which have
response characteristics similar to those of LDP, since their
flowering is only inhibited by long exposures to light containing mixtures of R and FR, they are not very responsive to
a brief night-break and they do not normally show R/FR reversibility (Vince-Prue, 1976). For this reason it has been
suggested that the mechanism requiring long daily exposures to
light and commonly associated with LDP might be termed a
light-dominant response since it is also observed in some SDP.
A particular problem with light-dominant responses is to
explain the requirement for FR (Chapter 4). In *Lolium
temulentum* at least, part of the requirement for FR arises
because Pfr is inhibitory at certain times in the photoperiodic cycle (Holland and Vince, 1971). However, prolonged
exposures to light containing both R and FR wavelengths are at
least as effective as treatments in which the Pfr values are
raised and lowered by alternations of R and FR light at the
appropriate times and the need for long daily exposures to
continuous or quasi-continuous light containing both R and FR

wavelengths (or at wavelengths of about 710 nm, Blondon and
Jacques, 1970) appears to be the overriding factor. For this
reason, it was proposed that light-dominant responses may
depend on a reaction which involved interconversions between
the two forms of phytochrome (i.e., cycling of the phytochrome
system) but that there is also a rhythm of sensitivity to Pfr
phytochrome which inhibits induction at certain times (Jose
and Vince-Prue, 1978). In this context, it is interesting to
note that one hypothesis for photoperiodic perception in SDP
also proposes that there is a reaction of phytochrome, perhaps
involving cycling, in which continuous light prevents the
coupling or release of a rhythm plus a reaction of Pfr which
prevents induction at a certain phase of this rhythm (Jose and
Vince-Prue, 1978, Lumsden and Vince-Prue, 1984 and see Chapter
8 in this volume). Other hypotheses have been advanced, for
example that there is a circadian change in sensitivity to an
HIR reaction of phytochrome rather than to Pfr (see Chapter 4
in this volume). There remains the problem of how an HIR
might be generated in light-grown plants since the most
generally accepted hypothesis explaining the HIR requires a
high content of destructible phytochrome (Schäfer, 1976) which
would not be present in fully de-etiolated plants (Chapter 2
in this volume). It is clear that the nature of photoperception in these light-dominant responses requires a better
understanding of the operation of the phytochrome system in
light-grown plants.

CONCLUDING REMARKS

This introductory chapter has addressed some, but by no means
all, of the topics covered in more detail in the chapters
which follow, many of which present views of the flowering
process that differ from those put forward here. It is,
therefore, appropriate to conclude with a brief summary of the
questions and problems discussed in this volume (Table 2).
These include a consideration of the effects of light on the
induction, evocation, initiation and development of flowers:
the location and identity of the photoreceptors and how they
function: the products of the photoreactions both with respect
to localised changes in the leaf during photoperiodic induction and the identity of the transmissible stimuli involved in
evocation. Finally, attention is given to the nature of the
interactions between processes. Flowering is a complex
response to a variety of stimuli and interactions between
environmental factors such as temperature and light, as well
as between light-dependent processes such as photoperiodism
and photosynthesis, are of the greatest importance and are
considered in some detail.

TABLE 2 *Light and Flowering*

---

1. Signals and responses

   duration induction initiation
   quantity development

2. Receptors and perception mechanisms

   where? what? how?

3. Products of the photoreactions

   localised changes
   transmissible stimuli

4. Interactions

   between photoreactions
   with non-photochemical reactions

The flowering process remains an enigma but the following contributions combine to shed some light on a complex problem and to highlight those areas where our ignorance remains greatest.

REFERENCES

Barber, J. (1983). *In* "The Biology of Photoreception" (eds. D. J. Cosens and D. Vince-Prue). pp. 19–52. Cambridge University Press, Cambridge

Blondon, F. and Jacques, R. (1970). *C.R. Hebd. Seances Acad. Sci.* 270, 947–950

Borthwick, H.A., Hendricks, S.B. and Parker, M.W. (1952). *Proc. Natl. Acad. Sci. USA* 38, 929–934

Bünning, E. (1973). "The Physiological Clock" Springer-Verlag, Heidelberg

Cockshull, K.E. (1976). *J. Hortic. Sci.* 51, 441–450

Cockshull, K.E., Horridge, J.S. and Langton, F.A. (1979). *J. Hortic. Sci.* 54, 337–338

Cockshull, K.E. and Hughes, A.P. (1972). *J. Hortic. Sci.* 47, 113–127

Deitzer, G.F., Hayes, R. and Jabben, W. (1979). *Plant Physiol.* 64, 1015–1021

Holland, R.W.K. and Vince, D. (1971). *Planta* 98, 232–243

Jose, A.M. and Vince–Prue, D. (1978). *Photochem. Photobiol.* 27, 209–216

Langton, F.A. and Cockshull, K.E. (1978). *Rep. Glasshouse Crops Res. Inst. 1977*, 177–186

Lumsden, P., Thomas, B. and Vince–Prue, D. (1982). *Plant Physiol.* 70, 277–282

Lumsden, P. and Vince–Prue, D. (1984). *Physiol. Plant.* 60, 427–432

Nakayama, S., Borthwick, H.A. and Hendricks, S.B. (1960). *Bot. Gaz.* 121, 237–243

Ohtani, T. and Kumagai, T. (1980). *Plant Cell Physiol.* 21, 1335–1338

Papenfuss, H.D. and Salisbury, F.B. (1967). *Plant Physiol.* 42, 1562–1563

Pittendrigh, C.S. (1972). *Proc. Natl. Acad. Sci. USA* 69, 2734–2737

Salisbury, F.B. (1981). *Plant Physiol.* 67, 1230–1238

Saunders, D.S. (1982). *In* "Biological Timekeeping" (ed. J. Brady). *Soc. Exp. Biol. Seminar Ser.* 14, pp. 65–87. Cambridge University Press, Cambridge

Schäfer, E. (1976). *In* "Light and Plant Development" (ed. H. Smith). pp. 45–49. Butterworths, London

Schwabe, W.W. (1968). *J. Exp. Bot.* 19, 108–113

Shropshire, W. (1973). *Solar Energy* 15, 99–105

Smith, H. (1982). *Annu. Rev. Plant Physiol.* 33, 481–518

Summerfield, R.J. and Wien, H.C. (1979). *In* "Advances in Legume Science" (eds. A.H. Bunting and R.J. Summerfield). pp. 17–36. HMSO, London

Takimoto, A. (1967). *Bot. Mag. Tokyo* 80, 241–247

Takimoto, A. and Ikeda, K. (1961). *Plant Cell Physiol.* 2, 213–229

Tcha, K.H., Jacques, R. and Jacques, M. (1976). *C.R. Hebd. Seances Acad. Sci. Ser. D.* 283, 341–344

Vince, D. (1960). *J. Hortic. Sci.* 35, 161–175

Vince–Prue, D. (1975). "Photoperiodism in Plants". McGraw Hill, London

Vince–Prue, D. (1976). *In* "Light and Plant Development" (ed. H. Smith). pp. 347–369. Butterworths, London

Vince–Prue, D. (1979). *In* "La Physiologie de la Floraison" (eds. P. Champagnat and R. Jacques). pp. 92–127. C.N.R.S. Paris

Vince–Prue, D. (1981). *In* "Plants and the Daylight Spectrum" (ed. H. Smith). pp. 223–242. Academic Press, London

Vince–Prue, D. (1983a). *Philos. Trans. R. Soc. Lond. B.* 303, 523–536

Vince–Prue, D. (1983b). *In* "Strategies of Plant Reproduction. BARC Symposium 6" (ed. W. Meudt). pp. 73–97. Allanheld Osmun, Totowa

Vince–Prue, D. (1983c). *In* "Encyclopedia of Plant Physiology" (eds. W. Shropshire, Jr. and H. Mohr). New Series Vol. 16B, pp. 457–490. Springer–Verlag, Heidelberg

Vince–Prue, D. and Canham, A.E. (1983). *In* "Encyclopedia of Plant Physiology" (eds. W. Shropshire, Jr. and H. Mohr). New Series Vol. 16B, pp. 518–544. Springer–Verlag, Heidelberg

Vince–Prue, D. and Cockshull, K.E. (1981). *In* "Physiological Processes Limiting Plant Productivity". (ed. C. B. Johnson). pp. 175–197. Butterworths, London

Weaver, R.J. (1972). "Plant Growth Substances in Agriculture". W. H. Freeman and Company, San Francisco

Chapter 2

ACTION OF PHYTOCHROME IN LIGHT-GROWN PLANTS

E. SCHÄFER, B. HEIM, E. MÖSINGER, AND V. OTTO

Institut für Biologie II, Schänzlestrasse 1,
D-7800 Freiburg, Federal Republic of Germany.

INTRODUCTION

At least three different photoreceptors (phytochrome, a blue
UV-A and a UV-B photoreceptor) control the transition from
skotomorphogenesis to photomorphogenesis (cf. Mohr and Schäfer
1983). The control of photoperiodism by phytochrome and a
blue UV-A photoreceptor is also well documented (Vince-Prue,
1975). In this chapter we will restrict the discussion to the
phytochrome system.
    Action spectroscopy and biochemical extraction have demons-
trated unambiguously that phytochrome is present and active in
etiolated as well as in mature green plants. Although physiological experiments indicate that the properties of phytochrome in light- and dark-grown plants may be different,
differences at the molecular level have not been fully
established.
    In this review we will summarize firstly our recent know-
ledge about the properties of phytochrome in etiolated seedlings and discuss the relevance of the observed phytochrome
light and dark reactions to an interpretation of the so-called
induction responses and the high-irradiance responses (HIR).
In the second part, the light and dark reactions of the phytochrome in light-grown seedlings will be described and the
action of phytochrome in end-of-day responses as well as under
continuous irradiation will be discussed.

LIGHT AND THE FLOWERING PROCESS
ISBN 0.12.721960.9

PROPERTIES OF PHYTOCHROME IN ETIOLATED SEEDLINGS

Light and Dark (Thermal) Reactions of Phytochrome in Etiolated Seedlings

Phytochrome can easily be isolated from etiolated seedlings and its light reactions studied *in vitro*. The overall photo-transformations (Pr --> Pfr and Pfr --> Pr) follow first order kinetics in both directions (Butler *et al.*, 1964). Similar first order reactions are also found *in vivo* if optical artefacts can be excluded (Schmidt *et al.*, 1973; Seyfried *et al.*, 1983).

Recently, phytochrome with a molecular weight of 124 kD has been extracted from *Avena sativa* L. (Vierstra and Quail, 1983) and rye (*Secale cerale* L.) (Kerscher and Nowitzky, 1982) showing properties expected from difference spectra obtained *in vivo* (Baron and Epel, 1982). The molar photoconversion cross-sections of phytochrome as measured *in vivo* were found to be almost identical with those measured *in vitro* (Seyfried and Schäfer, unpublished results).

Several thermal (i.e., non-photochemical) reactions have been established in etiolated mono- and dicotyledonous seedlings: Pr synthesis, Pfr destruction, Pfr --> Pr dark reversion (not observed in monocotyledons and Centrospermae), Pr turnover and Pfr-induced destruction of Pr.

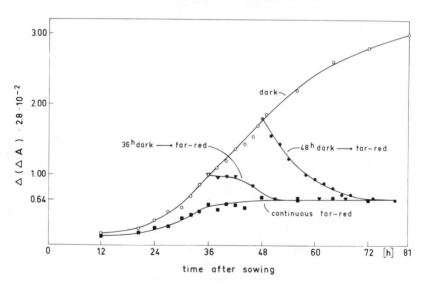

Fig. 1. Time course of change in total phytochrome for various times of onset of continuous FR in cotyledons of Sinapis alba *seedlings (Schäfer et al., 1972).*

Whereas Pr synthesis seems to follow zero order kinetics (Schäfer *et al.*, 1972; Schäfer, 1978), the other dark reactions seem to follow first order kinetics (cf. Pratt, 1979). This led to the concept of steady state regulation of phytochrome level under continuous irradiation (Fig. 1). The various phytochrome reactions (excluding Pfr --> Pr dark reversion) are summarized in models of phytochrome system shown in Fig. 2.

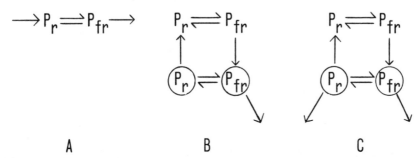

A   B   C

Fig. 2. Schematic phytochrome models. Model A summarizes light reactions and dark reactions of Pr synthesis and Pfr destruction. This model is mainly used to explain the induction reactions (Schäfer et al., 1972). Model B (the cyclic phytochrome model) involves in addition, two different states of phytochrome. This model is based on immunocytological experiments and pelletability data and is used to explain the HIR (Schäfer, 1975). Model C also includes Pfr-induced Pr destruction (Jabben and Holmes, 1983).

Induction vs HIR in Etiolated Seedlings

Since this topic has been discussed several times (Schäfer, 1975; Mohr and Schäfer, 1983; Schäfer and Mohr, 1984; Mancinelli and Rabino, 1978), we will only summarize the major conclusions briefly:

It has been demonstrated that model A can account for many induction responses if Pfr is assumed to be the controlling factor of the phytochrome system (cf. Mohr and Schäfer, 1983). On the other hand, some contradictory results have been obtained, leading to the concept of phytochrome paradoxes (Hillman, 1972). These problems can be overcome if the existence of a stable phytochrome pool is assumed (Brockmann and Schäfer, 1982). Recent spectrophotometric analysis of phytochrome destruction in etiolated systems supports this concept of a small fraction of stable phytochrome (Jabben *et al.*, 1980; Heim *et al.*, 1981; Brockmann and Schäfer, 1982). Furthermore Heim and Schäfer (1984) have demonstrated that the phytochrome-mediated HIR can not be explained on the basis of

the same signal transduction, starting from Pfr, as proposed
for the induction response (see Fukshansky and Schäfer, 1983;
Schäfer *et al.*, 1984b for discussion). Besides the action of
the spectrophotometrically detectable Pfr there has to be
another form of Pfr (model B), or a photochemical intermediate, as a second controlling factor.

PROPERTIES OF PHYTOCHROME IN LIGHT–GROWN SEEDLINGS

Until the development of the radio–immunoassay (RIA) for
phytochrome (Hunt and Pratt, 1979) and the use of the herbicide Norflurazon[1] (Jabben and Deitzer, 1978a), few reports of
measurements of phytochrome from green tissues were available.
The high chlorophyll content in light–grown plants does not
allow *in vivo* spectrophotometric measurements. Norflurazon-
treated plants are photobleached and contain almost no chlorophyll, without showing any significant changes in their responsiveness to photomorphogenetic, inductive light pulses or
continuous irradiation (Beggs *et al.*, 1980; Gorton and Briggs,
1980). Nevertheless, the more reliable data for the analysis
of phytochrome kinetics would be expected by using the RIA.
However, this assay is an *in vitro* assay and can not, at the
present time, distinguish between Pr and Pfr; moreover,
immunological differences between phytochrome from light- and
dark-grown plants cannot be excluded.
    Recently Gottmann and Schäfer (1983) obtained good agree-
ment between spectrophotometric and immunochemical results for
Ptot kinetics.

Spectral Properties of Phytochrome in Light-Grown Seedlings

In vivo difference spectra of phytochrome in white tissues are
always very similar to those reported for etiolated seedlings.
No significant immunochemical and spectral differences between
phytochrome extracted from etiolated and green pea seedlings
have been found (Shimazaki *et al.*, 1981). On the other hand
such differences have been reported for phytochrome isolated
from oat seedlings (Quail, personal communication; Pratt,
personal communication; Thomas, personal communication). This
indicates that the molecular properties of phytochrome,
chromophore and the protein determinant groups in etiolated
and green tissues are very similar (see Jabben and Holmes,
1983, for further discussion).

[1] Norflurazon (= SAN 9789) : 4–chloro-5-(methylamino)-2-(α,α,
α,-trifluoro–m–tolyl-3(2H)) pyridazinone.

Thermal Reactions of Phytochrome in Light-Grown Seedlings

The level of phytochrome measurable in light—grown seedlings
is ten to fifty times less than in etiolated seedlings of the
same age (Hunt and Pratt, 1980; Jabben *et al.*, 1980; Gottmann
and Schäfer, 1983). The question arises whether this low
level of phytochrome reflects a steady state situation, i.e. a
balance between synthesis and destruction or whether there is
a stable phytochrome pool.

Synthesis of phytochrome. Phytochrome re—accumulation as Pr
starts with a lag phase of about 3 h when plants, which have
been grown under continuous white light, are returned to darkness (Fig. 3). There has been some debate as to whether this
lag phase in Ptot accumulation is due to a balance between
synthesis and destruction or to a change in the rate of phytochrome *de novo* synthesis (cf. Jabben and Holmes, 1983). The

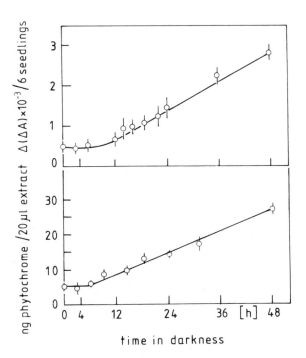

*Fig. 3. Kinetics of phytochrome accumulation in the dark
after a 5 min RG9-light pulse given to 6-d old light-grown
Avena sativa seedlings. Phytochrome measured as Δ(ΔA)) in
Norflurazon (2x10⁻⁴ M) treated seedlings (upper part); phytochrome measured using the RIA in green (H₂O-treated) seedlings
(lower part). RG9-light = long wavelength FR light.*

de novo synthesis of phytochrome can be measured by determining the activity of translatable mRNA coding for the phytochrome apoprotein. This analysis allows a comparison of the
rate of phytochrome synthesis during irradiation and after a
light–dark transition.

Gottmann and Schäfer (1982) observed that in *Avena* seedlings there is no detectable activity of mRNA coding for the
phytochrome apoprotein during white light irradiation.
Activity increases after a light–dark transition and reaches
its maximum value about 18 h later. The conclusion that light
controls Pr synthesis in *Avena* seedlings was confirmed by
analysing the *in vivo* incorporation of ^{35}S (given as ^{35}SO$_4$)
into phytochrome during 24 h dark or white light treatment
(Fig. 4) (Gottmann and Schäfer, 1983).

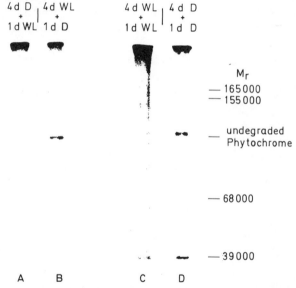

*Fig. 4. Autoradiographs of immunoprecipitates of extracts
from 5-d old* Avena sativa *L. seedlings. The seedlings were
grown for 4 d in white light (WL) or darkness (D) and then
transferred to a radioactive medium (*^{35}SO$_4$*) for a further day
in white light (A: C:) or in darkness (B: D:). The electrophoresis gel contained 5% (w/v) acrylamide. The positions of
unlabelled marker proteins are indicated.*

It has been observed that phytochrome synthesis is decreased in etiolated seedlings after a R (Fig. 5) or FR light
pulse (Gottmann and Schäfer, 1983). Control of phytochrome
levels by light has also been observed in herbicide treated
plants, indicating that phytochrome regulates its own

synthesis. Colbert *et al.*, (1983) confirmed these observations. The seed batch used in the latter experiments was less sensitive to Pfr and, therefore, showed a different response to R and FR. Using the classic R/FR reversibility experiment, these authors were able to show unequivocally that phytochrome controls its own synthesis.

The data in Fig. 5 show that the mRNA activity decreases very rapidly after a 5 min R pulse and increases again after a

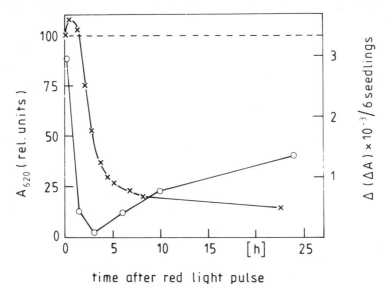

time after red light pulse

Fig. 5. Time course of the phytochrome apoprotein specific mRNA activity in the dark obtained for 4-d old dark-grown Avena *seedlings after a 5 min R pulse. The measured points (O) are densitometrical measurements of the autoradiographs. For comparison the time course of total phytochrome (X) measured spectrophotometrically is also plotted in this figure.*

4 h dark period, even though the amount of Pfr spectrophotometrically detectable should be high enough for full suppression of phytochrome synthesis. This indicates that phytochrome may not only control the decrease in synthesis after a dark − light transition but also the rate of resynthesis after a light − dark transition. It has been demonstrated spectrophotometrically, and by measuring mRNA activity, that the resynthesis of phytochrome in herbicide−treated plants is also under phytochrome control (Fig. 6) (Otto *et al.*, 1983). The astonishing conclusion which may be drawn from these data is that the Pfr level at a light − dark transition (which is dependent on light quality) controls the rate of Pr synthesis

in the dark over a very long period.

No measurable activity of translatable mRNA coding for the phytochrome apoprotein is observed in white-light grown *Avena* seedlings (Gottmann and Schäfer, 1982, 1983). In contrast to this, in light-grown *Zea mays* (Smith, 1981) and *Sorghum* seedlings (Sauter, pers. comm.), the level of Ptot is higher under a continuous irradiation with white light which has a low R : FR photon ratio than under light which has a high R : FR photon ratio. This is clearly important for phytochrome levels under continuous irradiation with white light.

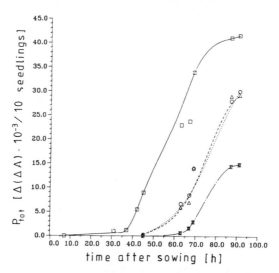

Fig. 6.   Ptot as a function of the time after sowing (Avena sativa). *Measurements began after the light treatment. Plants received 36 h D + 6 h WL followed by 5 min R (X); 5 min R + 5 min RG9-light (Δ); or 5 min RG9-light (O). Dark control ([ ]).*

Furthermore, in dicotyledonous seedlings, spectrophotometric data indicate that, in many cases, the rate of Pr synthesis after a white light — dark transition is very similar to that observed in etiolated seedlings (Jabben *et al.*, 1980). Further measurements in mono- and dicotyledonous seedlings are necessary to assess how important autoregulation of phytochrome synthesis is for an understanding of phytochrome kinetics in light-grown plants.

Phytochrome destruction and dark reversion. In light-grown Avena seedlings, the rate of destruction of phytochrome which has been synthesized during a dark period has been analysed under continuous irradiation (Hunt and Pratt, 1980; Gottmann

and Schäfer, 1983). The rate of destruction of this synthesized phytochrome was always rapid and comparable to that
measured for etiolated *Avena* seedlings. During continuous
irradiation the rate of destruction must be much slower to
account for the low levels of phytochrome and the observed
very low rates of phytochrome synthesis. This conclusion is
confirmed by direct spectrophotometric measurements of the
rate of Pfr (and Pr) destruction immediately after a light –
dark transition (Jabben and Deitzer, 1978b; Jabben, 1980;
Jabben *et al.*, 1980).

A re-investigation of Pfr destruction in etiolated seedlings showed biphasic destruction kinetics (Heim *et al.*, 1981)
indicating two pools of phytochrome, one exhibiting fast destruction (t½ ~ 30–60 min, labile phytochrome), the other
exhibiting slow destruction (t½ ~ 5–24 h, stable phytochrome).
This assumption of two different phytochrome pools has been
supported by an analysis of Pfr destruction after non-
saturating red light pulses (Heim *et al.*, 1981; Brockmann and
Schäfer, 1982).

Pfr->induced Pr destruction which has been described for
etiolated *Avena* (Dooskin and Mancinelli, 1968; Stone and
Pratt, 1979) and *Amaranthus caudatus* seedlings (Schäfer, 1981)
can also be observed in light grown *Avena* and *Zea* (Jabben,
1980), *Cucurbita pepo, Pharbitis nil* (Jabben *et al.*, 1980) and
Amaranthus (Schäfer, 1981).

Pfr ->Pr dark reversion, which is known to exist in
etiolated seedlings of several dicotyledonous species, seems
not to occur generally in light-grown seedlings (Jabben *et
al.*, 1980; cf. Jabben and Holmes, 1983). Dark reversion in
cauliflower heads (Butler *et al.*, 1963; Hillman, 1967; Spruit,
1970) seems not to occur immediately after a light – dark
transition, but only after a dark period of several hours
(Johnson and Hilton, 1978).

As a summary, we have to differentiate between two states
of the phytochrome system:

1. etiolated seedlings: predominantly labile phytochrome (up
   to 97%) characterized by fast destruction (Pr and Pfr) and,
   in some cases, dark reversion as well as regulation of Pr
   synthesis.

2. light-grown seedlings: predominantly stable phytochrome
   (up to 80%) characterized by very slow destruction (Pr and
   Pfr), no dark reversion and a very slow rate of Pr synthesis.

The two transient periods are de-etiolation and re-
etiolation. During de-etiolation, labile phytochrome will be
rapidly destroyed and – as shown for *Avena* – the rate of Pr

synthesis will be decreased. During re-etiolation, stable
phytochrome will be slowly destroyed and the synthesis of Pr
will start after a prolonged lag phase depending on the amount
of Pfr at the beginning of the dark period (Otto *et al.*,
1983). The resynthesized phytochrome shows the characteristics of labile phytochrome, including fast destruction (Hunt
and Pratt, 1980; Gottmann and Schäfer, 1983), and the occurrence of Pfr -> Pr dark reversion (Johnson and Hilton, 1978).

Phytochrome Controlled Responses in Light-grown Seedlings

In light-grown seedlings, as in etiolated seedlings, we can
distinguish two types of response; the end-of-day response and
the continuous light response.
   The end-of-day response of light-grown plants is equivalent
to the so-called induction response of etiolated seedlings.
Both require short irradiation periods and obey the Bunsen-
Roscoe law of reciprocity. The phytochrome-mediated control
of hypocotyl length (Wildermann *et al.*, 1978a; Beggs *et al.*,
1981) or internode length (Downs *et al.*, 1957; Kasperbauer,

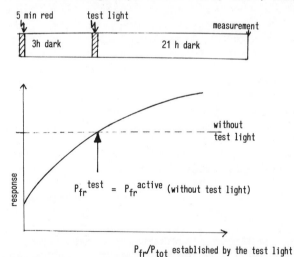

Fig. 7a. Scheme of irradiations and of the amount of the
response applying the null point method. White-light-grown
Sinapis alba *plants received a saturating R pulse. After 3 h*
of darkness another light pulse was given which established
different amounts of Pfr. If these plants showed the same
response as the control plants of the same age which received
only the first R pulse the null point is reached and it is
supposed that the same amount of active Pfr is present at this
time.

1971) by light pulses at the beginning of a dark period has
been described several times. We will concentrate on the
problem of whether these responses are mediated by labile or
stable phytochrome. A first conclusion can be drawn from an
analysis of loss of reversibility kinetics (see Fukshansky
and Schäfer, 1983; Schäfer *et al.*, 1983 for detailed discussion). The response induced by producing Pfr by a R pulse at
the end of a light period is still partially reversible by a
subsequent FR pulse over a prolonged dark period (Downs *et
al.*, 1957; Wildermann *et al.*, 1978b; Schäfer *et al.*, 1984a).

This indicates that Pfr is active over a long period (up to
16 h as tested by Downs *et al.*, 1957) and may be taken as
evidence that Pfr, which controls the response, has a half-
life of several hours.

A more direct test uses the null point method which was
originally introduced by Hillman. A null point test carried
out for light-grown *Sinapis* seedlings shows clearly that the

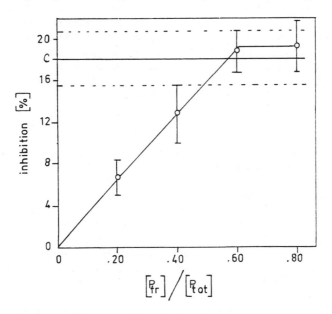

*Fig. 7b. An example of a null point experiment : inhibition of
hypocotyl length during a 24-h dark period as a function of
Pfr/Ptot established at the beginning of the dark period.
Various Pfr/Ptot ratios were established using sub-saturating
exposures to R given after a saturating RG9 light to transform
all Pfr remaining from the first light pulse to Pr. 48 h D +
6 h WL + 5 min R + 3 h D + 5 min RG9 light + 5 min R pulse
(sub-saturating) + 21 h D. The inhibition for plants not
treated with the second R pulse is indicated with a C.*

phytochrome which controls hypocotyl growth is stable (Fig. 7a, b).

In many light-grown plants it has been demonstrated that stem growth during continuous irradiation is under the control of Pfr or Pfr/Ptot. Detailed comparative action spectroscopy has been carried out for hypocotyl growth of etiolated and light-grown *Sinapis* seedlings (Beggs *et al.*, 1980; Holmes and Schäfer, 1981; Beggs *et al.*, 1981). It was observed that the responsiveness to FR (peak of action of HIR in etiolated seedlings) decreases with increasing de-etiolation, whereas the responsiveness to R increases leading to about a ten-fold higher effectiveness of continuous R in light-grown compared with dark-grown seedlings.

These observations and the fact that continuous R can be substituted for by hourly R pulses (Schäfer *et al.*, 1981; Heim and Schäfer, 1982) led Jabben and Holmes (1983) to the conclusion that the response to continuous irradiation may also be mediated by stable phytochrome. The major problem underlying this assumption is the lack of an interpretation of the irradiance dependence of the responses. The irradiance dependence and the position of the peaks in the action spectra for etiolated seedlings indicate that labile phytochrome is the active form (Schäfer, 1975; Schäfer *et al.*, 1982).

In parallel with the irradiance dependence of the response, irradiance dependence of Pfr and Pfr/Ptot has been observed (Heim and Schäfer, 1982, 1984; Jabben *et al.*, 1982). The latter has been explained on the basis of competition between the light reactions and a fast dark reaction, which is probably dark reversion (Schäfer and Mohr, 1984). It has been concluded that this fast dark reaction cannot account for the HIR of etiolated seedlings (Schäfer *et al.*, 1984b).

If the fast dark reactions are missing in green seedlings, a higher effectiveness of R would be expected, which is in agreement with recent observations (Beggs *et al.*, 1981). But, in addition, a R-irradiance-response curve should reflect simply Pr - Pfr photoconversion if no dark reactions are present. This conclusion is not supported by recent experiments (Fig. 8). Whereas, for 623 and 650 nm, continuous irradiation could be substituted for by hourly light pulses, this was only partially possible for 694 and almost impossible for 715 nm light. This indicates that phytochrome cycling under continuous irradiation is also important for light-grown seedlings. Therefore, the interpretation of irradiance dependence must remain open.

CONCLUSION

The observation of stable and labile phytochrome raises the question of which phytochrome is the active form for each type of response. The action of FR in HIR of etiolated seedlings will be controlled by labile phytochrome in all cases. In other cases it is not clear whether stable or labile phytochrome controls the response under investigation, although, in light-grown plants, stable phytochrome is predominantly present and will probably control the response in most instances.

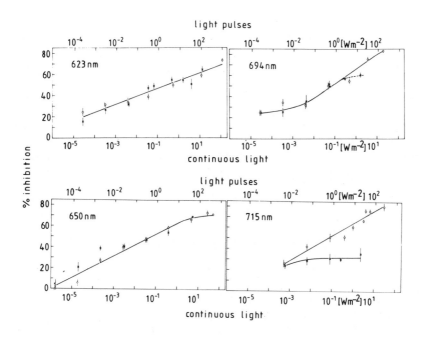

Fig. 8. Irradiance-response curves for inhibition of hypocotyl growth of 54-h old WL grown herbicide treated Sinapis alba seedlings after 24 h of continuous (O) or hourly pulsed (X) irradiation. The wavelength of the light used is indicated in the figure. The abscissa for the light pulses (upper scale) is shifted compared with that of continuous light (lower scale) to have data points with the same total exposure of continuous or pulsed light above each other.

The mechanism of autoregulation of phytochrome synthesis allows a rapid loss of labile phytochrome during de-etiolation leading rapidly to the light-grown system. Autoregulation of phytochrome during re-etiolation seems to be more sophisticated: a normal night does not lead to strong Pr synthesis, only prolonged dark periods allow a restart of Pr synthesis forming labile phytochrome which will finally lead to the capacity to respond in a classic HIR.

ACKNOWLEDGEMENT

The authors wish to thank I. Schomerus for the first class technical help in some experiments. This work was supported by Deutsche Forschungsgemeinschaft (SFB 206).

REFERENCES

Baron, O. and Epel, B.L. (1982). *Photochem. Photobiol.* 36, 79–82

Beggs, C.J., Holmes, M.G., Jabben, M. and Schäfer, E. (1980). *Plant Physiol.* 66, 615–618

Beggs, C.J., Geile, W., Holmes, M.G., Jabben, M. and Schäfer, E. (1981). *Planta* 151, 135–140

Brockmann, J. and Schäfer, E. (1982). *Photochem. Photobiol.* 35, 555–558

Butler, W.L., Lane, H.C. and Siegelman, H.W. (1963). *Plant Physiol.* 38, 514–519

Butler, W.L., Hendricks, S.B. and Siegelman, H.W. (1964). *Photochem. Photobiol.* 3, 521–528

Colbert, J.T., Hershey, H.P. and Quail, P.H. (1983). *Proc. Natl. Acad. Sci. USA* 80, 2248–2252

Dooskin, R.H. and Mancinelli, A.L. (1968). *Bull Torrey Bot. Club* 95, 474–487

Downs, R.J., Hendricks, S.B. and Borthwick, H.A. (1957). *Bot. Gaz.* 118, 199–208

Fukshansky, L. and Schäfer, E. (1983). *In* "Encyclopedia of Plant Physiology". (eds W. Shropshire, Jr. and H. Mohr). New Series Vol.9. pp. 69–95. Springer-Verlag, Heidelberg

Gorton, H.L. and Briggs, W.R. (1980). *Plant Physiol.* 66, 1024–1026

Gottmann, K. and Schäfer, E. (1982). *Photochem. Photobiol.* 35, 521–525

Gottmann, K. and Schäfer, E. (1983). *Planta* 157, 392–400

Heim, B., Jabben, M. and Schäfer, E. (1981). *Photochem. Photobiol.* 34, 89–93

Heim, B. and Schäfer, E. (1982). *Planta* 154, 150–155

Heim, B. and Schäfer, E. (1984). *Plant Cell Environ.* 7, 39–44

Hillman, W.S. (1976). *Annu. Rev. Plant Physiol.* 18, 301–324

Hillman, W.S. (1972). *In* "Phytochrome" (eds K. Mitrakos and W. Shropshire, Jr.). pp. 573–584. Academic Press, New York

Holmes, M.G. and Schäfer, E. (1981). *Planta* 153, 267–272

Hunt, R.E. and Pratt, L.H. (1979). *Plant Physiol.* 64, 327–331
Hunt, R.E. and Pratt, L.H. (1980). *Plant Cell Environ.* 3, 91–95
Jabben, M. and Deitzer, G.F. (1978a). *Photochem. Photobiol.* 27, 799–802
Jabben, M. and Deitzer, G.F. (1978b). *Planta* 143, 309–313
Jabben, M. (1980). *Planta* 149, 91–96
Jabben, M., Heim, B. and Schäfer, E. (1980). *In* "Photoreceptors and Plant Development" (ed J. De Greef). pp. 145–158. Antwerp Univ. Press, Antwerp
Jabben, M., Beggs, C.J. and Schäfer, E. (1982). *Photochem. Photobiol.* 35, 709–712
Jabben, M. and Holmes, M.G. (1983). *In* "Encyclopedia of Plant Physiology" (eds W. Shropshire, Jr., and H. Mohr). New Series, Vol. 27, pp. 704–722. Springer-Verlag, Heidelberg
Johnson, C.B. and Hilton, J. (1978). *Planta* 144, 13–17
Kasperbauer, M.J. (1971). *Plant Physiol.* 47, 775–778
Kerscher, L. and Nowitzky, S. (1982). *FEBS Lett.* 146, 173–176
Mancinelli, A.L. and Rabino, I. (1978). *Bot. Rev.* 44, 129–180
Mohr, H. and Schäfer, E. (1983). *Philos. Trans R. Soc. Lond.* B. 303
Otto, V., Mösinger, E., Sauter, M. and Schäfer, E. (1983). *Photochem. Photobiol.* 38, 693–700
Pratt, L.H. (1979). *Photochem. Photobiol. Rev.* 4, 59–124
Schäfer, E. (1975). *J. Math. Biol.* 2, 41–56
Schäfer, E. (1978). *Photochem. Photobiol.* 27, 775–780
Schäfer, E. (1981). *In* "Plants and the Daylight Spectrum" (ed H. Smith). pp. 461–480. Academic Press, London
Schäfer, E., Marchal, B. and Marmé, D. (1972). *Photochem. Photobiol.* 15, 457–464
Schäfer, E., Lassig, T.-U. and Schopfer, P. (1982). *Planta* 154, 231–240
Schäfer, E. and Mohr, H. (1984). *Ber. Dtsch. Bot. Ges.* (In press)
Schäfer, E., Fukshansky, L. and Shropshire, W. Jr. (1983). *In* "Encyclopedia of Plant Physiology". (eds W. Shropshire Jr. and H. Mohr). New Series, Vol. 16A, pp. 39–95. Springer-Verlag, Heidelberg
Schäfer, E., Ebert, C. and Schweizer, M. (1984a). *Photochem. Photobiol.* 39, 95–100
Schäfer, E., Heim, B. and Löser, G. (1984b). *Ber. Dtsch. Bot. Ges.* (In press)
Schmidt, W., Marmé, D., Quail, P. and Schäfer, E. (1973). *Planta* 111, 329–336
Seyfried, M. and Schäfer, E. (1983). *Plant Cell Environ.* 6, 633–640
Seyfried, M., Fukshansky, L. and Schäfer, E. (1983). *App. Optics* 22, 492–496

Shimazaki, Y., Moriyasu, Y., Pratt, L.H. and Furuya, M. (1981). *Plant Cell Physiol.* 22, 1165–1174

Smith, H. (1981). *Nature (Lond.)* 293, 163–165

Spruit, C.J. (1970). *Meded. Landbouwhogesch. Wageningen* 70–114, 1–18

Stone, H.J. and Pratt, L.H. (1979). *Plant Physiol.* 63, 680–682

Vierstra, R.D. and Quail, P.H. (1983). *Plant Physiol.* 72, 264–267

Vince-Prue, D. (1975). "Photoperiodism in Plants" McGraw Hill, London

Wildermann, A., Drumm, H., Schäfer, E. and Mohr, H. (1978a). *Planta* 141, 211–216

Wildermann, A., Drumm, H., Schäfer, E. and Mohr, H. (1978b). *Planta* 141, 217–223

Chapter 3

THE PHOTOPERIODIC INDUCTION OF FLOWERING IN
SHORT-DAY PLANTS

K. E. COCKSHULL

Glasshouse Crops Research Institute, Worthing Road,
Littlehampton, West Sussex, BN16 3PU, U.K.

Flowering in short-day plants (SDP) is induced when they
receive an adequate duration of darkness in each daily cycle.
Darkness apparently permits timing processes to begin, which,
if they proceed for long enough, lead to the synthesis or
release of factors which induce flowering (floral stimuli).
The main influence of light, therefore, is to inhibit induction. It presumably suppresses timing processes, may
directly inhibit the production of floral stimuli when given
after a period of darkness, and may promote the synthesis of
floral inhibitors. Light also has an important promotory
effect on flowering because of its influence on the rate of
photosynthesis in the main light period. Higher irradiances
in this period provide additional energy and substrates for
growth and the more rapid initiation and development of
flowers.

Three main problems arise when considering the effects of
light on the flowering of SDP. First, the wide range of
light sources and units of measurement that have been used by
different authors make it difficult to compare the effectiveness of different light treatments. To overcome this in the
present chapter, these different units have been converted to
a common basis, viz. irradiance in the photosynthetically-
active waveband (PAR; 400–700 nm), using the conversion
factors shown in Table 1. Similar factors have been produced
by various authors (e.g., Bickford and Dunn, 1972; McRee,
1972; Anon, 1982) and appear to be accurate to within about
10%. Although it would have been more useful to have chosen

LIGHT AND THE FLOWERING PROCESS
ISBN 0.12.721960.9

TABLE 1   *The following factors were used to convert lux and
other units to mW m^{-2} PAR.*

Light source	Factor (mW m^{-2} PAR per) lux
"Cool-White" fluorescent (CWF)	2.9
"Daylight" fluorescent (DLF)	3.9
Incandescent lamp (INC)	4.2
Natural light (NL)	4.0

1 foot candle = 10.76 lux   ;   1 erg cm^{-2} = 1 mJ m^{-2}

the photon flux density in some specific waveband as the
common basis, conversion factors were not available for all
the light sources and units encountered in the experiments
discussed.

The second problem is the enormous volume of results that
have been obtained using a great number of different SDP. To
make this more manageable, discussion has been restricted to
the responses of selected cultivars of just four species, viz.
Chrysanthemum morifolium (syn. *Dendranthema morifolium*) cv
Polaris, *Glycine max* cv Biloxi, *Pharbitis nil* cv Violet, and
Xanthium strumarium (syn. *X pensylvanicum*).

The third problem is that we still have no means of
assaying the actual quantity of stimulus produced in response
to any treatment. Our best estimate, therefore, is to assay
the changes that the stimulus evokes in the apical meristems
even though these will be affected by effects on the translocation of the stimuli, on the supply of assimilates to the
meristems and on the competence of the meristems themselves to
respond.

LIGHT AND THE PROMOTION OF INDUCTION

The main way in which light promotes induction is through the
influence of the irradiance of the main light period. This
was first demonstrated in *Glycine* (Borthwick and Parker, 1938)
but has since been demonstrated in *Chrysanthemum* (Cockshull
and Hughes, 1971), *Pharbitis* (Marushige and Marushige, 1966),
and *Xanthium* (see Salisbury, 1969). In general, the irradiance conditions at the time of induction are particularly
important suggesting that primary products of the light period

are required. These are probably products of photosynthesis, for increases in photoperiodic sensitivity in *Pharbitis* are accompanied by increases in chlorophyll content and photosynthetic activity (Marushige and Marushige, 1966). In *Xanthium*, however, although sucrose could substitute for the absence of high irradiance light (Liverman and Bonner, 1953) it could not substitute for the absence of CO_2 during the main light period (Ireland and Schwabe, 1982).

In *Chrysanthemum*, the daily total of radiant energy received is an important modifying influence on both photoperiodic induction in SD and on autonomous induction in LD (Fig. 1). Flower initiation in *Pharbitis* is also autonomously induced in LD under moderate light conditions, occurring within 30 days when plants are grown in continuous light at an irradiance of about 50 W m^{-2} (Shinozaki, 1972).

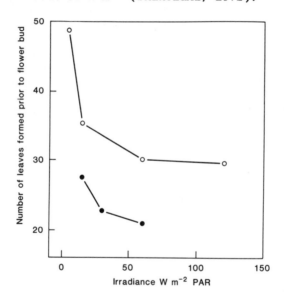

Fig. 1. The effect of irradiance in the main light period on time of flower initiation in Chrysanthemum morifolium *cv Polaris. O, continuous light LD (data from Cockshull, 1979); ●, 8 h light - 16 h dark SD (Cockshull, unpublished data).*

LIGHT AND THE INHIBITION OF FLOWERING

The inhibition of induction by light usually requires much less energy than its promotion and effective irradiances are often in the mW m^{-2} range, especially when light is given for some hours. Inhibition by light is of great practical interest because it provides a means of controlling the duration of vegetative growth and thus of controlling plant size and the yield of flowers or fruits (Vince–Prue and Cockshull, 1981). Under natural conditions, the duration of darkness is determined by the times of sunset and sunrise but light from artificial sources can be used to modify this by extending the day or by interrupting the dark period (night-break treatments).

"Dusk-to-Dawn" Lighting

The presence of light signals that the plant is not in darkness but how is the change to darkness detected? Changes in light quality do occur at the beginning and end of the natural day (e.g. Salisbury, 1981) but these are apparently not essential for detecting dusk and dawn as the transition from light to dark and vice versa is abrupt in most experimental procedures and yet serves as an adequate signal.

One approach to this problem has been to transfer plants from a high irradiance to different, low irradiance treatments given for the same duration as a long inductive dark period ("dusk-to-dawn" lighting), the object being to determine the irradiance at which the plant responds as though in darkness. Salisbury (1963) grew plants of *Xanthium* in natural light for

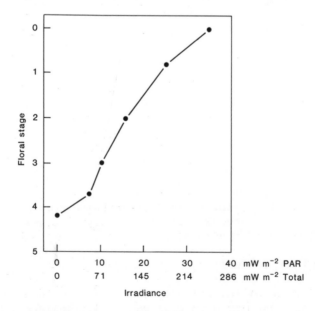

Fig. 2. The effect of irradiance of "dusk-to-dawn" lighting for 16 h (incandescent light source) on floral induction in Xanthium *(Data from Salisbury, 1963).*

8 h and then used incandescent lamps to give different
irradiances for 16 h. His irradiance measurements were made
with an Eppley thermopile, responsive to radiant energy of all
wavelengths from 300 to 3000 nm, and approximately 14% of the
emission from an incandescent lamp that is detectable by such
an instrument, falls in the 400 – 700 nm waveband (see
Bickford and Dunn, 1972; Fig. 4–12).

The results indicated that flower initiation was completely
suppressed at 35 mW m^{-2} while at 7 mW m^{-2} the response
approximated that in darkness, suggesting that this irradiance
failed to act as a light signal (Fig. 2). Intermediate
irradiances permitted intermediate degrees of flower initiation giving neither the full inhibition expected of light nor
the full induction expected of darkness. It was shown from
other experiments (Salisbury, 1963), that transfer from a high
irradiance to 14 mW m^{-2} did not inhibit dark timing, which
suggests that a later step in the inductive process was inhi-

TABLE 2   *The minimum irradiance required to produce maximum
inhibition of flowering when given for the duration of an
inductive dark period (i.e. "dusk-to-dawn" lighting).*

	Irradiance mW m^{-2} PAR		Total energy per "night" J m^{-2} PAR	Light source	Reference
Chrysanthemum					
'White Pink Chief'	46		2650	INC	1
'Polaris'	150		8100	INC	2
Glycine					
'Biloxi'	0.46		23	INC	3
various cv	84		4200	INC	4
Pharbitis	25		1440	DLF	5
Xanthium	0.46		20	INC	3
	34		2938	INC	6
	35		2016	INC	7

1. Cathey and Campbell, 1975; 2. Cockshull and Horridge, unpublished; 3. Parker *et al.*, 1946; 4. Major and Johnson, 1974;
5. Takimoto and Ikeda, 1959b; 6. Liverman and Bonner, 1953;
7. Salisbury, 1963.

bited at this irradiance. The light sensitivity of this later
step could account for the graded nature of the whole response
to "dusk-to-dawn" lighting, for the possibility that dark
timing also began on transfer to 35 mW m^{-2}, a fully inhibitory
irradiance, was not tested.

Similar quantitative responses to "dusk-to-dawn" lighting
have been observed in *Pharbitis* (Takimoto and Ikeda, 1959b;
Table 7), in ten cultivars of *Glycine* (Major and Johnson,
1974) and in *Chrysanthemum* (Cockshull and Horridge, unpublished). From these and other experiments it is possible to
calculate the minimum irradiance which will give complete inhibition of flowering (Table 2). In the case of *Chrysanthemum*
(Cathey and Campbell, 1975) and *Glycine* (Major and Johnson,
1974) the data probably include effects on flower development
as well as on induction. With *Xanthium*, the statement of
Liverman and Bonner (1953) that 1.5 f.c. (INC) was approximately twice that needed to suppress induction when given all
night, was used to calculate the effective irradiance. This
agrees with that obtained by Salisbury (1963) but is substantially greater than that cited by Parker *et al.* (1946). With
the exception of the data of Parker *et al.*, the minimum
effective irradiance in each species falls within the range
from 25 to 150 mW m^{-2}. It is also of some interest that 100
mW m^{-2} of a predominantly FR light suppressed induction in
Pharbitis when given from "dusk-to-dawn" (Takimoto and Ikeda,
1959b; Table 7).

"Dusk-to-dawn" treatments are fully effective, therefore,
at comparatively low irradiances but because they can exert
their effects at any time in the night they may not readily be
related to the effects of twilight.

Twilight Lighting

The effects of twilight have been investigated more directly
either by transferring plants from different irradiances of
twilight to darkness or by using artificial light sources to
give short extensions to the natural daylength.

If plants of *Pharbitis* were transferred to darkness when
the twilight irradiance fell to 2000 mW m^{-2}, flowering was
promoted as compared with plants that remained under natural
conditions, but transfer at 400 mW m^{-2} was without effect
(Takimoto and Ikeda, 1960b). The data suggest that some
component of induction, presumably dark timing, was being
suppressed by the higher twilight irradiance and that the
suppression had been removed by the time the lower irradiance
was reached. This range of twilight irradiances was traversed
in less than 34 min under natural conditions at the time of
the experiment. When plants were transferred to a 4 h day-

length extension (DLF) followed by 12 h darkness, 1950 mW m^{-2} suppressed flowering while 390 mW m^{-2} was equivalent to darkness (Takimoto and Ikeda, 1960d). These values are similar to

TABLE 3 *The maximum irradiance of natural twilight or of a short (<4 h) daylength extension that produced no detectable inhibition of induction at either the beginning or the end of an inductive night. Also, the minimum irradiance of such treatments to effect either some inhibition or complete inhibition of induction.*

	Max. irradiance without effect mW m^{-2} PAR	Min. irradiance (mW m^{-2} PAR) to effect some inhibition	to effect complete inhibition	Light source	Ref.
A. Beginning of Night					
Glycine	800	—	—	NL	1
	39	195	780	DLF	1
Pharbitis	400	2000	—	NL	2
	—	2000	5000	WWF	3
	390	780	>1950	DLF	4
Xanthium	40	200	—	NL	1
	4	43	780	DLF	1
	6.1	3.3	12.5	R	5
	10	25	91	R+FR	5
B. End of Night					
Glycine	4.0	40	—	NL	1
	3.9	39	39	DLF	1
Pharbitis	<4.0	4.0	—	NL	2
	<3.9	3.9	39–780*	DLF	4
Xanthium	3.9	43	>1950	DLF	1

1. Takimoto and Ikeda, 1961; 2. Takimoto and Ikeda, 1960b; 3. Lumsden and Vince-Prue, 1984; 4. Takimoto and Ikeda, 1960d; 5. Salisbury, 1981. *Effectiveness depends upon whether the night is <11 h or >12 h in length.

those obtained with twilight. In other transfer experiments
(Lumsden and Vince-Prue, 1984), the onset of circadian timing
was suppressed at 5000 $mW\ m^{-2}$ ("warm-white" fluorescent, WWF)
and delayed at 2000 $mW\ m^{-2}$ but not for the full duration of
the 2 h treatment.

The effects of transfer at either dusk or dawn and to or
from either natural light or short daylength extensions are
summarised in Table 3. This shows the minimum irradiance that
caused complete inhibition of flowering and the minimum irradiance that caused some inhibition of flowering. As observed
with "dusk-to-dawn" lighting, intermediate irradiances tended
to have intermediate effects. Table 3 also shows the maximum
irradiance used that had no effect on induction and so was
still equivalent, therefore, to darkness.

Induction in *Glycine* and *Pharbitis* is relatively insensitive to light at the beginning of the night, for a higher
irradiance is required to suppress induction at dusk than at
dawn and, in addition, quite high irradiances are apparently
undetected at dusk. The effective irradiance at dawn is
similar to that effective from dusk-to-dawn in these two
species. The position is less clear with *Xanthium*. Salisbury
(1981) found dark timing was suppressed at 12.5 $mW\ m^{-2}$ when a
predominantly R source was used to give a short daylength
extension; a much lower effective irradiance than in the other
two species. He had earlier found that dark timing was not
suppressed by a similar irradiance from incandescent lamps
when given from "dusk-to-dawn" (Salisbury, 1963). The reason
for this discrepancy may be related to light quality for if R
and FR were given together at similar irradiances, as in the
emission from an incandescent lamp, then timing was not
suppressed until a higher irradiance (c 91 $mW\ m^{-2}$; 600 - 697
nm) was reached (Salisbury, 1981).

The data suggest that the onset of dark timing at dusk is
controlled by changes in irradiance, as concluded by Vince-
Prue (1981), but that light quality may influence the effective irradiance, at least in *Xanthium*. Vince-Prue (1981) also
suggested that there was a threshold irradiance for triggering
timing, but there is little evidence for that view for, as
shown here, intermediate irradiances give intermediate responses. Light treatment at dawn could either suspend timing
or directly inhibit later steps in induction such as the
release or synthesis of floral stimuli. The differences in
sensitivity to light at dusk and dawn lend some support to the
view that different processes are affected at these two times.
Eventually, however, timing must also be suspended at dawn
when an adequate irradiance or duration of light is achieved.
There is also growing evidence that the production of floral
stimuli does not cease on return to light following an

adequate period of darkness, for flowering in *Chrysanthemum*
(Cockshull *et al.*, 1982), *Glycine* (Hadley *et al.*, 1984) and
Vigna unguiculata (Hadley *et al.*, 1983) is related to the mean
diurnal temperature. In these plants, therefore, low temperatures during the period of darkness, which might be expected to retard synthesis of stimuli, can be compensated for
by higher temperatures during the light period, when synthesis
has supposedly ceased.

Lighting at Different Times in the Night

The data presented so far suggest that sensitivity to irradiance changes between dusk and dawn. Further evidence of
this was obtained by Takimoto and Ikeda (1960d) who divided a
16 h night into four 4 h periods and then, in each period,
examined the effect of irradiance on *Pharbitis*. The plants
proved to be insensitive to light in the first period, when
even an irradiance of 1950 mW m^{-2} was ineffective. In the
third period, however, the plants were especially sensitive to
light, for none flowered with just 39 mW m^{-2} and even 4 mW m^{-2}
stopped 44% of them from flowering (Fig. 3). The response was
quantitatively related to the irradiance in each period, even

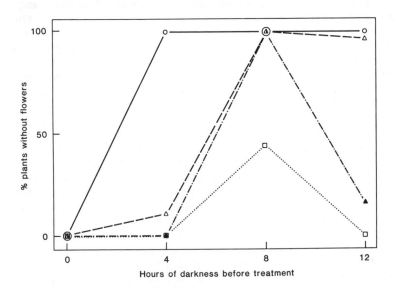

Fig. 3. *The effect of irradiance on the inhibition of induction in* Pharbitis *when light from "daylight" fluorescent lamps
was given for 4 h at different times in a 16 h dark period.*
O, *1950;* Δ, *390;* ▲, *39; and* □ *4 mW m^{-2} PAR. (Data from
Takimoto and Ikeda, 1960d).*

in the first, where although no plants were stopped from
flowering at 1950 mW m^{-2}, none actually formed terminal
flower buds, and the proportion of plants with them increased
as the irradiance was reduced to 390 mW m^{-2}.

Similar patterns of sensitivity have been demonstrated in
Glycine and *Xanthium* (Parker *et al.*, 1946). Short light
treatments, lasting less than 9 min, suppressed induction
almost completely when given at a low energy level after 7 to
8 h of darkness. Their effectiveness was less when given
earlier or later but was restored at these times if additional
energy was provided. With *Xanthium*, an irradiance of 6.1 mW
m^{-2} or less was considerably more effective in inhibiting
induction when given for 2 h in the middle of a 16 h night
than when given at its start (Salisbury, 1981). These changes
in sensitivity to irradiance account for the classical night-
break response when light of short duration and constant
irradiance is given at different times in the night.

Night-Break Treatments

The existence of a period of great sensitivity to light about
7 to 8 h after the onset of darkness has been demonstrated in
Chrysanthemum (Cathey and Borthwick, 1964), *Glycine* (Parker *et
al.*, 1946), *Pharbitis* (Takimoto and Hamner, 1964), and
Xanthium (Parker *et al.*, 1946; Salisbury and Bonner, 1956).
The relationship between this period of sensitivity and the
critical night length is not clear. With extended periods of
darkness, light can inhibit flowering even when given many
hours after the critical night length has been exceeded, and
when given after 8 h, it can render the following dark period
ineffective even though this may exceed the critical length by
some hours (Wareing, 1954; Takimoto and Hamner, 1964; Papenfuss and Salisbury, 1967). The evidence suggests the involvement of an endogenous circadian rhythm which is started by the
transfer to darkness (Takimoto and Hamner, 1964).

The night—break responses of SDP have been described as low
irradiance responses but Parker *et al.*, (1946) first demonstrated that they were dependent on the total energy delivered
and that there was reciprocity between duration and irradiance. It would be more accurate, therefore, to describe
these responses as requiring low energies, as high irradiances
must be used in order for brief durations to be effective.
Table 4 shows that *Xanthium* is especially sensitive and
requires a very small energy input to inhibit induction.
Pharbitis is less sensitive and *Chrysanthemum* requires up
to 100 times more energy than *Xanthium*. It seems unlikely
that differences in the optical properties of leaves could
account for the whole of this variation. *Glycine* may also be

quite sensitive, though an irradiance of 4,200 mW m^{-2} was required for 1800 s in order to inhibit induction when the

TABLE 4 *The minimum irradiance required to produce maximum inhibition of flowering when given near the middle of an inductive dark period (i.e., night-break).*

	Irradiance mW m^{-2} PAR	Duration s	Total energy per night J m^{-2} PAR	Light source	Ref.
A. Brief night-break					
Chrysanthemum					
'Honeysweet'	18 722	60	1 123	CWF	1
	74 890	60	4 493	CWF	1
Pharbitis	3 300	75	248	R	2
Xanthium	2 350	20	47	R	3
	18 000	4	72	INC	4
B. Long night-break					
Chrysanthemum					
'Polaris'	400	18 000	7 200	INC	5
'Honeysweet'	903	4 800	4 334	INC	6
	1 806	2 880	5 201	INC	6
Glycine	131	540	71	R	3
Pharbitis	39	14 400	562	DLF	7
Xanthium	3.3	7 200	24	R	8
	6	7 200	43	R	8

1. Cathey and Borthwick, 1964; 2. Takimoto and Hamner, 1965; 3. Parker *et al.*, 1946; 4. Salisbury and Bonner, 1956, 5. Cockshull and Horridge, 1979; 6. Borthwick and Cathey, 1962; 7. Takimoto and Ikeda, 1959b; Table 8; 8. Salisbury, 1981.

dark period was extended to 39 h. (Wareing, 1954).
    The data suggest that floral induction in *Chrysanthemum*, *Pharbitis*, and *Xanthium* is inhibited as readily by a brief night break as by a long one, provided sufficient energy is

given. A measure of reciprocity holds even when exposure
times longer than 2000 s are used and may hold for *Chrysanthe-*
mum and *Pharbitis* even with "dusk-to-dawn" lighting (Table 2).
When reciprocity has been tested directly, however, it has
usually been found that energy is used more efficiently given
as a low irradiance over a long period than as a high
irradiance over a short period. For example, 180 J m^{-2} were
more effective in inhibiting flowering of *Pharbitis* when
delivered over 7200 s than 120 s (Takimoto and Ikeda, 1960c),
and 3000 J m^{-2} were more effective over 4800 s than 600 s in
Chrysanthemum (Borthwick and Cathey, 1962; Table 2). In
Chrysanthemum also, the efficiency of usage of a given energy
total is increased further if the light is pulsed or cycled,
so that periods of light and dark alternate for the duration
of the night break (Borthwick and Cathey, 1962).

As with the other inhibitory effects of light, energies
lower than the minimum required for full inhibition of induction, give intermediate responses, e.g. *Chrysanthemum* (Cathey
and Borthwick, 1964; Kadman-Zahavi and Yahel, 1971; Cockshull,
1979), *Glycine* (Parker *et al.*, 1946), *Pharbitis* (Takimoto and
Hamner, 1965) and *Xanthium* (Parker *et al.*, 1946).

Radiant energy of any wavelength in the 400 – 700 nm waveband will inhibit flowering in *Glycine* and *Xanthium* but least
energy is required in the 580 – 680 nm waveband (Parker *et
al.*, 1946). It is not easy to demonstrate photoreversible
control of flowering in green plants (e.g. Takimoto and
Hamner, 1965) but examples are known for all four species in
which the effects of brief R treatments have been at least
partially reversed by a subsequent FR treatment under certain
conditions (Cathey and Borthwick, 1957; Hamner, 1969; Vince-
Prue and Gressel, 1984; Salisbury, 1969). There is some
evidence, therefore, that phytochrome is the photoreceptor for
brief night-break treatments. It is less certain that it is
involved at other times, however, for although the energy
required to photoconvert phytochrome does change rhythmically
in darkness, the changes do not parallel those involved in the
sensitivity to light and the periodicities of the two
responses differ (King *et al.*, 1982).

Long Daylength Extensions

Long extensions to a short main photoperiod inhibit induction
of SDP, the degree of inhibition usually being quantitatively
related to the irradiance of the extension as demonstrated by
Borthwick and Parker (1938) with *Glycine*. In this species, 45
mW m^{-2} (INC) for 8 h completely suppressed induction when it
followed an 8 h day. A long daylength extension may suppress
the onset of time measurement for the whole duration of the

extension or for sufficient part of it to render the ensuing
dark period too short to permit induction. Time measurement
in *Pharbitis* is probably linked to a circadian rhythm (see
Chapter 8 in this volume), for transfer from high irradiance
continuous light to 39 mW m^{-2} (DLF) for 8 h did initiate a
rhythm of responsiveness to a subsequent brief night-break,
whereas transfer to 975 mW m^{-2} did not and transfer to 195 mW
m^{-2} had an intermediate effect (Takimoto, 1967). These
irradiances are lower than those that affect induction when
given as short daylength extensions (Table 3). It is also
possible that a low irradiance daylength extension does not
affect dark timing but acts later, when the plant has entered
a phase of greater sensitivity to light. If this were so, it
might be expected that lower irradiances would be required for
long daylength extensions given at the end of the night, as
with the responses to twilight, but this aspect does not seem
to have been tested.

Light quality has a profound influence on the effectiveness
of a daylength extension. Exposure of *Glycine* or *Xanthium* to
either R (450 mW m^{-2}) or R + FR for the first half of a 16 h
night completely suppressed flowering though FR alone (450 mW
m^{-2}, 700 – 800 nm) was ineffective. In *Fragaria* x *ananassa*,
in contrast, although R + FR reduced flowering, R was ineffective while FR had some effect in the first half of the
night. Both R and R + FR were effective, however, in the
second half of the night (Vince–Prue and Guttridge, 1973). It
was suggested that the Pfr/Ptot ratio must be high early in
the night to inhibit *Glycine* and *Xanthium* but low early in the
night and high later to inhibit *Fragaria*. The latter changes
are analogous to those required for the promotion of flowering
in some LDP. This prompted the suggestion that *Fragaria*
flowered because the R treatment failed to promote a process,
such as the formation of an inhibitor, and not because it
failed to prevent the formation of a promoter (Vince–Prue and
Guttridge, 1973).

Chrysanthemum responds in a similar manner to *Fragaria*
(Cockshull and Prue, 1980), as do some genotypes of *Glycine*
(Buzzell, 1971) when tested at one irradiance. Further experiments showed that the efficacy of the R treatment in the
first half of the night was greatly enhanced if its irradiance
was increased (Cockshull and Vince–Prue, unpublished). This
was achieved with no change in light quality and, therefore,
with no light-induced change in the Pfr/Ptot ratio. Maximum
effectiveness was obtained at about 30 000 mW m^{-2} whereas R +
FR was effective at 3000 mW m^{-2} or less.

There are some similarities in the response of *Pharbitis*,
for light deficient in FR (DLF) is also relatively ineffective
in the first half of the night. Takimoto and Ikeda, (1959b)

found an irradiance of 11 700 mW m^{-2} was required to suppress induction completely, which is just double that observed to suppress circadian timing when given as a short daylength extension (Lumsden and Vince–Prue 1984). Lower irradiances had intermediate effects. Furthermore, addition of FR (120 mW m^{-2}, 700 – 1200 nm) enhanced the effectiveness of FR–deficient light (50 mW m^{-2}) in the first half of the night (Takimoto and Ikeda, 1960a; Tables 2 and 3). Terminating either the R or R + FR extension with a short (5 min) high irradiance R treatment (3000 mW m^{-2}) completely suppressed flowering, suggesting that the circadian rhythm of responsiveness to a night–break began on transfer to either extension, and that the addition of FR must have acted to inhibit some other component of induction. The observation that predominantly FR light (8 h) also suppressed flowering even though it was followed by an inductive 16 h dark period (Takimoto and Ikeda, 1959a, b) supports this view. In *Xanthium*, however, addition of FR reduced the effectiveness of R because it permitted timing to begin at a higher R irradiance than in its absence (Salisbury, 1981).

The responses of *Chrysanthemum* and *Pharbitis* to long daylength extensions with R are difficult to explain on the basis of phytochrome action. If the action of R is to produce a high Pfr/Ptot ratio, then it appears that this can be inhibitory in the first half of the night, though much more energy is required than in the second half. If the same pigment is involved at all times, then these changes in the saturation energy might imply massive changes in the numbers either of phytochrome molecules or of screening molecules present, neither of which seems likely. Furthermore, the energy required to inhibit induction in *Pharbitis* seedlings, is greatly in excess of that believed to produce maximum conversion of Pr to Pfr (i.e. 82.5 J m^{-2}, Takimoto and Hamner, 1965).

CONCLUSIONS

1. The evidence suggests that all effects of light on the induction of SDP are quantitative responses to radiant energy. The inhibitory effects are not readily related therefore, to the Pfr/Ptot ratio of phytochrome alone but require a mechanism which also uses information about the energy or photon flux density to produce a graded response. This response could involve the formation of either promoters or inhibitors of flowering.

2. The inductive processes commence following transfer from a high irradiance to either darkness or to a low irradiance that

permits dark timing. Induction can then be suppressed by return to light at any time before the critical dark period is exceeded, provided it is of adequate irradiance. In *Glycine* and *Pharbitis*, suppression requires a higher irradiance at the beginning of the night than later. This may indicate that two different processes are affected, e.g. the onset of dark timing and the production of floral stimuli. Irradiances that are effective given from dusk-to-dawn are similar to those effective at dawn alone in these two species. There is also evidence from these two species that short light treatments can inhibit induction when given after the critical dark period has been exceeded provided sufficient energy is given.

3. All four species are most sensitive to light about 8 h after the onset of darkness. This night-break response exhibits some reciprocity between irradiance and duration, but the energy range over which light is effective varies greatly between species; while *Xanthium* requires less than 50 J m^{-2}, *Chrysanthemum* requires about 5000 J m^{-2}. In *Pharbitis*, the onset of dark timing seems associated with the release of a circadian rhythm of responsiveness to light which reaches maximum sensitivity about 8 h after its release.

4. Although all wavelengths of PAR are effective as a night break, less energy is required when the orange-red waveband is used. The effect of a brief interruption with R can be reversed by FR implying that phytochrome is the photoreceptor. In *Chrysanthemum* and *Pharbitis*, a daylength extension at dusk requires a high R irradiance to be effective but the effectiveness of a low R irradiance can be considerably enhanced by the simultaneous addition of FR. This does not appear to affect timing, although in *Xanthium*, the addition of FR to R allows timing to begin at higher R irradiances.

5. More attention needs to be paid to these quantitative relationships, especially in connection with the onset of timing at dusk and the inhibition of induction later in the night, in order to determine the mechanisms by which photon flux density is sensed and linked to these processes.

REFERENCES
Anon. (1982). "Artificial Lighting in Horticulture".
    Philips' Gloeilampenfabrieken, Eindhoven
Bickford, E.D. and Dunn, S. (1972). "Lighting for Plant
    Growth" Kent State University Press, Kent, Ohio
Borthwick, H.A. and Cathey, H.M. (1962). *Bot. Gaz.* 123,
    155–162

Borthwick, H.A. and Parker, M.W. (1938). *Bot. Gaz.* 100, 374–387

Buzzell, R.I. (1971). *Can. J. Genet. Cytol.* 13, 703–707

Cathey, H.M. and Borthwick, H.A. (1957). *Bot. Gaz.* 118, 71–76

Cathey, H.M. and Borthwick, H.A. (1964). *Bot. Gaz.* 125, 232–236

Cathey, H.M. and Campbell, L.E. (1975). *J. Am. Soc. Hortic. Sci.* 100, 65–71

Cockshull, K.E. (1979). *Ann. Bot. (Lond.)* 44, 451–460

Cockshull, K.E., Hand, D.W. and Langton, F.A. (1982). *Acta Hortic.* 125, 101–110

Cockshull, K.E. and Horridge, J.S. (1979). *Rep. Glasshouse Crops Research Inst. 1978,* 59–60

Cockshull, K.E. and Hughes, A.P. (1971). *Ann. Bot. (Lond.)* 35, 899–914

Cockshull, K.E. and Prue, D.V. (1980). *Rep. Glasshouse Crops Res. Inst. 1979.* 64–66

Hadley, P. Roberts, E.H., Summerfield, R.J. and Minchin, F. (1983). *Ann. Bot. (Lond.)* 51, 531–543

Hadley, P. Roberts, E.H., Summerfield, R.J. and Minchin, F. (1984). *Ann. Bot. (Lond.)* (In press)

Hamner, K.C. (1969). *In* "The Induction of Flowering" (ed. L.T. Evans) pp. 62–89. MacMillan Co., Melbourne

Ireland, C.R. and Schwabe, W.W. (1982). *J. Exp. Bot.* 33, 738–747

Kadman–Zahavi, A. and Yahel, H. (1971). *Physiol. Plant.* 25, 90–93

King, R.W., Schäfer, E., Thomas, B. and Vince–Prue, D. (1982). *Plant Cell Environ.* 5, 395–404

Liverman, J.L. and Bonner, J. (1953). *Bot. Gaz.* 115, 121–128

Lumsden, P.J. and Vince–Prue, D. (1984). *Physiol. Plant.* 60, 427–432

McCree, K.J. (1972). *Agric. Meteorol.* 10, 443–453

Marushige, K. and Marushige, Y. (1966). *Bot. Mag. Tokyo* 79, 397–403

Major, D.J. and Johnson, D.R. (1974). *Crop Sci.* 14, 839–841

Papenfuss, H.D. and Salisbury, F.B. (1967). *Plant Physiol.* 42, 1562–1568

Parker, M.W., Hendricks, S.B., Borthwick, H.A. and Scully, N.J. (1946). *Bot. Gaz.* 108, 1–26

Salisbury, F.B. (1963). *Planta* 59, 518–534

Salisbury, F.B. (1969). *In* "The Induction of Flowering". (ed. L.T. Evans) pp. 13–61. MacMillan Co., Melbourne

Salisbury, F.B. (1981). *Plant Physiol.* 67, 1230–1238

Salisbury, F.B. and Bonner, J. (1956). *Plant Physiol.* 31, 141–147

Shinozaki, M. (1972). *Plant Cell Physiol.* 13, 391–393

Takimoto, A. (1967). *Bot. Mag. Tokyo* 80, 241–247

Takimoto, A. and Hamner, K.C. (1964). *Plant Physiol.* 39, 1024–1030

Takimoto, A. and Hamner, K.C. (1965). *Plant Physiol.* 40, 865–872

Takimoto, A. and Ikeda, K. (1959a). *Bot. Mag. Tokyo* 72, 181–189

Takimoto, A. and Ikeda, K. (1959b). *Bot. Mag. Tokyo* 72, 388–396

Takimoto, A. and Ikeda, K. (1960a). *Bot. Mag. Tokyo* 73, 37–43

Takimoto, A. and Ikeda, K. (1960b). *Bot. Mag. Tokyo* 73, 175–181

Takimoto, A. and Ikeda, K. (1960c). *Bot. Mag. Tokyo* 73, 341–347

Takimoto, A. and Ikeda, K. (1960d). *Bot. Mag. Tokyo* 73, 468–473

Takimoto, A. and Ikeda, K. (1961). *Plant Cell Physiol.* 2, 213–229

Vince–Prue, D. (1981). *In* "Plants and the Daylight Spectrum" (ed. H. Smith) pp. 223–242, Academic Press, London

Vince–Prue, D. and Cockshull, K.E. (1981). *In* "Physiological Processes Limiting Plant Productivity" (ed. C. B. Johnson). pp. 175–197. Butterworths, London

Vince–Prue, D. and Gressell, J. (1984). *In* "Handbook of Flowering" (ed. A.H. Halevy). CRC Press, Boca Raton, Florida (In press)

Vince–Prue, D. and Guttridge, C.G. (1973). *Planta* 110, 165–172

Wareing, P.F. (1954). *Physiol. Plant.* 7, 157–172

Chapter 4

PHOTOPERIODIC INDUCTION IN LONG-DAY PLANTS

GERALD F. DEITZER

Smithsonian Environmental Research Center
12441 Parklawn Drive, Rockville, Maryland, 20852, U.S.A.

INTRODUCTION

Photoperiodic induction of flowering in long-day plants has
not been as extensively studied as that in short-day plants.
The reason for this is the relative insensitivity of most LDP
to floral promotion by a brief light interruption of a non-
inductive long dark period. Indeed, only a small number of
species of LDP are capable of induction with a single night
break of less than 30 min duration, and then only under very
specific conditions. Determination of the original action
spectra (Borthwick *et al.*, 1948; Parker *et al.*, 1950) for LDP
was carried out with *Hordeum vulgare* and *Hyoscyamus niger*
grown on marginally inductive 11.5- or 12-h photoperiods and
required nine repeated cycles of 15-min night breaks during a
four-week period. Neither plant could be induced with repeated 15-min R night breaks when grown under completely
non-inductive 8-h photoperiods, even when such breaks were
given continuously for the full four-week period (Lane *et al.*,
1965). However, both were induced when a 4-h FR night break
was given in the middle of the 16-h dark period and when the
8-h day was extended with 8 h of FR-containing light.
    This is in marked contrast to the response in most SDP
where, as in *Xanthium strumarium* for example, a single 2 to
3 min R night break is able to suppress flowering completely
(Downs, 1956). Also, whereas SDP often show an all-or-none
response to a night break (but see Chapter 3 in this volume),
many LDP are increasingly promoted as the duration of the
night break is increased (Kasperbauer *et al.*, 1963) often

LIGHT AND THE FLOWERING PROCESS
ISBN 0.12.721960.9

saturating only in continuous light (Harris, 1968). While no action spectra have been determined for the FR reversal of the R promotion by a night break in LDP, partial reversal was demonstrated for both *Hordeum* and *Hyoscyamus* (Downs, 1956). This, combined with the similarity of action spectra for the night-break effect on flowering in LDP and SDP, suggests that phytochrome is the photoreceptor molecule involved in night-break perception in both groups of plants.

When the daylength is extended with low irradiance light to induce flowering, the action spectrum in most LDP is very different from that determined for the night-break response (Imhoff *et al.*, 1979; Schneider *et al.*, 1967). It shows a peak of effectiveness in the FR region between 710 and 720 nm that conforms to neither the absorption spectrum maximum of Pr nor Pfr. It does, however, resemble the absorption spectrum maximum for the reaction centre of photosystem I (P700). Although such responses have been interpreted by many authors solely on the basis of phytochrome (Hartmann, 1966; Borthwick *et al.*, 1969; Schäfer, 1975) others have proposed an inter-action between phytochrome and photosynthesis (Schneider and Stimson, 1971, 1972).

While the nature of the photoreceptor for this day-extension response remains somewhat less clear than that for the night-break response, the positive enhancement of flower-ing by light in LDP does appear to be mediated by a mechanism different from that in SDP where light serves more to prevent the effectiveness of a prolonged dark period. This has led to the suggestion that such long-day responses be termed light-dominant (as opposed to dark-dominant in SDP) (Vince-Prue, 1979) to emphasize this essential difference. These light-dominant responses may be characterized by: (a) maximal enhancement with mixtures of R and FR light, to an extent greater than either alone, (b) a dependence on irradiance that is substantially in excess of that required for phytochrome photoconversion and (c) a change in responsiveness to R and FR during the course of the day (Evans, 1971).

This paper will attempt to re-examine night-break res-ponses, brief end-of-day responses and daylength extensions in LDP in terms of current thinking of how phytochrome functions in light-grown plants.

END-OF-DAY RESPONSE

Downs and Thomas (1982) have recently described a possible mechanism to explain the promotion of flowering in *Hyoscyamus* by daylength extensions of an 8-h short day with light from incandescent lamps. They confirm what has been reported extensively in the literature for a large number of plant species (see Vince-Prue, 1975 for a review) that plants grown under 16-h long days with incandescent light reach anthesis sooner than those grown under 16-h photoperiods with fluorescent light. They suggest that this is the result of the sequential stimulation of floral initiation by R light in the middle of the presumptive dark period and stimulation of later floral development by FR light at the end of the presumptive short day. This conclusion is based upon the fact that FR appears to be most effective when added at the end of the second ten (of 20) 16-h fluorescent photoperiods. Also, the effect of 5 min of FR could be obtained when added to the end of the second ten of 20 photoperiods, even when these last ten photoperiods were only 8 h long. This effect of FR was completely reversed by a subsequent R irradiation.

Since the stimulation of stem elongation was greater than that for floral stage, an attempt was made to dissociate the effects of FR on the two processes. Exogenously applied GA_3 was found markedly to stimulate stem elongation with little effect on floral stage development. This suggests that the rate of floral development in *Hyoscyamus* is, at least, not a simple function of the rate of stem elongation. However, there was also an effect of FR light on the GA_3-stimulated elongation after both 16-h long days and 8-h short days, indicating that FR given at the end of the day increased the sensitivity of the plant to exogenously applied GA_3.

The conclusion that there is both a low Pfr and a high Pfr requiring period involved in the induction of flowering in LDP is in accord with numerous observations made previously in *Hyoscyamus* (El Hattab, 1968), *Lemna gibba* G_2 (Ishiguri and Oda, 1972), *Lolium temulentum* (Holland and Vince, 1971; Evans, 1976; Vince, 1965) and *Anagallis arvensis* (Imhoff et al., 1979). The indication that the action spectra for daylength extensions reflects the combined action of R and FR at different times in the sequence of events leading to anthesis is also in agreement with previous suggestions (Vince, 1966; Jacques and Jacques, 1969; Blondon and Jacques, 1970; Imhoff et al., 1971) that both the high and low Pfr processes could be mediated by a constant photostationary state, provided that the level of Pfr was not too high. It was assumed, however, in these earlier studies that both processes were involved with floral initiation and not with subsequent floral development and many of these utilised a single (Evans, 1976) or only a few (Holland and Vince, 1971) LD cycles.

The evidence presented by Downs and Thomas (1982) for the end-of-day FR stimulation of subsequent floral development rests on its effectiveness when added to the last ten days of a 20-day period in either long or short days. As previously noted, the effect was most pronounced on stem elongation. The

conclusion that the response to FR is not simply an effect on
elongation, which in a plant already induced would result in
more rapid development, is based on the fact that added GA
stimulates only elongation. Unfortunately, since the results
from the various experiments cannot be quantitatively compared, it is difficult to evaluate this conclusion. For
example, the effect of adding FR at the end of the last ten
8-h days was an increase in elongation from 13 mm to 43 mm and
an increase in floral stage from 3.0 to 6.0 in one experiment
and from 2 to 4 mm and 2.0 to 3.1 floral stage in another.
GA_3 caused an increase in length from 2 to 40 mm with a concomitant reduction in floral stage from 2.0 to 1.3. Addition
of FR in the presence of exogenous GA_3 resulted in an increase
in length from 40 to 93 mm (two-fold) and an increase in
floral stage from 1.3 to 4.1. This does not, however, rule
out the possibility that endogenous GA might account for the
effects of the FR if there were an increase in the sensitivity
to GA as a consequence. Such an increased sensitivity is
indicated by the two-fold stimulation of elongation in response to FR in the 8-h short-day controls.

In *Anagallis* (Imhoff *et al.*, 1979), which is a caulescent,
non-rosette LDP, addition of 15 min FR to the end of two 9-h
photoperiods increased internode elongation, but did not result in flowering even when added for 3 h and given for seven
cycles. In *Lolium temulentum*, which is also a rosette plant
where stem elongation occurs following initiation, end-of-day
FR does not promote flowering (Vince, 1965), even after
several weeks of treatment. It is, therefore, suggested that
the R/FR reversible end-of-day promotion of flowering in the
rosette plant *Hyoscyamus* is more an effect on stem elongation
than a direct effect on floral development. To test this
possibility, the effect of this FR treatment should be
repeated using a growth retardant such as AMO 1618 (Cleland
and Zeevaart, 1970) to show that flowering can be enhanced
without concomitant elongation, rather than the reverse
approach with GA. This is especially true since it has been
demonstrated that photoperiodic induction in *Agrostemma
githago* involves both a change in sensitivity to GA and the
rate of turnover of endogenous GA (Jones and Zeevaart, 1980).
Transfer from short to long days is also accompanied by an
increase in elongation that is blocked by AMO 1618 and
reversed by addition of GA_{20}.

INTERMITTENT LIGHT

According to the hypothesis discussed above from Downs and
Thomas (1982), a sequence of ten short days given with a brief
R night break followed by ten short days ending with a brief

terminal FR treatment should be as effective as 20 days of
16-h incandescent photoperiods. While direct comparison
between experiments is again not possible, both 16-h incandescent photoperiods for 20 days and 16-h fluorescent photo
periods given for ten days followed by 8-h fluorescent photoperiods ending with FR do produce maximal flowering. Data of
Stolwijk and Zeevaart (1955) showing that photoperiod extensions are most effective when composed of a FR period followed
by a R period also tend to support the concept of sequential
effectiveness. In *Lolium* (Evans, 1976) the effect of 16 h of
incandescent light was, however, always significantly greater
than any combination of FR and R, including 4 h of FR + 12 h
R. Evans *et al.*, (1965) also reported that rapid flowering
could only be caused when R + FR was given simultaneously or
sequentially in short (10 and 30 min) cycles.

Cycles of incandescent light as short as 2 s (0.2 s light
and 1.8 s dark) given for 6 h in the middle of a 16-h dark
period in *Hyoscyamus* were much less effective than continuous
light (Schneider *et al.*, 1967). Cycles as long as 30 min
(3 min on/27 min off) were equally ineffective at promoting
flowering in *Hyoscyamus*, but 6 min of light every hour was
found to be equivalent to constant light in *Melilotus alba*
(Kasperbauer *et al.*, 1963) when given throughout 16-h dark
periods. Unfortunately no quantitative data were presented in
the paper and so comparison is difficult. In *Dianthus caryo-
phyllus* the total amount of light was found to be important;
the same flowering response was achieved irrespective of
whether the light was cycled or given continuously, as long as
the total energy was kept constant (Harris, 1972).

CONTINUOUS LIGHT

While the results with intermittent light are somewhat contradictory, it appears that, whether given continuously or as a
series of pulses, the quantity of energy required to induce
maximal flowering is substantially in excess of that required
for either end-of-day or night-break responses. Also, it
appears that light must be present for a long period in order
to be effective. Such long duration, high-energy requiring
responses have come to be called the high irradiance responses of photomorphogenesis (Hartmann, 1966; Borthwick *et
al.*, 1969). A number of physiological responses, including
seed germination, hypocotyl elongation, anthocyanin synthesis
and the control of flowering in both LDP and SDP, have been
described as being regulated through some HIR mechanism. All
share the common features of being strongly irradiance-
dependent, mediated by light that would establish a low
P_{fr}/P_{tot} phytochrome photoequilibrium and not readily R/FR

reversible. Most also fail to obey the Bunsen-Roscoe law of reciprocity (i.e. where irradiance x time = constant) except when light is provided as short pulses over a fixed duration (Mancinelli and Rabino, 1975). Failure of reciprocity is often interpreted as evidence for the participation of more than one photoreceptor in the sequence of events leading to the response. Where reciprocity can be demonstrated by pulsing the light, it suggests that only a single photoreceptor is involved but its action is required over a defined period of time. Since the results from the intermittent light experiments are inconclusive, the possibility of photoreceptor interactions should be seriously considered. Such an interaction almost certainly occurs in the B region of the spectrum (Mancinelli and Rabino, 1978) and may also occur in FR through an interaction with the P700 reaction centre chlorophyll of photosystem I (Schneider and Stimson, 1971, 1972). An alternative explanation that explains both the irradiance dependence and the failure of reciprocity solely on the basis of phytochrome by postulating the production of a separate pool of Pfr associated with a reaction partner (Hartmann, 1966; Borthwick et al., 1969; Schäfer, 1975), has been proposed, and is widely accepted in the literature.

Results obtained with Hordeum (Deitzer et al., 1979) show that maximal flowering, measured both as floral stage and apical elongation is obtained when FR is added to continuous fluorescent light. When FR was added to 12-h photoperiods, both the time of initiation and the rate of floral development were the same as those under continuous fluorescent light. This does not agree with the concept that FR acts primarily at the end-of-day to stimulate only floral development since both the addition of FR and an extension of the photoperiod caused exactly the same response. The specific increase in apex length was stimulated to the same extent in both and the results were additive when both treatments are given.

When the number of inductive 24-h photoperiods containing supplemental FR light was varied, each of the first three inductive periods resulted in maximal stimulation of the rate of elongation (ca. 12 fold that of the control) for a period proportional to the number of cycles given. After a burst of maximal elongation each reverted to the rate of the control. More than three cycles resulted in cessation of maximal elongation rate at the same time as the three cycle treatment, but now the rate after return to the control condition subsequently increased, saturating only under continuous inductive conditions (24 h + FR). The same number of cycles (3) appeared to be required to saturate the time that the transition from a vegetative apex to a reproductive apex occurred, although one cycle appeared to be disproportionately effective. However, after undergoing initiation following a single cycle, the floral apex did not develop further until well after the SD controls had initiated flowers.

Since three cycles appeared to saturate the initiation response and the rate of elongation during this period was linearly related to the amount of time an inductive stimulus was given, spectral changes were compared only during this 72-h period. When FR was added to 72 h of fluorescent light, there was about a two-fold stimulation of both apex elongation and floral stage, but no change in dry weight accumulation. When the FR was added for only a 6-h period at different times during the 72-h period, the ability of the plant to respond varied with circadian periodicity. Moreover, the addition of FR for only 6 h produced as much as 50% of the response obtained by adding FR throughout the 72-h period. Maximal stimulation occurred during the presumptive night, as would be expected for a daylength extension in a LDP.

A detailed examination of the response to 6 h FR was undertaken (Deitzer, 1983). A 6-h period during which there was maximal response to FR was chosen and the amount of FR was varied to create a range of R/FR energy ratios from 0.2 to 5.6. There was little or no promotion above the control level (R/FR = 5.6) with any ratio above 2.0. Maximal promotion was obtained with a ratio of 0.2, but there was no significant difference between points from 0.2 to 0.6. It may be worth noting that 50% of the maximal response was obtained with a R/FR ratio of 1.2, the ratio found for solar daylight throughout most of the day.

Having established that light with a R/FR ratio between 0.2 and 0.6 was maximally effective, a ratio of 0.5 was chosen for all subsequent experiments. An irradiance response curve, determined during a period of maximal response (15-21 h from the onset of the 72-h period), showed that the response was strongly irradiance dependent. Half-maximal response was obtained with a FR irradiance of 1.35×10^4 J m^{-2} (0.63 W m^{-2} for 6 h) with saturation occurring between 5 and 8×10^4 J m^{-2}. However, when a similar response curve was determined during a 6 h period of minimal response, the half-maximal response was found to be at 6.6×10^5 J m^{-2} and saturation could not be reached even with 10^6 J m^{-2}. Thus, the difference in the sensitivity of the plant to FR light changes by a factor of 50 fold during the course of the day.

Reciprocity was also tested (Deitzer, unpublished) and found to hold only for periods greater than 6 h. When the irradiance was doubled and the duration reduced to 3 h, the response was not significantly greater than the control. However, when given as pulses during the 6-h period, reciprocity was found to be valid as long as the pulses were

shorter than 2 min (1 min on/1 min off). There was some
indication that very short pulses, in the millisecond range,
were also less effective, but this requires further investigation.

Since 6 h of FR was capable of producing 50% of the response to 72 h of added FR, the possibility was considered that
the plant could integrate more than one 6-h pulse to produce
the full 72-h response. Therefore, one pulse was given for
6 h between hours 15 and 21 and this was followed by a second
6-h pulse at various times thereafter. The two pulses were
found to sum, but the second pulse was now most effective
between the hours 30 and 36 rather than between hours 42 and
48 as had been anticipated. Thus, the addition of FR not only
promotes flowering directly, but also affects the phase of the
time-keeping mechanism that controls the sensitivity of the
plant for such promotion (Deitzer et al., 1982). Whether or
not both can be ascribed to the same mechanism is not known
since there is no spectral information on the phase-shifting
response.

Finally the question of the participation of photosynthesis
in this response was tested utilizing the herbicide, Norflurazon (Jabben and Deitzer, 1978). Plants grown on this herbicide become photobleached as a consequence of the inhibition
of carotenoid synthesis and consequent lack of photoprotection
for chlorophyll (Hilton et al., 1969). While it was possible
to obtain flowering in Hordeum grown on this herbicide (Jabben
and Deitzer, 1979), it is technically very difficult to main-
tain such plants long enough to evaluate flowering. Therefore, the same experiment was carried out with Arabidopsis
thaliana growing in petri dishes in the presence or absence of
the herbicide. As can be seen in Fig. 1, a rhythm in response
to a 6-h addition of FR is evident in both treatments. Both
have the same period and phase, which is the same period and
phase as that reported in Hordeum, but the amplitude is increased by a factor of 2 in the herbicide-treated plants.
This enhancement by the herbicide is not completely understood, but it is thought to involve a FR effect on either the
uptake or the utilization of glucose. Nevertheless, this
provides very strong evidence that neither chlorophyll nor the
light reactions of photosynthesis are required for the photoperception of FR light, even though photosynthate may play a
quantitative role in its expression.

PHYTOCHROME IN LIGHT-GROWN PLANTS

Action spectra for the inhibition of hypocotyl elongation
(Beggs et al., 1980, 1981) by 24 h of continuous monochromatic
light in Sinapis alba seedlings show that both the FR and B

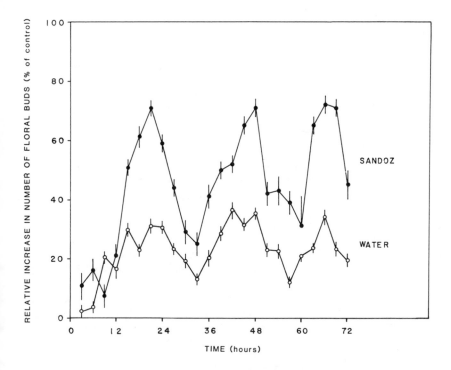

Fig. 1. Effect on flowering in Arabidopsis thaliana *of the addition of 6 h of FR (to establish a R/FR ratio = 0.5) to a continuous background of white fluorescent light (R/FR ratio = 5.6). Plants were grown either on agar alone (water) or on agar with 5 x 10^{-7} M Norflurazon (Sandoz). The points are plotted at the centre of each 6-h period and the error bars indicate the standard errors of the mean for 50 plants. Scale is a per cent response between 72 h of continuous fluorescent (0%) and 72 h of continuous fluorescent supplemented with FR (100%). (Previously unpublished).*

peaks are lost as a consequence of growth for 54 h in white light. A 30–min end–of–day irradiation was also only effective when given to light–grown plants and showed only a single broad peak between 500 and 700 nm with no B or FR activity. Since Hartmann (1966) based his conclusion that the HIR was explicable solely on the basis of phytochrome on the action spectrum for hypocotyl elongation in dark–grown lettuce seedlings, it must be concluded that his explanation is not valid for light–grown plants. Based on these results Jabben and Holmes (1983) have concluded that phytochrome–controlled elongation rates are a function only of the Pfr/Ptot ratio, or the concentration of Pfr, and that the irradiance dependence

arises from competing light and dark reactions. Thus, end-
of-day and continuous-light responses would be mediated by the
same phytochrome mechanism. As evidence for this, 5 min of
light every hour was found to be as effective as continuous
light for the inhibition of elongation in *Sinapis* and the R
light pulses were reversible by FR light. This also suggests
that the Pfr formed by the R light pulses is very stable
during the intervening dark periods. Measurements of the
kinetic behaviour of phytochrome in light-grown plants (cf.
Chapter 2 in this volume) utilizing Norflurazon to remove
chlorophyll (Jabben and Deitzer, 1978) have led to the
conclusion that phytochrome exists as two distinct pools (Heim
et al., 1981). These two pools are characterized by the
stability of their Pfr to destruction. It was found that, in
plants grown in the light, the stable phytochrome predominated
while in etiolated (or re-etiolated) plants, the labile pool
predominated. These pools may be similar to those proposed by
Clarkson and Hillman (1968) as bulk and active pools, except
that both the labile (bulk) and stable (active) pools may be
equally active. The labile pool undergoes rapid destruction
with a half-life of the order of 1 h, while the half-life of
the stable pool is about 5 h in *Amaranthus caudatus*. It is
proposed that the stable pool of phytochrome is physiologically active in light-grown plants.

Dark reversion, which does not occur in monocotyledons,
possibly also does not occur in light-grown dicotyledons
(Jabben, 1980), except after prolonged incubation in the dark,
and following a red-light pulse after several hours in the
dark. This reversion, however, appears to be a property of
the labile phytochrome synthesized during darkness.

CONCLUSION

Both Downs and Thomas (1982) and Jabben and Holmes (1983)
argue that there is no need to invoke an HIR mechanism to
explain the promotion of flowering in LDP by FR daylength
extensions. Both conclude that manipulation of either the
concentration of Pfr or the Pfr/Ptot ratio is all that is
required to explain the response. Downs and Thomas suggest
that there are two sequential phytochrome-mediated events, a
high Pfr-requiring step occurring toward the middle of a
presumptive long dark period that produces initiation,
followed by a low Pfr-requiring step that occurs at the end-
of-day and results in a promotion of floral development.
Light given throughout the dark period would satisfy both if
it were long enough in duration to overlap the two periods of
sensitivity, and if it contained sufficient amounts of both R
and FR to trigger both responses. The former requirement would

explain the failure of reciprocity and the latter would explain the apparent action spectrum peak at 710–720 nm.

Jabben and Holmes, on the other hand, assume only a single high Pfr-requiring response to explain the inhibition of hypocotyl elongation in light–grown seedlings and in their model the irradiance dependence arises from competing light and dark reactions in the stable pool of phytochrome. The action spectrum peak at 710–720 nm in dark-grown seedlings is assumed to be a function of fast Pfr destruction from the labile pool relative to the rate of synthesis. The HIR responses in both light- and dark-grown plants are, therefore, assumed to operate through the stable Pfr pool, and in that sense, the mechanism is the same as that described by Hartmann (1966).

Perhaps one should be somewhat cautious in accepting interpretations of data based on stem extension to explain mechanisms that control floral initiation. This is especially true since the conclusions of Jabben and Holmes (1983) are based on the inhibition of elongation while those of Downs and Thomas (1982) are based on promotion of elongation and the concomitant promotion of flowering. Neither appears to be capable of explaining all of the results in the literature. The critical question that must be answered is why the FR peak at 710–720 nm persists in the action spectrum for floral promotion in light–grown plants. The work reported in Fig. 1 strongly suggests that the reason is not because it is mediated by chlorophyll.

REFERENCES

Beggs, C.J., Geile, W., Holmes, M.G., Jabben, M., Jose, A.M. and Schäfer, E. (1981). *Planta* 151, 135–140

Beggs, C.J., Holmes, M.G., Jabben, M. and Schäfer, E. (1980). *Plant Physiol.* 66, 615–618

Blondon, F. and Jacques, R. (1970). *C.R. Seances Acad. Sci. Ser. D.* 270, 947–950

Borthwick, H.A., Hendricks, S.B. and Parker, M.W. (1948). *Bot. Gaz.* 110, 103–118

Borthwick, H.A., Hendricks, S.B., Schneider, M.J., Taylorson, R.B. and Toole, V.K. (1969). *Proc. Natl. Acad. Sci. USA* 64, 479–486

Clarkson, D.T. and Hillman, W.S. (1968). *Plant Physiol.* 43, 88–92

Cleland, C.F. and Zeevaart, J.A.D. (1970). *Plant Physiol.* 46, 392–400

Deitzer, G.F. (1983) In "Strategies of Plant Reproduction BARC Symposium 6" (ed. W.J. Meudt). pp. 99–115. Allenheld Osmun, Totowa

Deitzer, G.F., Hayes, R. and Jabben, M. (1979). *Plant Physiol.*
    64, 1015–1021
Deitzer, G.F., Hayes, R. and Jabben, M. (1982). *Plant Physiol.*
    69, 597–601
Downs, R.J. (1956). *Plant Physiol.* 31, 279–284
Downs, R.J. and Thomas, J.F. (1982). *Plant Physiol.* 70,
    898–900
El Hattab, A.H. (1968). *Meded. Landbouwhogesch. Wageningen* 68,
    1–111
Evans, L.T. (1971). *Annu. Rev. Plant Physiol.* 22, 365–394
Evans, L.T. (1976). *Aust. J. Plant Physiol.* 3, 207–217
Evans, L.T., Borthwick, H.A. and Hendricks, S.B. (1965). *Aust.
    J. Biol. Sci.* 18, 745–762
Harris, G.P. (1968). *Ann. Bot. (Lond.)* 32, 187–197
Harris, G.P. (1972). *Ann. Bot. (Lond.)* 36, 345–352
Hartmann, K.M. (1966). *Photochem. Photobiol.* 5, 349–366
Heim, B., Jabben, M. and Schäfer, E. (1981). *Photochem.
    Photobiol.* 34, 89–93
Hilton, J.L., Scharen, A.L., St. John, J.B., Moreland, D.E.
    and Norris, K.H. (1969). *Weed Sci.* 17, 541–547
Holland, R.W.K. and Vince, D. (1971). *Planta* 98, 232–243
Imhoff, C., Brulfert, J. and Jacques, R. (1971). *C.R. Seances
    Acad. Sci. Ser. D.* 273, 637–740
Imhoff, C.H., Lecharny, A., Jacques, R. and Brulfert, J.
    (1979). *Plant Cell Environ.* 2, 67–72
Ishiguri, Y. and Oda, Y. (1972). *Plant Cell Physiol.* 13,
    131–138
Jabben, M. (1980). *Planta* 149, 91–96
Jabben, M. and Deitzer, G.F. (1978). *Photochem. Photobiol.*
    27, 799–802
Jabben, M. and Deitzer, G.F. (1979). *Ber. Dtsch. Bot. Ges.*
    92, 575–584
Jabben, M. and Holmes, M.G. (1983). *In* "Encyclopedia of Plant
    Physiology" (eds W. Shropshire, Jr. and H. Mohr). New
    Series, Vol. 27. pp. 704–722. Springer–Verlag, Heidelberg
Jacques, M. and Jacques, R. (1969). *C. R. Seances Acad. Sci.
    Ser. D.* 269, 2107–2109
Jones, M.G. and Zeevaart, J.A.D. (1980). *Planta* 149, 269–273
Kasperbauer, M.J., Borthwick, H.A. and Hendricks, S.B. (1963).
    Bot. Gaz. 124, 444–451
Lane, H.C., Cathey, H.M. and Evans, L.T. (1965). *Am. J. Bot.*
    52, 1006–1014
Mancinelli, A.L. and Rabino, I. (1975). *Plant Physiol.* 56,
    351–355
Mancinelli, A.L. and Rabino, I. (1978). *Bot. Rev.* 44, 129–180
Parker, M.W., Hendricks, S.B. and Borthwick H.A. (1950). *Bot.
    Gaz.* 111, 242–252
Schäfer,E. (1975). *J. Math. Biol.* 2, 41–56

Schneider, M.J. Borthwick, H.A. and Hendricks, S.B. (1967). *Am. J. Bot.* 54, 1241–1249

Schneider, M.J. and Stimson, W.R. (1971). *Plant Physiol.* 48, 312–315

Schneider, M.J. and Stimson, W.R. (1972). *Proc. Natl. Acad. Sci. USA.* 69, 2150–2154

Stolwijk, J.A.J. and Zeevaart, J.A.D. (1955). *Verh. K. Ned. Akad. Wet.* 58, 386–396

Vince, D. (1965). *Physiol. Plant.* 18, 474–482

Vince, D. (1966). *Photochem. Photobiol.* 5, 449–50

Vince-Prue, D. (1975). "Photoperiodism in Plants". McGraw Hill, London

Vince-Prue, D. (1979). *In* "La Physiologie de la Floraison" (eds P. Champagnat and R. Jacques). pp. 91–127. CNRS, Paris

Chapter 5

LIGHT AND AUTONOMOUS INDUCTION

ABRAHAM H. HALEVY

Department of Ornamental Horticulture,
The Hebrew University of Jerusalem, Rehovot, Israel.

In plants having autonomous induction (self-inductive plants),
flower initiation and development occur without any requirement for a specific photoperiod or temperature. Some may
produce flowers continuously if conditions are suitable for
growth (e.g., rose), others however, show distinct periodicity, initiating flowers and flowering at specific seasons
(e.g., apples, citrus).

Some self-inductive plants produce flowers only at certain
meristems, while continuing to produce vegetative growth at
others (e.g., most trees, apple, orange). In other plants,
flowers are initiated autonomously on every growing shoot
after a certain size is attained (e.g., rose, carnation,
paeony). In the first group, light and other environmental
factors may affect both flower initiation and development
while in the second group, the effect is usually only on
flower development (or the prevention of flower bud abortion).

High irradiances are associated with increased flower
production in most self-inductive plants. In many species,
flowers are produced mainly on exposed plants or branches,
while those branches that are shaded or are below the leaf
canopy remain vegetative. Horticulturists have been well
aware of this fact for centuries and developed growing and
pruning techniques which best utilize light energy and increase flower and fruit production. This light effect has
been attributed in most cases to the level of photosynthesis
and, thus, to the availability of assimilates for growth and
development (Jackson and Sweet, 1972).

Two interesting cases of the effect of light on sex ex-

pression of plants may illustrate this effect. Jack-in-the-
pulpit (*Arisaema triphyllum*, Araceae), is a perennial herbaceous plant which usually produces a single annual shoot
from an overwintering corm. *Arisaema* individuals do not have
genetically fixed genders but have the ability to change sex
in successive years (Bierzychudek, 1982). In a given year a
plant may produce either a vegetative shoot, a male inflorescence or a female one. In locations with high light and in
soil high in nutrients, mainly female individuals are found.
Staminate individuals are concentrated in shaded areas, and
vegetative plants in even darker places (Lovett-Doust and
Cavers, 1982; Meeuse, 1984). After a series of experiments,
which included trimming of leaves and changing the growing
conditions of individual plants, it was concluded that all
factors that increase biomass production favour femaleness.
Indeed it was found that the plant's decision for the next
year is based on the size of the corm. Large corms will
produce female plants, smaller ones will produce male plants,
and the smallest will remain vegetative.

The adaptive value of the sex-changing behaviour in
Arisaema seems to be based on the cost of reproduction. The
female plant spends large amounts of energy and nutrients in
producing the flowers, fruits and seeds which account for 44%
of the total dry weight of the plant. Male individuals
produce only flowers which account for about 12% of the total
weight, while sterile plants conserve all their available
resources for the next season. This species behaves, therefore, as though flowering and the pattern of floral composition are a function of resource allocation.

In several species of *Catasetum* and *Cycnoches* orchids,
female flowers occur in open sites and male in more shaded
areas. It has been shown by Gregg (1978) that the sex of
these orchids is a function of light intensity and the size of
the pseudobulb. Plants with large pseudobulbs are female,
those with smaller ones are male and the smallest are
vegetative. The effects of these two factors are additive and
exposure of plants with large pseudobulbs to full sunlight
results in production of the highest percentage of female
flowers. Transitional flowers and racemes were obtained, when
the plants were removed from sun to shade or vice versa when
the racemes were 2–3 cm long. It seems, however, that the
effect is not simply mediated through the level of photosynthesis and accumulation of metabolites, since capping only
the racemes with aluminium foil in sun-grown plants of
Catasetum expansum, promoted the production of male rather
than female flowers by these plants (Gregg, 1975). This
observation also indicates that perception of the light
stimulus by the racemes themselves is necessary.

Flower bud abortion (blasting) is a common phenomenon in winter-forced greenhouse irises. It usually occurs at the stage of greatest stem elongation, showing cessation of flower bud growth first, followed by atrophy. The iris, unlike tulip, hyacinth or daffodil, has insufficient storage reserves in the bulb to support flower development to anthesis and current photosynthesis at later stages is very important (Fortanier and van Zevenbergen, 1973). Insufficient light is a major cause of this problem. However, by reducing the CO_2 level in the atmosphere under high light it was demonstrated (Mae and Vonk, 1974; Vonk and Ribot, 1982) that, apart from the non-specific effect of light, there is also a specific effect on promotion of flower development which is independent of photosynthesis. Likewise, darkening for 7 days at the sensitive stage, drastically reduced translocation of both ^{14}C and ^{32}P to the flower buds indicating a specific effect of light on the allocation of metabolites. These results support the nutrient diversion hypothesis of flower development (Sachs, 1977).

Further support for the nutrient diversion hypothesis has been obtained from experiments with roses. Bush roses initiate terminal flowers autonomously on every growing shoot after a certain number of nodes are produced. A pre-condition for flower initiation is, of course, the release of the lateral buds from correlative inhibition; an inhibition which is mainly due to apical dominance (Zieslin and Halevy, 1976; Cockshull and Horridge, 1977). The initiated flower buds may then continue their development to anthesis or abort. Light affects these two processes of flower formation.

Light is an absolute requirement for sprouting of buds located at the base of the plant (renewal cane). Sprouting of axillary buds located at the lower part of individual branches is also promoted by light (Khayat and Zieslin, 1982), even when correlative inhibition is abolished by decapitating the branch above the buds and removing the subtending leaf. Upper buds, which are much less inhibited (Zieslin, et al., 1976), may sprout following decapitation even in darkness. However, the sprouting of intact lateral buds below the flower is suppressed by the natural shade of the canopy. The R : FR ratio at the canopy level where these buds are located, affects their breaking ability for higher ratios of R : FR (0.8 and up) enhance sprouting (Mor and Halevy, 1984).

It is well known that flower production of roses is enhanced by high irradiances. Low irradiances cause an increase in the incidence of flower bud atrophy and the production of blind shoots (Zieslin and Halevy, 1975). These responses have generally been attributed to the effect of light on photosynthesis and the availability of assimilates for flower bud development but, when only one young shoot or its tip was darkened while the rest of the plant was held in full light, flower bud abortion was still promoted in the darkened shoot (Zieslin and Halevy, 1975; Mor and Halevy, 1980). We have demonstrated that the young shoots are totally dependent on translocation of metabolites from mature leaves (Mor and Halevy, 1979). Darkening of only the young tip greatly reduced the amount of ^{14}C assimilates translocated to the tip, so promoting the degeneration and death of the young flower bud. Darkening the tip also enhanced the ability of the young developing leaves to compete with the flower bud for the available assimilates.

When monochromatic light was given directly to the tip of a darkened shoot, by means of optical fibres, translocation of ^{14}C-labelled assimilates to the tip was greatly enhanced and flower abortion was prevented (Mor et al., 1980). Thus light greatly affects the sink activity of the flower bud and photoperception occurs in the shoot tip itself. Enhancement of the mobilizing ability of the shoot tip by light is independent of photosynthesis, since holding shoots in light in CO_2-free air or spraying them with inhibitors of photosynthesis did not diminish the promoting effect of light on the import of assimilates and flower bud development.

The light reaction that promotes the sink activity of the flower bud has some characteristics of the high irradiance reaction of photomorphogenesis. It requires continuous illumination and red (R) light is more effective than far-red

TABLE 1. *Effect of monochromatic, low-energy light given to darkened shoot tips of rose on translocation of ^{14}C-labelled assimilates to the shoot tip. Light was applied intermittently by means of optical fibres for 48 h. Translocation is expressed as the relative specific activity (RSA), which is calculated as % radioactivity recovered in the shoot tip (of the total that left the source leaf) divided by the dry weight of the tip as % of the total dry weight of the plant. (From Mor et al., 1980).*

Light treatment to shoot	Irradiance $W\ m^{-2}$	RSA
Full light control	45	14.5
Dark control	0	4.4
R, 660 nm	2	38.2
FR, 728 nm	1.5	11.1
B, 455 nm	0.3	7.9

(FR) or blue (B) (Table 1). However, the augmentation of R with FR to a ratio of about 1:1 enhances the effect of R. Similar characteristics of the light reaction were observed in experiments in which light enhanced ^{14}C-sucrose uptake by isolated buds grown *in vitro*.

The results with roses clearly demonstrate a specific effect of light on the allocation of assimilates to flower buds. The importance of metabolite diversion for flower development is strengthened by experiments with growth substances. In both iris (Vonk and Ribot, 1982) and rose (Mor *et al.*, 1980), as well as in tomato (Leonard *et al.*, *1983*) the application of cytokinins or gibberellins to the flower buds promoted their development and the preferential transport of ^{14}C assimilates to them, thus overcoming the deleterious effects of insufficient light.

In gladiolus, flowers are always initiated after a certain number of foliage leaves (usually 8-9 leaves in *G. grandiflora*) have been formed. A blind mature gladiolus plant is thus not a vegetative plant but a plant in which the flower bud has aborted, or more often withered - a phenomenon called blasting. Failure to flower and a reduction in the number of florets per spike are common in winter-grown gladiolus for both reduced light intensity and short days induce flower blasting (Shillo and Halevy, 1976a, b). The effect of these factors depends upon the stage of development of the inflorescence. During early stages of development, the entire inflorescence is affected and low light causes atrophy of the entire flowering stem; later on, when all florets have been initiated, only individual florets are affected.

A specific effect of photoperiod on flowering of gladiolus has also been reported. It was generally found that flowering was somewhat advanced by SD, but that percentage flowering, the length of the spike and the number of florets per spike were decreased by SD (Shillo *et al.*, 1981). Low intensity light (100 lx; incandescent lamps) applied as a night-break delayed flowering by a few days, but greatly reduced the incidence of blindness and increased the number of florets. It was initially suggested that LD promoted flower development indirectly; by delaying flowering, the number of days the plants were exposed to light at the sensitive stages of development was increased and thus the total light energy intercepted by the plant was also increased (Shillo and Halevy, 1976c). It was later found, however, that flowering time was not affected by LD in some cultivars and yet flowering percentage and quality were greatly promoted. This indicated a specific photoperiodic effect on flower development, independent of the effect of light integral (Shillo *et al.*, 1981).

A study of the changes in fresh and dry weights of the

various organs revealed that SD accelerated flower development
and advanced anthesis but reduced the final size of the
flowers, while LD increased the weight and size of leaves and
flowers (Shillo and Halevy, 1981). Initial growth of the corm
was similar under both photoperiods but, while corm growth
continued throughout the growing period under SD, it was
checked under LD when flowers developed at an enhanced rate,
and did not resume growth until after anthesis (Fig. 1). At

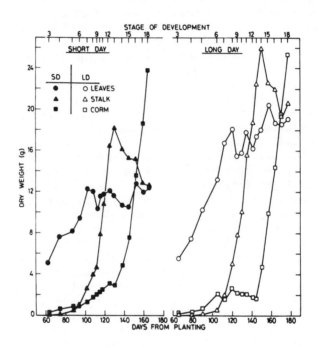

*Fig. 1. The effect of photoperiod on dry weight of leaves,
flower stalk and corms of gladiolus cv Spic and Span, at
various dates after planting and at various stages of development. (Stages 1 to 8 - one to eight expanded foliage leaves,
9 - spike emergence, 10, 11 - spike extension and growth, 13 -
half the florets open (anthesis), 15 - wilting of last floret)
(Shillo and Halevy, 1981).*

the stage of accelerated flower development in LD, the allocation of assimilates was directed towards the flower and away
from the corm (Fig. 2).

By following the distribution of ^{14}C-labelled assimilates

it was established that there are two competing sinks in the
developing gladiolus, the inflorescence and the new corms
(Robinson et al., 1980). The relative strength of the two
sinks varies with development. The young inflorescence is a
very weak sink which becomes increasingly stronger until
flowering, after which its strength declines. Photoperiod
directly affects the distribution of assimilates between these
two sinks by increasing the strength of the flower sink in LD
and that of the corm sink in SD. It was found that SD also
promoted corm development in the absence of flowers in vegetative plants raised from cormels (Shillo and Halevy, 1981).

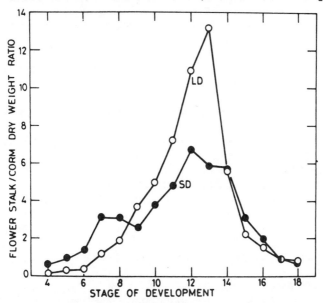

*Fig. 2. The effect of photoperiod on distribution of dry
matter between the flower stalk and corm of gladiolus cv Spic
and Span at various stages of development. Results are expressed as the ratio of dry weight of the flower stalk to the
corm at each development stage (see legend to Fig. 1) (Shillo
and Halevy, 1981).*

This may indicate that SD specifically promote corm growth,
thus increasing the competition for assimilates between the
flower and the corm. This process may further enhance flower
blasting when photosynthates are in limited supply. Thus, it
is clear that although gladiolus is a day-neutral plant for
flowering, photoperiod has a pronounced effect on flower
development by affecting the partitioning of assimilates
between the flower and the corm. A similar effect of photoperiod on corm and flower formation has been found for

Ranunculus asiaticus (van de Pol and Stroet, unpublished).
The promotive effect of light on ^{14}C-sucrose uptake by isolated rose buds *in vitro* has been mentioned above (Mor *et al.*,
1980). Recently it was reported that light has a direct
effect on *de novo* flower initiation *in vitro* from thin layers
of tobacco cells, by promoting the uptake and utilization of
sucrose (Cousson and Tran Thanh Van, 1983).

It seems, therefore, that there is a triple effect of light
on flowering in autonomously induced plants; a general non-
specific effect on photosynthesis and on the availability of
assimilates, a specific effect on directing the available
metabolites towards the flower sink, and an activation of
inhibited meristems that may later produce flower buds.

REFERENCES

Bierzychudek, K. (1982). *Ecol. Monogr.* 52(4), 335–351
Cockshull, K.E. and Horridge, J.S. (1977). *J. Hortic. Sci.*
    52, 421–427
Cousson, A. and Tran Thanh Van, K. (1983). *Plant Physiol.* 72,
    33–36
Fortanier, E.J. and van Zevenbergen, A. (1973). *Neth. J.*
    Agric. Sci. 21, 145–162
Gregg, K.B. (1975). *Selbyana* 1, 101–113
Gregg, K.B. (1978). *Selbyana* 2, 212–223
Jackson, D.I. and Sweet, G.B. (1972). *Hortic. Abst.* 42, 9–24
Khayat, E. and Zieslin, N. (1982). *J. Exp. Bot.* 33, 1286–1292
Leonard, M., Kinet, J.M., Bodson, M. and Bernier, G. (1983).
    Physiol. Plant. 58, 85–89
Lovett-Doust, J.L. and Cavers, P.B. (1982). *Ecology* 63,
    797–808
Mae, T. and Vonk, C.R. (1974). *Acta Bot. Neerl.* 23, 321–331
Meeuse, B.J.D. (1984). *In* "Handbook of Flowering" (ed. A.H.
    Halevy). Vol. 1, CRC Press, Boca Raton, Florida, USA (In
    press)
Mor, Y. and Halevy, A.H. (1979). *Physiol. Plant.* 45, 117–182
Mor, Y. and Halevy, A.H. (1980). *Plant Physiol.* 66, 990–995
Mor, Y. and Halevy, A.H. (1984). *Physiol. Plant.* (In press)
Mor, Y., Halevy, A.H. and Porath, D. (1980). *Plant Physiol.*
    66, 996–1000
Robinson, M., Harav, I., Halevy, A.H. and Plaut, L. (1980).
    Ann. Bot. (Lond.) 45, 113–122
Sachs, R.M. (1977). *HortScience* 12, 220–222
Shillo, R. and Halevy, A.H. (1976a). *Sci. Hortic. (Amst.)* 4,
    131–137
Shillo, R. and Halevy, A.H. (1976b). *Sci. Hortic. (Amst.)* 4,
    139–146
Shillo, R. and Halevy, A.H. (1976c). *Sci. Hortic. (Amst.)* 4,
    154–162

Shillo, R. and Halevy, A.H. (1981). *Sci. Hortic. (Amst.)* 15, 187–196

Shillo, R., Valis, G. and Halevy, A.H. (1981). *Sci. Hortic. (Amst.)* 14, 367–375

Vonk, C.R. and Ribot, S.A. (1982). *Plant Growth Reg.* 1, 93–105

Zieslin, N. and Halevy, A.H. (1975). *Sci. Hortic. (Amst.)* 3, 383–391

Zieslin, N. and Halevy, A.H. (1976). *Bot. Gaz.* 137, 291–296

Zieslin, N., Haaze, H. and Halevy, A.H. (1976). *Bot. Gaz.* 137, 297–300

Chapter 6

LIGHT AND VERNALIZATION

K. NAPP—ZINN

*Botanisches Institut, Universität zu Köln,
Gyrhofstrasse 15, D-5000 Köln 41, W. Germany.*

INTRODUCTION: A THEORY OF PHASIC DEVELOPMENT

Fifty years ago the matter seemed quite simple: according to
Lysenko's theory of phasic development every plant, with
regard to flowering, should irreversibly pass first through a
temperature—sensitive phase (thermophase) and then a light
sensitive phase (photophase). After certain experiments, particularly with winter wheats, Lysenko (1932a, b, 1934, 1936,
1951) concluded "the photophase cannot start before or during
the thermophase. The plant can only pass the photophase after
it has accomplished the thermophase" (Lysenko, 1951: p.52).
  Since then things have become much more complicated, and
even Lysenko himself seems to have lost confidence in his own
theory. [In his report of meetings with Lysenko, Mathon
(1977: p.15), mentions a conversation in summer 1959 during
which Lysenko declared three times "I am not convinced (sure)
myself that the phases exist".] Today we know that there are
only a few plants which behave exactly in the manner that
Lysenko proposed. The most important example of this kind is
the biennial henbane (*Hyoscyamus niger*) originally introduced
into the physiology of flowering by Correns (1903, 1904) and
subsequently studied exhaustively by Melchers, Lang, and their
collaborators. Biennial henbane is ready for vernalization
[vernalization is understood here as the induction of ripeness
to flower by temperatures below the optimum for growth] only
after a juvenile phase of 10 days (Sarkar, 1958) and can be
induced by LD only after at least 7 days of vernalization
(Lang, 1951). It is interesting to note that Lysenko never
considered this plant that obeys his theory so nicely.

LIGHT AND THE FLOWERING PROCESS
ISBN 0.12.721960.9

LIGHT AND VERNALIZATION IN COLD-REQUIRING PLANTS

Cold-requiring plants show a large spectrum of interactions between light and cold treatments. Earlier observations on this subject have been summarised by Chouard (1960), Napp-Zin (1961a, 1973), Purvis (1961), Lang (1965), and Picard (1968) among others. The scarcity of information in those reviews seems to have had a stimulating effect. Since then, more tha 100 papers have been published in this field and it is not possible to review them all. Instead I shall here try to distinguish several types of interaction and to illustrate them by examples. Let us first consider the replacement of vernalization by light treatments.

Light Instead of Vernalization

Daylength - short day vernalization. Short-day vernalization (i.e. the induction of ripeness to flower by SD instead of cold) has been discussed since the 1930's. For two decades Petkus winter rye (e.g. Purvis and Gregory 1937), was the focus of discussion. Later, Gott, Gregory and Purvis (1955) showed that continuous light was more effective than SD, but in the experiments of Hartman (1964, 1966) 2 weeks of SD at 1(or 25 °C, given to 10-16 day old seedlings, accelerated development towards flowering more than did continuous light. Krekule (1964) also observed SD vernalization in some winter wheat varieties, and Mokhtare and Limberg (1977) did so in Iranian winter barleys.

Wellensiek (1953) was apparently the first to discover a similar phenomenon in a dicotyledon, namely *Campanula medium*. Other examples of this kind are *Scabiosa succisa* (= *Succisa pratensis;* Chouard, 1957), *Symphyandra hofmanni* (Mathon, 1960b), *Salvia pratensis* (Listowski, 1965a) and *Coreopsis grandiflora* (Ketellapper and Barbaro, 1966).

For reasons which cannot be discussed here in detail, Wellensiek (1953) and Hartman (1964) concluded that verna-lization by cold and by SD concerned different processes. In none of the examples quoted was it shown (e.g. by giving night breaks) that flowering was accelerated specifically by SD. In many other cases SD vernalization was unsuccessful, e.g. in winter rye (Listowski, 1958; Listowski and Jeśmianowicz, 1959), many varieties of winter wheat (Gott, 1961; Krekule, 1964), *Arabidopsis thaliana* (Laibach, 1951), and *Oenothera biennis* var. sulfurea (Picard, 1965).

Daylength - long-day vernalization. In several other plants LD (or continuous light) and vernalization may substitute for each other, e.g. *Scabiosa columbaria, Campanula longestyla,* and *C. caespitosa* (Mathon, 1960a, b), and *Chondrilla juncea* (Cuthbertson, 1966). This type of response is best represented by certain late flowering genotypes of *Pisum sativum* containing the gene *Sn* (Barber, 1959; Wellensiek, 1969; Murfet and Reid, 1974; Reid and Murfet, 1975, 1977; Murfet, 1977; Berry and Aitken, 1979; Reid, 1981). Other Papilionaceae behave in more or less the same way, e.g. *Lupinus luteus* (Rahman and Gladstones, 1972), several *Medicago* species, particularly *M. rugosa* (Clarkson and Russell, 1975), and some grasses such as *Festuca arundinacea* (Blondon, 1972).

By means of SD and night interruptions, Wellensiek (1981) showed that the replacement of vernalization by LD (at least in *Silene armeria*) was a photoperiod effect, and not simply a response to light quantity. Although Barber (1959) and Murfet (1977) both concluded "that vernalization and long days act in a competitive manner" in pea, Barber suggested that both factors destroyed a flower inhibitor produced by *Sn*, while Murfet proposed that both factors led to suppression of *Sn* activity which results in inhibitor formation.

Light quality. There is little information on the most favourable wavelengths of light for replacing vernalization. In the case of *Sn* peas, Reid and Murfet (1977) observed two contrasting reactions. When supplementary light was given as an extension of 16 h photoperiods, far-red light proved more effective than red light. If, however, short photoperiods were supplemented by night interruptions, red (2 h) was more efficient than far-red. They concluded "that there are two light-dependent reactions..., one operating through the phytochrome system with high levels of Pfr suppressing production of flower inhibitor by the *Sn* gene and a second requiring continuous illumination with wavelengths above 700 nm". The latter also seems true for *Blitum capitatum*, where Lona and Faccini (1976) succeeded in overcoming the vernalization requirement by giving photoperiods of 8 h fluorescent light + 16 h far-red light (>700 nm). An observation by Pavlov (1958) that red was better than blue light in a winter wheat is only of historical interest now.

Irradiance. The role of irradiance of light in substituting for vernalization was studied in particular by Chouard and co-workers at Gif-sur-Yvette (France). *Geum urbanum* (Chouard and Tran Than Van, 1964) and cold-requiring clones of *Dactylis glomerata* (Blondon and Chouard, 1965; Blondon, 1966) and *Festuca arundinacea* (Blondon, 1970, 1971, 1972) flowered without cold when they were given either LD (*Dactylis*) or continuous light (*Festuca*) at high irradiances, mostly above 14,000 lx. It is probable that the role of light in photosynthesis

is concerned here, as supported by the observation that rich
mineral nutrition is necessary at the same time. Inouye and
Ito (1968) and Adachi *et al.* (1970) grew a total of four
Japanese cultivars of naked winter barley (*Hordeum vulgare*
var. nudum) on artificial medium containing sucrose and
mineral salts. Under these conditions vernalization could be
replaced by darkness even at temperatures up to 30°C, again
underlining the importance of nutritional factors.

THE INTERACTION OF VERNALIZATION WITH LIGHT

The following sections deal with the interaction of vernalization and the light conditions before, during, and after a
cold treatment. Many plants from temperate zones, for which
vernalization is favourable, react most rapidly to a cold
treatment if SD prevails prior to and LD subsequent to vernalization (Blondon and Chouard, 1965). This imitates the
seasonal variations in temperature and daylength in their
original countries.

Light Before Plant Vernalization

Photoperiod. With regard to their reactions to the photoperiod prevailing before a cold exposure, vernalizable plants
may be divided into several groups. Those of the first group
prefer SD before vernalization, as expected. Members of this
group are *Rumex obtusifolius* (Listowski and Jackowska, 1964;
Listowski, 1964, 1966a) [strictly speaking, the best combination for *Rumex obtusifolius* is LD − SD − vernalization − SD
− LD], *Salvia pratensis* (Listowski, 1965a), and *Trifolium
arvense* (Listowski, 1966b). In such cases LD or continuous
light may cause inhibition of flowering that can be overcome
by a subsequent cold treatment. In contrast, flowering of the
members of a second group is enhanced by LD or continuous
light before vernalization (as compared with SD); this is true
for *Symphyandra hofmanni* (Mathon, 1960b), *Oenothera biennis*
var. sulfurea (Picard, 1965), *Potentilla supina* (Listowski,
1965b), *Cardamine pratensis* (Pierik, 1967b), and certain
winter wheats such as cv Odesskaya 16 and Bezostaya 1 (Babenkc
et al., 1974). Pierik (1967a), in contrast to earlier
authors, could not find any influence of pre−vernalization
daylength on the flowering of *Lunaria annua*.

Quality. Apparently, nothing has been published so far about
the role of light quality given before vernalization. The
results of experiments with *Arabidopsis thaliana* (strain
Stockholm) and various types of Philips coloured fluorescent
lamps indicate that previous light quality has little if any

importance (Napp–Zinn, unpublished data).

Irradiance. Varying the relative light levels between 25% and 100% of the maximum irradiance during the six last weeks before vernalization did not influence the effect of the cold treatment in *Lunaria annua* (Pierik 1967a). But in similar experiments with *Cardamine pratensis* by the same author (1967b), 100% relative light level furthered flowering most, and 25% least. A third cruciferous plant behaves in just the opposite way. For the winter–annual strain Stockholm of *Arabidopsis thaliana*, low light between sowing and 40 days of vernalization at $2^{\circ}C$ proved significantly more favourable than a three–fold higher irradiance (Napp–Zinn, 1960b).

Light During Vernalization

Photoperiod. During the last two decades several further examples have been added to the contradictory observations summarised earlier (Napp–Zinn, 1961a). Vernalization of the winter wheat *Hodoninska holice* for 35 days (with the remainders of the caryopses removed) was more efficient when combined with 16 h LD (than with 8 h SD). Vernalization in darkness was ineffective, but light could be substituted for by sucrose, perhaps indicating a nutritional role for light (Krekule, 1961). Hartmann (1968) did similar experiments with seven other varieties of winter wheat (but without removal of the rest of the caryopses). With vernalization for 69 days, it did not matter whether LD or SD were given during the cold treatment, but with 34 days of cold 8 h SD were better than 16 h LD in the case of the three or four latest varieties. With the winter wheat varieties Odesskaya 16 and Bezostaya 1, continuous light during vernalization shortened the time until readiness for reproduction by up to 25 days compared with darkness (Babenko *et al.*, 1974).

LD, SD + night breaks, or continuous light during the cold treatment may reduce the vernalization effect in several dicotyledons (e.g., celery, Pressman and Negbi, 1980, and increase it in others. The latter is true for strains of *Pisum sativum* containing the *Sn* gene (Murfet and Reid, 1974) and for several strains of *Arabidopsis thaliana* (Napp–Zinn, 1960a, b). The *Arabidopsis* strain Stockholm shows effects of the pre–vernalization light intensity only after plant vernalization in the light (Napp–Zinn, 1960b). This means that the favourable effect of low light intensity before vernalization is annulled by darkness during the cold treatment. *Oenothera biennis* var. sulfurea, would die under these conditions within 2 weeks, but whether LD or SD prevails during vernalization does not matter in this species (Picard, 1965).

Light quality. In *Cardamine pratensis*, a slight promotion of flowering by LD during cold treatment could only be observed when incandescent light was used. Under fluorescent light, subsequent flowering was not influenced by daylength (Pierik, 1967b). In *Lunaria annua*, daylength and lamp types during vernalization did not matter at all (Pierik, 1967a).

Irradiance. In experiments with *Lunaria annua* and *Cardamine pratensis*, Pierik (1967a, b) varied the irradiance between 4.1 and 18 W m^{-2} during vernalization for 8 weeks. In *Lunaria*, 40–50% of those plants which were 8–weeks old at the start of the cold treatment flowered irrespective of irradiance, while none of those which were 7–weeks old did so. In *Cardamine*, the results depended upon plant age: no 10–week old plants flowered after vernalization at 4.1 W m^{-2}, but all did so after vernalization at 18 W m^{-2}; at 38 weeks the difference was much smaller.

Light After Vernalization

Photoperiod. It has long been known that the manifestation of vernalization effects under various photoperiods depends upon the specific daylength requirements for flower initiation in the plants concerned. Most are LDP (Wellensiek, 1970), some are DNP or SDP. Before entering into details, I should like to stress that vernalization requirements and photoperiodic requirements may be governed, at least in certain cases, by different genes. This was shown, for example, by experiments of Keim *et al.*, (1973) who crossed two LD requiring winter wheats (cv. Lancer and Warrior) with a day–neutral summer wheat (Sonora 64). The photoperiodic responses of vernalized plants may, therefore, be more or less fortuitous.

Photoperiod - long-day plants. Among LDP several subtypes may be distinguished. Plants of the first subtype flower only under LD conditions, including continuous light. Those of a second subtype <u>prefer</u> a brief SD exposure between vernalization and LD conditions; while those of the third subtype flower earliest under LD, but eventually show the greatest relative vernalization effect under SD. In other words, even at higher post–vernalization temperatures, the critical daylength is decreased as an after–effect of vernalization. There are, of course, still transitional subtypes and practically all subtypes are represented among the 32 legume species studied by de Ruiter and Taylor (1979). After 21 days of vernalization at 3°C, six of 14 *Trifolium* species, two of three *Lotus* species, three of five *Vicia* species and *Ornithopus sativus* did not flower under 8 h SD, but many others

(e.g. all the *Medicago* species) did. Some flowered earlier
under SD than without vernalization, and vice versa.
   Among those plants with an absolute LD requirement are the
sugar-beet, cv Kleinwanzleben E (Margara, 1960), and many of
the winter wheat varieties studied by Balkova (1973). [Aston-
ishingly, in these experiments many cultivars needed longer
vernalization when subsequently kept under CL than under 14-16
h LD.] Other plants show a quantitative LD requirement and
are also able to flower under SD after longer vernalization,
although later. This is true for some winter wheat varieties
(Balkova 1973), *Lunaria annua* (Pierik, 1967a), the winter-
annual *Arabidopsis* strain Stockholm (Chintraruck and
Ketellapper, 1969), late pea genotypes (Wellensiek, 1973),
Calceolaria x *herbeohybrida* (Rünger, 1978), and *Apium
graveolens* var. dulce cv Florida (Pressman and Negbi, 1980).
Rünger showed that photoperiodism really is involved in
Calceolaria, for SD + night breaks were similar to LD in their
effect. On the other hand, in *Arabidopsis* it seems to be
simply a question of light quantity. This is seen in its
response to varying light intensity under LD conditions after
seed vernalization (Chintraruck and Ketellapper, 1969).
   LDP which respond favourably when some SD are intercalated
between vernalization and LD exposure include the winter wheat
Hodoninska holice (Krekule, 1961) [Hartmann's (1968) experiments with the winter wheat Fanal are not conclusive in this
respect, as SD were combined with the cool temperatures of
March and April in the open.], *Hordeum bulbosum* (Ofir and
Koller, 1974), the Argentine winter rye Remeco (Sivori and
Gimenez, 1981), and *Rumex obtusifolius* (Listowski, 1964,
1966a).
   Some LDP whose critical daylength decreases as the cold
treatment is prolonged are several winter wheats (Babenko *et
al*., 1971; Balkova, 1973), *Potentilla supina* (Listowski,
1965b), *Chondrilla juncea* (Cuthbertson, 1966), and a strain of
Scabiosa columbaria (Ballet *et al*., 1962).

Photoperiod - day neutral plants. Plants which flower at the
same time after vernalization irrespective of the prevailing
daylength include *Cardamine pratensis* (Pierik, 1967b), *Apium
graveolens* cv Prazsky obrovsky (Hanisova and Krekule, 1975),
and certain chrysanthemum varieties (Mason, 1957).

Photoperiod - short day plants. Many other chrysanthemum
varieties behave as SDP after vernalization (Mason, 1957).

Light quality. There seems to be hardly any information about
light quality after vernalization. I am only aware of my own
purely orientating trials with the winter-annual strain Stock-

holm of *Arabidopsis thaliana* under Philips coloured fluorescent tubes (550 W m^{-2}) which have already been referred to
briefly (Napp-Zinn, 1969). After seed or plant vernalization
for 26–81 days, plants usually flowered earliest when white
light was given after vernalization and latest under red
light. Blue and green lamps gave intermediate results. To
some extent vernalization compensated for unfavourable light
quality, irrespective of the plant age at the beginning of the
cold treatment.

Irradiance. There are several reports of effects of light
irradiance after vernalization. Higher irradiances favour the
manifestation of the vernalization response, particularly
after incomplete vernalization, in the winter-annual *Arabidopsis* strain Stockholm (Napp-Zinn, 1960b) and *Cardamine
pratensis* (Pierik, 1967b), but not in *Lunaria annua* (Pierik,
1967a). Some observations on iris cv Wedgwood (Sano, 1975)
and wheat (Jones *et al*., 1975) led to the conclusion that, it
is the nutritional role of light (i.e., photosynthesis) that
is important.

Light and the Stabilization of the Vernalized Condition

Light and darkness during cold and heat treatments. The most
detailed experiments have probably been done with the winter-
annual *Arabidopsis* strain Stockholm, where the results may be
summarized as follows: with seed vernalization, light promotes
stabilization and prevents de-vernalization whether applied
during the cold exposure, the heat treatment or during an
intercalated neutral treatment at 20°C (Napp-Zinn, 1960a;
Chintraruck and Ketellapper, 1969). During a heat treatment,
LD is more stabilizing than SD in *Arabidopsis* (Bose, 1974). In
henbane, complete devernalization by heat is also possible
under SD (Lang and Melchers, 1947): devernalization in LD was
not tried for this species. Increasing duration of preculture
under light may also stabilize plant vernalization in *Arabidopsis* and plants older than 35 days at the beginning of the
cold exposure can no longer be devernalized. In many
respects, *Lactuca serriola* behaves similarly: devernalization
is only possible after fruit vernalization and only in the
absence of light (Marks and Prince, 1979). The question has
been raised, whether stabilization by light has anything to do
with photoperiodic induction. According to Devay (1967)
phytochrome, in winter wheat, is only synthesized during
vernalization, and destroyed by devernalization.

Devernalization by short-day and by low irradiance. As we
have seen, SD after vernalization may accelerate flowering

under subsequent inductive conditions in several LDP, while
the LDP, *Hyoscyamus niger*, retains the vernalized condition
under SD for several or many months (Lang and Melchers, 1947;
Sarkar, 1958). In contrast, other plants may be devernalized
by SD immediately after plant vernalization, e.g., by six
weeks of 8 h SD in sugar-beet cv Kleinwanzleben E (Margara,
1960), or two to three weeks at 8 h SD in *Oenothera biennis*
var. sulfurea (Picard, 1965). According to Chintraruck and
Ketellapper (1969), the effect of partial seed vernalization
(1-4 weeks at $4^{o}C$) can also be annulled by SD in *Arabidopsis*
Stockholm, but this is not conclusive as the plants were not
transferred to LD after SD exposure.

Devernalization under light of low intensity was first
observed by Schwabe (1955, 1957) in *Chrysanthemum*. Similarly,
in pea genotypes with the *Sn* gene, the devernalizing effect of
nine days at $30^{o}C$ under 8 h SD increased with decreasing light
intensity and was greatest in darkness (Reid and Murfet,
1978).

INDUCTION OF COLD REQUIREMENT IN EARLY SUMMER-ANNUAL PLANTS

The earliest summer-annual strains of *Arabidopsis thaliana* do
not respond to vernalization when grown under LD at 5000 -
6000 lx. With such strains some vernalization response can be
observed in plants grown in SD or under low light intensity
(400 lx) before and/or after cold treatment (Napp-Zinn,
1962a). Similar phenomena were observed by Mokhtare and
Limberg (1977) in Iranian alternative barleys (*Hordeum
vulgare*) whose SD inhibition was reduced by subsequent
vernalization.

In an early variety of *Pisum sativum*, (cv Kleine Rhein-
länderin), flowering can be delayed by removing the cotyledons
shortly after soaking. This effect may be reduced by either
LD or vernalization (Haupt and Nakamura, 1970).

CONCLUSIONS

The conclusions reached at the end of this review are somewhat
discouraging. On the one hand, there is still too little information, especially about the roles of wavelength and light
intensity, to allow a clear-cut picture to emerge. On the
other hand, there are many divergent, if not contradictory,
results with regard to vernalization-daylength interactions.
The reasons for the latter situation appear to be partly real
and partly a consequence of experimental approaches.

There are strong arguments for the supposition that vernalization may mean different things in different species and
even in different genotypes of one and the same species: e.g.

in *Pisum*, one gene (*Sn*) is known to control both vernalization and LD requirements at the same time, while in *Triticum* several genes are responsible for daylength sensitivity, and several others for vernalization requirements (Keim *et al.*, 1973; Law, 1979). In the case of most winter cereals and of cold-requiring *Arabidopsis* strains there are genotypes whose need for vernalization depends upon the dominant allele of one gene, others where it depends upon the recessive allele of another gene, and still others where both kinds of genes are combined, and it may depend upon external conditions whether their interactions must be described in terms of epistasy or of additivity (Napp–Zinn, 1957, 1961b, 1962b, 1969, 1979). For more than 80 years grafting experiments have pointed in the same direction: in some cases a flower-promoting substance seems to be transmitted from an annual or vernalized stock to a cold-requiring scion, while in others an inhibitor seems to be transmitted (cf. Napp–Zinn, 1973).

From the experimental, or methodological, point of view, it is unsatisfactory that the photoperiodic nature of daylength effects has only rarely been proven. In only a restricted number of cases were putative photoperiodic effects tested by SD + night break controls, and only rarely was a shorter daylength compensated for by a higher light intensity.

These conclusions, however, would be incomplete if I did not include some suggestions and guidelines for future research.

1. In the future, physiological experiments should preferably be done with genetically well-studied genotypes whose cold requirement depends exclusively upon one gene locus, like Petkus winter rye, biennial henbane, or certain lines of *Arabidopsis thaliana* [Unfortunately most of the work with *Arabidopsis thaliana* has been done with the strain Stockholm whose vernalization requirement depends on at least four gene loci, with partly dominant and partly recessive alleles responsible for the cold requirement (Napp–Zinn, 1962b, 1979).]

2. Where there are known interactions between light and vernalization, action spectra should be determined, something which apparently has never been done.

3. When the influences of light intensity and daylength are investigated, both should be varied in a reciprocal manner, i.e., in such a way that the product of both remains constant.

Looking at such gaps, in spite of hundreds of publications, including my own, one feels tempted to end with a well known quotation – so much to do, so little done.

ACKNOWLEDGEMENT

As far as results of my own research are included in this
review, it has been supported by Deutsche Forschungsgemeinschaft to whom sincere thanks are due. Thanks also to Dr.
Angela Franz for going through the manuscript.

REFERENCES

Adachi, K., Inouye, J. and Ito, K. (1970). *J. Fac. Agric.
Kyushu Univ.* 16, 77–84

Babenko, V.I., Biryukov, S.V. and Komarova, V.P. (1971).
Fiziol. Rast. 18, 932–940

Babenko, V.I., Biryukov, S.V. and Komarova, V.P. (1974).
S-kh. Biol. 9, 648–653

Balkova, A. (1973). *Genet. Slechteni* 9, 271–276

Ballet, A., Mathon, Ch.–C. and Grossin, F. (1962). *C.R. 87e
Congr. Soc. Sav.* 1093–1097

Barber, H.N. (1959). *Heredity* 13, 33–60

Berry, G.J. and Aitken, Y. (1979). *Aust. J. Plant Physiol.* 6,
573–587

Blondon, F. (1966). *C.R.Hebd. Seances Acad. Sci. Ser. D.* 263,
48–51

Blondon, F. (1970). *C.R.Hebd. Seances Acad. Sci. Ser. D.* 270,
3063–3066

Blondon, F. (1971). *C.R.Hebd. Seances Acad. Sci. Ser. D.* 272,
2896–2899

Blondon, F. (1972). *C.R.Hebd. Seances Acad. Sci. Ser. D.* 274,
218–221

Blondon, F. and Chouard, P. (1965). *C.R.Hebd. Seances Acad.
Sci. Ser. D.* 260, 6966–6969

Bose, K.K. (1974). Thesis, University of Cologne

Chintraruck, B., and Ketellapper, H.J. (1969). *Plant Cell
Physiol.* 10, 271–276

Chouard, P. (1957). *C.R.Hebd. Seances Acad. Sci.* 245,
2520–2522

Chouard, P. (1960). *Annu. Rev. Plant Physiol.* 11, 191–238

Chouard, P. and Tran Than Van, M. (1964). *C.R.Hebd. Acad.
Sci.* 259, 4783–4786

Clarkson, N.M. and Russell, J.S. (1975). *Aust. J. Agric. Res.*
26, 831–838

Correns, C. (1903). *Ber. Dtsch. Bot. Ges.* 21, 195–201

Correns, C. (1904). *Ber. Dtsch. Bot. Ges.* 22, 517–524

Cuthbertson, E.G. (1966). *Aust. J. Agric. Res.* 17, 457–464

Devay, M. (1967). *Acta Agron. Acad. Sci. Hung.* 16, 289–295

Gott, M.B. (1961). *Aust. J. Agric. Res.* 12, 547–565

Gott, M.B., Gregory, F.G. and Purvis, O.N. (1955). *Ann. Bot.
(Lond.)* 19, 87–126

Hanisova, A. and Krekule, J. (1975). *J. Hortic. Sci.* 50, 97–104

Hartman, Th.A. (1964). *Neth. J. Agric. Sci.* 12, 132–155

Hartman, Th.A. (1966). *Neth. J. Agric. Sci.* 14, 89–102

Hartmann, W. (1968). *Flora, Abt. A*, 159, 35–39

Haupt, W. and Nakamura, E. (1970). *Z. Pflanzenphysiol.* 62, 270–275

Inouye, J. and Ito, K. (1968). *Plant Cell Physiol.* 9, 137–142

Jones, H.G., Ford, M.A. and Plumley, R. (1975). *Photosynthetica* 9, 24–30

Keim, D.L., Welsh, J.R. and McConnell, R.L. (1973). *Can. J. Plant Sci.* 53, 247–250

Ketellapper, H.J. and Barbaro, A. (1966). *Phyton (Vicente Lopez)* 23, 33–41

Krekule, J. (1961). *Biol. Plant.* 3, 180–191

Krekule, J. (1964). *Biol. Plant.* 6, 299–305

Laibach, F. (1951). *Beitr. Biol. Pflanz* 28, 173–210

Lang, A. (1951). *Züchter* 21, 241–243

Lang, A. (1965). *In* "Encyclopedia of Plant Physiology" (ed. W. Ruhland). Vol. XV/1, pp. 1380–1536. Springer-Verlag, Berlin

Lang, A. and Melchers, G. (1947). *Z. Naturforsch.* 2b, 444–449

Law, C.N. (1979). *In* "La Physiologie de la Floraison" (eds. P. Champagnat and R. Jacques). pp. 215–216. Coll. Int. C.N.R.S., No. 285, Paris

Listowski, A. (1958). *Züchter* 28, 314–320

Listowski, A. (1964). "Observations on the Interaction between External Conditions and Development of Some Perennial Plants". Mimeographed typescript

Listowski, A. (1965a). *Bull. Soc. Bot. Fr.* 112, 208–219

Listowski, A. (1965b). *Acta Soc. Bot. Pol.* 34, 1–26

Listowski, A. (1966a). *In* "Differentiation of Apical Meristems and some Problems of Ecological Regulation of Development in Plants" Proc. Symp. Praha – Nitra, of 1964, pp. 261–269. Czech. Acad. Sci., Praha

Listowski, A. (1966b). *Acta Soc. Bot. Pol.* 35, 455–459

Listowski, A. and Jackowska, I. (1964). *Acta Soc. Bot. Pol.* 33, 705–717

Listowski, A. and Jesmianowicz, M. (1959). *Züchter* 29, 276–279

Lona, L. and Faccini, O. (1976). *Ateneo Parmense, Acta Nat.* 12, 375–378

Lysenko, T.D. (1932a). *Bull. Yaroviz.* 2/3, 16–34

Lysenko, T.D. (1932b). *Bull. Yaroviz.* 4, 1–57

Lysenko, T.D. (1934). *Semenovodstvo* 2, 20–31

Lysenko, T.D. (1936). "The Theoretical Bases of Yarovization" (in Russian) 2nd Edn. Moscow

Lysenko, T.D. (1951). "Agrobiologie" Kultur und Fortschritt, Berlin (East)

Margara, J. (1960). Thesis, University of Paris

Marks, M.K. and Prince, S.D. (1979). *New Phytol.* 82, 357-364

Mason, D.T. (1957). *Univ. Reading, Dept. Hort. Tech. Bull.* 1, 1-7

Mathon, C.-Ch. (1960a). *Bull. Soc. Bot. Fr.* 107, 92-93

Mathon, C.-Ch. (1960b). *Phyton (Vicente Lopez)* 14, 167-174

Mathon, C.-Ch. (1977). "Ecologie et Biogeographie. Initiation a l'Ecologie du Developpement" Fac. Sci. Univ. Poitiers

Mokhtare, F. and Limberg, P. (1977). *Z. Acker-Pflanzenb.* 145, 85-102

Murfet, I.C. (1977). In "The Physiology of the Garden Pea" (eds J.F. Sutcliffe and J.S. Pate). pp. 385-430, Academic Press, London

Murfet, I.C. and Reid, J.B. (1974). *Z. Pflanzenphysiol.* 71, 323-331

Napp-Zinn, K. (1957). *Z. Vererbungsl.* 88, 253-285

Napp-Zinn, K. (1960a). *Planta* 54, 409-444

Napp-Zinn, K. (1960b). *Planta* 54, 445-452

Napp-Zinn, K. (1961a). In "Encyclopedia of Plant Physiology" (ed W. Ruhland). Vol. XVI, pp. 24-75. Springer-Verlag, Berlin

Napp-Zinn, K. (1961b). *Züchter* 31, 128-135

Napp-Zinn, K. (1962a). *Naturwissenschaften* 49, 473-474

Napp-Zinn, K. (1962b). *Z. Vererbungsl.* 93, 154-163

Napp-Zinn, K. (1969). In "The Induction of Flowering" (ed L. T. Evans). pp. 291-304. Macmillan, Melbourne

Napp-Zin, K. (1973). In "Temperature and Life" (eds H. Precht, J. Christophersen, H. Hensel and W. Larcher). pp. 171-194, 264-292. Springer-Verlag, Berlin

Napp-Zinn, K. (1979). In "La Physiologie de la Floraison" (eds P. Champagnat and R. Jacques). pp. 217-220. Coll. Int. C.N.R.S., No. 285, Paris

Ofir, M. and Koller, D. (1974). *Aust. J. Plant Physiol.* 1, 259-270

Pavlov, P. (1958). *Izv. Inst. Rasteniev.* 5, 279-302

Picard, C. (1965). *Ann. Sci. Nat., 12e Ser. Bot.* 6, 197-314

Picard, C. (1968). "Aspects et Mecanismes de la Vernalisation" Masson et Cie, Paris

Pierik, R.L.M. (1967a). Thesis, Landbouwhogesch. Wageningen

Pierik, R.L.M. (1967b). *Z. Pflanzenphysiol.* 56, 141-152

Pressman, E. and Negbi, M. (1980). *J. Exp. Bot.* 31, 1291-1296

Purvis, O.N. (1961). In "Encyclopedia of Plant Physiology" (ed W. Ruhland). Vol. XVI. pp. 76-122. Springer-Verlag, Berlin

Purvis, O.N. and Gregory, F.G. (1937). *Ann. Bot. (Lond.)* 1, 569–592

Rahman, M.S. and Gladstones, J.S. (1972). *Aust. J. Exp. Agric. Anim. Husb.* 12, 638–645

Reid, J.B. (1981). *Aust. J. Plant Physiol.* 8, 319–327

Reid, J.B. and Murfet, I.C. (1975). *J. Exp. Bot.* 26, 860–867

Reid, J.B. and Murfet, I.C. (1977). *J. Exp. Bot.* 28, 1357–1364

Reid, J.B. and Murfet, I.C. (1978). *Ann. Bot. (Lond.)* 42, 945–956

Rünger, W. (1978). *Sci. Hortic.* 9, 71–81

Ruiter, J.M. de and Taylor, A.O. (1979). *N.Z. J. Exp. Agric.* 7, 153–156

Sano, Y. (1975). *J. Jpn. Soc. Hortic. Sci.* 44, 66–72

Sarkar, S. (1958). *Biol. Zentralbl.* 77, 1–49.

Schwabe, W.W. (1955). *J. Exp. Bot.* 6, 435–450

Schwabe, W.W. (1957). *J. Exp. Bot.* 8, 220–234

Sivori, E.M. and Gimenez, D.O. (1981). *Phyton (Buenos Aires)* 40, 159–168

Wellensiek, S.J. (1953). *Ned. Versl. Kon. Ned. Akad. Wet.* 62, 115–118

Wellensiek, S.J. (1969). *Z. Pflanzenphysiol.* 60, 388–402

Wellensiek, S.J. (1970). *Proc. 18th Int. Hortic. Congr.* 5, 21–29

Wellensiek, S.J. (1973). *Sci. Hortic.* 1, 177–192

Wellensiek, S.J. (1981). *Z. Pflanzenphysiol.* 103, 189–198

PHOTOPERCEPTION AND TRANSDUCTION OF DAYLENGTH SIGNALS

Chapter 7

LIGHT AND PHOTOPERIODIC TIMING

R. W. KING

CSIRO Division of Plant Industry, P.O. Box 1600
Canberra City, A.C.T. 2601, Australia.

INTRODUCTION

When seasonal climatic change is severe, plants may initiate
processes of reproduction, leaf fall or dormancy well in
advance of seasonal extremes in order to survive. This pre-
planning may involve a response to temperature but more often
the time cue is provided by change in daylength. Increasingly
it appears that the photoreceptor may be the pigment phytochrome but the nature of the underlying timer is more conten-
tious. It is possible for endogenous oscillatory clocks –
circadian (about 24 h) rhythms – to provide a basis for photoperiodic timing. The pattern of re-setting of their phase by
photoperiod is consistent with the involvement of a rhythm in
measuring the duration of light/dark cycles. On the other
hand, on a diurnal basis, timekeeping can also be explained
using a single hourglass or input-response timer.

Here most attention is directed to rhythmic timers in order
to highlight not only the supporting evidence but also to show
shortcomings and aspects requiring re-interpretation. In particular it is questioned whether there are dual actions of
light; one on rhythm re-phasing and the other on induction –
an external coincidence model as argued by Bünning, (e.g.,
1973). Is this dual action of light the explanation of the
rhythmic effect of brief light interruptions (5-15 min) on
flowering responses – they interact with the rhythm at its
different phases but without causing re-phasing? Or, alternatively, is the effect of brief light interruptions to be
explained in part or totally as phase resetting? To invoke a

single action of light on re-phasing alone does allow for
response to both light-off and on signals and it greatly
simplifies their interpretation. Examination of these
questions provides the focus for the information presented
subsequently. More general comment is available in reviews of
Cumming and Wagner (1968), Vince-Prue (1975) and Hillman
(1976).

PHOTORECEPTOR INPUT

The leaf is the main site of the photoresponse for the control
of flowering as discussed by Zeevaart (Chapter 10, this
volume). Further, events in the leaf can be accurately timed.
For example, in the SDP *Pharbitis nil*, photosensitive events
in the cotyledon can pass a threshold by about 11 h (Fig. 1,
critical night length). This photoresponse/timer interaction
is satisfied within a further 1-2 h, although this is not to

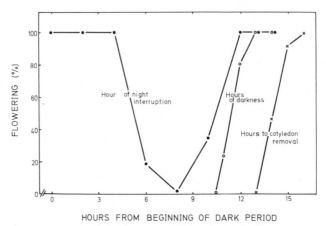

HOURS FROM BEGINNING OF DARK PERIOD

*Fig. 1. Timing of events of flowering in the cotyledon of
Pharbitis (i) sensitivity to night interruption (ii) critical
night length (iii) export of stimulus to flowering. (Adapted
from Ogawa and King, 1979).*

say that the timekeeper then stops running. Subsequent dark
reactions involving floral stimulus generation are completed
between 13 to 15 h (Fig. 1). After this time removal of the
cotyledon no longer depresses apical flowering response.
Clearly, whether or not time masurement continues, timed
responses have gone to saturation by 15 h.

    Of even greater significance is the demonstration of pro-
cessing of timing cues without a terminating (dawn) light
signal. Light terminating darkness at say 10 h stops the
flowering response (critical dark or night interruption res-

ponses, Fig. 1). However, the dark period was 16 h in the cotyledon removal experiment so that the stimulus must have been exported in darkness (Fig. 1). Stimulus export, even in darkness, has been reported before both for *Pharbitis* (Zeevaart, 1962; King *et al.*, 1968) and *Xanthium strumarium* (Searle, 1961). Clearly, the main requirement is for a light-off (dusk) signal at the start of the dark period, which sets up timing in these short-day plants. In contradiction to Bünning's concepts (see Bünning, 1973) there is no inductive requirement for the coincidence of a light-on (dawn) signal with a specific period or phase of time measurement.

One feature Bünning built into his model of dual action of light was that there were dual photoreceptors. This was to distinguish photoreceptor action on re-setting the timer from its action inductively – the coincidence action of light. Thus, to deny external coincidence also allows more freedom (simplification) in discussion of the nature of the photo-receptor.

PHOTORECEPTION

Phytochrome is apparently an effective photoreceptor in phase setting of overt rhythms such as leaf gas exchange in *Bryo-phyllum fedtschenkoi* (Harris and Wilkins, 1978), dark respi-ration in *Lemna paucicostata* (see Hillman, 1976) and for leaf movements (see Bünning, 1973). Action spectra show maxima in the red region. Also, R/FR photoreversibility has been demon-strated through the use of brief repeated irradiations. For flower opening of *Pharbitis* and for leaf movement of *Samanea saman*, photoreversibility of rhythm rephasing has been estab-lished after a single brief red irradiation (see Chapter 17 in this volume and Satter *et al.*, 1981).

For photoperiodic responses of both LDP and SDP, action spectra for the effect of night interruptions on flowering show maxima in the red and they are generally photoreversible (Vince-Prue, 1975). That rhythmic sensitivity to inter-ruptions is seen in non-chlorophyllous seedlings excludes any role for photosynthetic pigments (King *et al.*, 1982). Thus, it appears that phytochrome also mediates rhythmic sensitivity to brief night interruptions.

Does phytochrome re-phase rhythms of flowering? Such a role is likely from its action on phasing of overt rhythms (see above). Furthermore, in the SDP *Lemna* and *Chenopodium rubrum*, quite low irradiances of red light are effective in re-phasing. Red/far-red photoreversal has not been estab-lished but there is a lesson in the studies of Harris and Wilkins (1978). They demonstrated photoreversibility for phase shifting of the CO_2 output rhythm in leaves of *Bryo-*

phyllum but only with repeated daily cycles.

In discussions of photocontrol, the site of photoresponse needs to be identified. For induction of flowering the leaf is the usual site of photoperiodic response and there follows transmission of a signal to the shoot apex (Fig. 1). The leaf is also the site of rhythmicity in photoresponse for *Cheno-podium* (King, 1975).

LIGHT, RHYTHMS AND PHASE CONTROL

A now classic illustration of rhythmic involvement in flowering was reported by Cumming *et al.*, (1965) with the SDP *Chenopodium*. When seedlings of *Chenopodium* are exposed to a single dark period of varied duration interrupting continuous white light their capacity to flower fluctuates rhythmically for at least 3 cycles and with a period of 30 h. The light—off signal sets the phase and the time of the light—on signal determines whether or not flowering will result. There are many reports of similar rhythmic flowering responses to the duration of light and darkness (see Cumming and Wagner, 1968; Vince-Prue, 1975; Hillman, 1976).

Light acts on these rhythms to set their phase as demon-

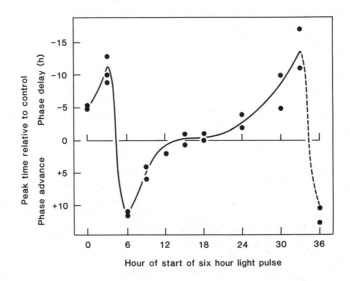

Fig. 2. Re-phasing of the rhythmic flowering response of Chenopodium *by a 6 h light pulse at different phases of the free-running oscillation. (Adapted from King and Cumming 1972a).*

strated for *Chenopodium* using a phase response curve as shown
in Fig. 2. This curve was derived from measured re-phasing of
the flowering rhythm by 6 h light pulses given at various
times during a dark period of varied duration. It is the
timing of both dawn and dusk signals which is important (see
King and Cumming, 1972a). Further, because of the non-linear
nature of this re-phasing profile, after repeated daily cycles
a 6 h photocycle re-sets or forces the oscillation to a point
of least net change as defined by the zero re-phasing point at
12–18 h (Fig. 2). Thus, in repeated 6 h photoperiods, flowering results because the light–inhibited phase (trough of the
rhythm) falls at 9 to 15 h and, hence, in darkness (rhythm
peak at hour 18 or at normal dawn time).

In contrast to the response to 6 h photoperiods, for longer
interruptions the oscillator is re-set at dusk to give constant phase setting by the light–off signal. The first peak of
the oscillation then falls at a fixed time (13 h) in darkness
(Fig. 3). As a consequence the light-sensitive phase of the

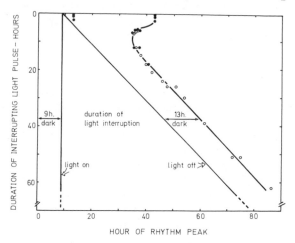

*Fig. 3. Re-phasing of the rhythm of flowering by a red (O) or
fluorescent (O) light period of 5 min to 62 h duration
commencing at 9 h. Time in darkness to the first peak of the
oscillation. (After King and Cumming, 1972a).*

oscillation falls in darkness in shorter photoperiods (ca 11
h) but longer photoperiods move the dawn signal back and
flowering is progressively depressed. Thus these patterns of
re-phasing of flowering rhythms show how, in *Chenopodium*, an
endogenous rhythm can provide a continuously consulted
"flowering clock" which can be synchronized to solar and,
hence, to seasonal time.

Not only for *Chenopodium* but also for *Pharbitis* (Takimoto

and Hamner, 1964; Lumsden *et al.*, 1982) and *Xanthium*
(Papenfuss and Salisbury, 1967) prolonged photoperiods (> 9 h)
lead to setting the timer to a fixed phase following the dusk
signal. The oscillation probably does not stop in these
conditions but, as shown by Peterson and Jones (1979), it may
cycle around (approach) a limit point. Rhythmic expression
becomes non-detectable in light but in darkness there is rapid
re-setting to a fixed phase on the light/dark transition.
Clearly in LDP this continued cycling even in light could
confer the rhythmic sensitivity seen to changes in light
quality (see Deitzer, Chapter 4 this volume).

Not all rhythmic flowering responses are so dominated by
the dusk signal. For soybean (*Glycine max*) both dusk and dawn
signals influence expression of its rhythm of flowering
(Blaney and Hamner, 1957). Even if dark period length is
maintained or increased, the flowering of soybean declines if
the duration of the light cycle exceeds 10 to 15 h. This is
precisely the type of response expected if repeated cycles
were to set up resonance with a rhythm with a natural period
of about 24 h. However, as noted above, such inhibition in
prolonged irradiations is not found for all SDP (e.g., *Chenopodium*, *Pharbitis*, *Xanthium*).

The demonstration that the shape of the phase response
curve can change with photocycle duration for *Chenopodium*
(cf. Figs. 2, 3) emphasizes the need for complete phase control information for each species and for all photoperiods.
In addition, these relationships for *Chenopodium* show that the
response to light-on/light-off signals can change from sensing
both signals in a 6 h photocycle to sensing only light-off
timing in a 12 h cycle. Clearly, therefore, it would be
misleading to emphasize any simple control by dawn and/or
dusk signals. The timing of these signals is no more important than the continued light input that makes a 12 h photocycle from a 6 h one. This comment is considered again
later.

There are many aspects of rhythm re-phasing yet to be
examined if we are to explain fully differences in photoperiodic responses between species. It can be expected that
species will differ in the period length of their free-running
rhythm and this should alter the direction and rate of their
re-phasing responses (see Daan and Pittendrigh, 1976).
Similarly, differences in re-phasing will result because of
differences between species in the symmetry of their phase
response curves and the balance of phase delays and advances
(see Chapter 17 this volume). Perhaps the shape of the phase
response curves determines ability to sense shortening and
lengthening photocycles and, hence, confers long-short-day
sensing and short-long-day sensing. On the other

hand, there may be two distinct biochemical sequences, the one dependent on prior satisfaction of the other as seems to be the case in *Bryophyllum diagremontanum* (see Chapter 10 in this volume). In the extreme, one or two intercalated long- and short-day cycles show inhibitory and promotory effects and it has been suggested that separate responses occur in the different daylengths (Schwabe, 1959). However, this suggestion must be treated with great caution. When only a few daily cycles are involved then there may be insufficient time to reset the rhythm to its new phase before it is shifted back again. Considerable phase confusion will be generated much like the jet-lag of the trans-Atlantic traveller.

A further area where caution must be exercised is in comparing rhythm phases between LDP and SDP. Such comparisons may reflect nothing more than different photoperiodic treatments preceding transfer to inductive photoperiods. It is clear that for *Chenopodium* the rapidity of re-phasing by repeated cycles and, hence, the degree of flowering will depend on when the first photocycle impinges on the rhythm. The effect of starting time on the rate of phase adjustment has precisely this action in *Lemna* as shown by Hillman (1964). He found that a rhythm almost 180° out of phase resulted following a 2.5 h delay in starting the second light pulse of a 10.5 h skeleton photoperiod. Clearly great care must be exercised in interpreting how and why rhythm phases differ and how changes in daylength interact with rhythm phase.

RESPONSE TO BRIEF LIGHT INTERRUPTIONS

It is now almost fifty years since Hamner and Bonner (1938) first reported inhibition of flowering of a SDP by brief light interruptions of darkness. Evidence from action spectra and of R/FR photoreversibility demonstrate that this photoresponse involves phytochrome (see Vince-Prue, 1975). That maximum sensitivity to red light interruptions only occurs in the middle of darkness (Fig. 1) was taken initially as evidence of disappearance of Pfr by this time. Hence, the proposed timing action suggested for phytochrome - the reversion-as-a-timer hypothesis (see Vince-Prue, 1975). Inability to measure phytochrome changes in green tissue made it difficult to test this model but this problem has been resolved by the use of non-green but photoperiodically responsive tissue. In *Pharbitis*, for example, Pfr has been shown to disappear rapidly during the early hours of an inductive dark period as shown in Fig. 4. These measurements are for both the total spectrophotometrically detectable phytochrome and also for the phytochrome that is physiologically active in the control of flowering as detected using a null response technique. Not

only do these two methods show reasonable agreement but Pfr
loss in darkness clearly occurs much earlier than the time
when red light interruptions become inhibitory to flowering
(Fig. 4).

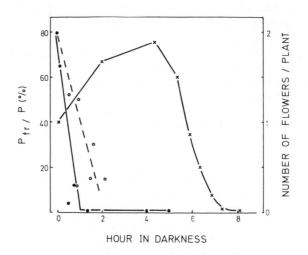

HOUR IN DARKNESS

*Fig. 4. Timing of change during darkness in Pfr in cotyledons
of Pharbitis (●, spectrophotometric, and 0, physiological
assay) and in sensitivity to red light interruption of
darkness (X). (Adapted from King et al., 1978).*

Pfr loss may not always be as rapid (e.g., Cumming *et al.*,
1965; Evans and King, 1969; King and Cumming, 1972b; Evans,
1976; King *et al.*, 1978; Kato, 1979) but its timing cannot
explain the appearance of sensitivity to night interruptions.
It must be concluded that it is response to phytochrome input
that changes or, in other words, brief night interruptions
tell you what stage (phase) the timer is at. In prolonged
dark periods sensitivity to such interruptions may actually
change rhythmically (Fig. 5 and see Vince—Prue, 1975) and
there is a parallel with the response to dark periods of
varied duration. The implication is, therefore, that the
stage of the rhythm determines timing of response. How this
response is controlled is as yet unclear but it apparently
involves both changes at the biochemical level and at the
level of the initial photochemical events involving phytochrome phototransformation (King *et al.*, 1982).
    What is not clear is how light/timer interactions affect
the flowering response. If only prolonged irradiations re-
phase a rhythm then the responses to brief interruptions must
involve a second or dual action of light as implied in
Bünning's (e.g., 1973) external coincidence model. However,

for some rhythms brief interruptions can induce rhythm
re-phasing as discussed earlier. Further, for flowering

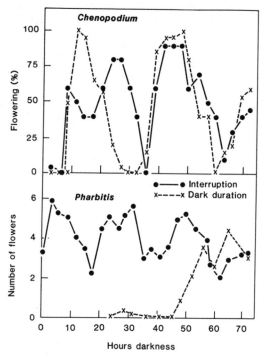

Fig. 5. Effect on flowering of Chenopodium *and* Pharbitis *of
the duration of a single dark period and of the time of a
brief red (5 min) interruption of 72 h dark. Data for*
Chenopodium *from B. G. Cumming used to derive Fig. 9 of*
Cumming *et al., (1965). Data for* Pharbitis *from King et al.,
(1982).*

rhythms brief red interruptions do not always reproduce the
rhythmic pattern of response seen to dark period duration
(Fig. 5). Also, the rhythmic sensitivity to interruptions
seen for etiolated seedlings of *Pharbitis* (Fig. 5) is
initiated or reset by the single 5 min pulse given at the
start of the dark period. When the initiating 5 min
irradiation is delayed the oscillation shifts to the same
extent (King *et al.*, 1982), so this initiating irradiation is
clearly controlling rhythm phase.

    Possibly the most decisive evidence of light interruptions
acting on re-phasing involves the use of brief (15 min) light
pulses as skeleton photoperiods for the control of flowering
of *Lemna* (Hillman, 1964; Oda, 1969). As is also seen in

insects (e.g. Pittendrigh, 1966; cf. Saunders, 1982) skeleton
photoperiods perfectly simulate a complete photoperiod up to
about 11 h and they also provide perfect simulation of photoperiods greater than 14 h (Oda, 1969). In between 11 and
14 h, however, there is considerable depression of flowering
with the oscillator receiving ambiguous information about
which of the two signals to read as the shorter period. In
Drosophila this "bistability" or phase jump can be predicted
in its entirety by summating the individual phase responses to
the two skeleton pulses (Pittendrigh, 1966).

On the assumption that brief interruptions do re-set
flowering rhythms then light interruptions during darkness of
a normal light/dark cycle would result in a bistability or
ambiguity in the middle of darkness leading to inhibition of

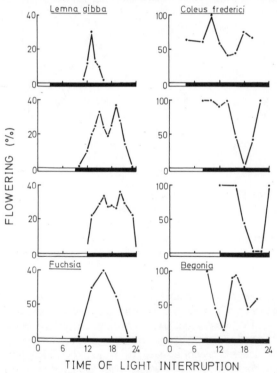

TIME OF LIGHT INTERRUPTION
IN DAILY PHOTOCYCLE

*Fig. 6. Sensitivity of flowering to interruptions of darkness
at different times for repeated cycles of various photoperiods. Duration of interruption 2 h for* Lemna gibba *(Oota,
1981), 1 h for* Fuchsia *cv Lord Byron (Vince-Prue, 1975), 0.5
to 1 h for* Coleus frederici *(Halaban, 1968) and 3 h for*
Begonia boweri *(Zimmer, 1970).*

flowering, especially when the photoperiod is short. The
light break becomes part of a skeleton, albeit asymmetric,
photocycle. Earlier and later interruptions in asymmetric
photocycles will actually act as extensions of the dawn and
dusk signals. By careful perusal of the literature (Fig. 6)
it is actually possible to illustrate such complex changes in
sensitivity to light breaks, changes that are consistent with
action of light as false dawn and dusk signals or as an
ambiguous signal.

Night interruptions in a longer dark period could be expected to show rhythmicity (Fig. 5) but based on a regular
cycling in the degree of phase re-setting. At this time it is
not clear why the response of *Chenopodium* is not always the
same for brief interruptions and for termination by continuous
exposure to light (Fig. 5). However, the experimental proto-
cols do differ. The brief red interruption is always followed
by a further prolonged period of darkness. Thus, the diver-
gence seen in Fig. 5 may actually point to phase re-setting.

Some experimental evidence does not appear to accord with
phase re-setting effects of brief light pulses. Four to six
hours of light may be required to re-initiate a flowering
response (Vince-Prue, 1975). Overt rhythms of leaf movement
in *Pharbitis* and soybean may not be reset by brief light
pulses (5-10 min) yet flowering is inhibited by such light
interruptions (Brest *et al.*, 1971; Bollig, 1975). Also, the
rhythm of flowering of *Chenopodium* is apparently not re-phased
by a single brief (5 min) light interruption (Fig. 7 and

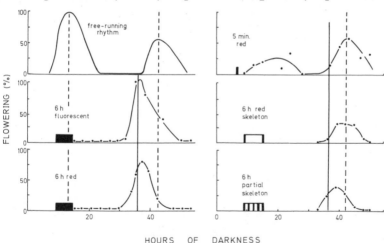

HOURS OF DARKNESS

*Fig. 7. Effect of skeleton or partial 6 h light pulses on
re-phasing the free-running rhythm of flowering of* Chenopodium.
(Adapted from King and Cumming, 1972b).

Cumming *et al.*, 1965) but these results may not be decisive.
The site and nature of receptors may differ between the
flowering response and some leaf movement rhythms (Bünning,
1973). Also, a cumulative or summated effect on phasing by 5
min light pulses can be seen for *Chenopodium* when these pulses
are repeated five times every 1.5 h over the period of a 6 h
skeleton photoperiod (Fig. 7). Furthermore, a single 5 min
interruption can induce re-setting or transient change in
phasing of the rhythm of flowering in etiolated seedlings of
Pharbitis (King *et al.*, 1982; Lumsden *et al.*, 1982). Thus,
perhaps there is no absolute lower limit to the duration of
light required for phase re-setting. The real difference may
be between species and in the degree of prior preconditioning
as it affects sensitivity for re-phasing of the oscillation.

TIMERS IN CONFLICT

In the absence of a biochemical basis of understanding it is
not possible to resolve how photoperiodic time measurement is
carried out. Although repetitive or non-rhythmic processes
based on an hourglass principle cannot be excluded as timers
in diurnal cycles, it is the evidence of free-running rhythms,
their reproducibility, ubiquity and re-phasing properties
which makes them more appealing conceptually. Further, for
Chenopodium at least, its rhythm of flowering is so phased
that all its photoperiodic response can be accounted for (King
and Cumming, 1972a, and see Bollig *et al.*, 1976). Also, the
complicated responses to skeleton photoperiods as in *Lemna*
(Hillman, 1964; Oda, 1969) and to asymmetric skeletons
(Fig. 7) both point to rhythmic control of flowering. However, the interactions between light and rhythms require
re-examination. The external coincidence concepts developed
by Bünning (see Bünning, 1973) required two light reactions,
the one controlling rhythm phase and the other highlighting
changes in sensitivity to light. Brief light breaks, it was
argued, highlighted the phase of this rhythmic sensitivity
without inducing re-phasing. Such light was essential for
triggering the response whilst longer irradiations were
required for re-phasing.

With time a number of facts have emerged which are
apparently at odds with this external coincidence model. For
instance, there may be a common photoreceptor. A single
photoresponse mediated by phytochrome may control both sensitivity to brief light pulses and light re-phasing responses.
It must be questioned, in fact, whether brief irradiations may
not also have a re-phasing effect (see King *et al.*, 1982;
Lumsden *et al.*, 1982). Certainly some rhythm re-phasing can
occur with brief 5-25 min irradiations in skeleton photo-

periods or in single partial photoperiods. Also, when brief
light pulses are compared with continuous light to terminate
darkness there may be considerable deviation from the expected
rhythmic pattern of response of flowering at least in
Chenopodium (Fig. 5). Perhaps the most telling arguments
against dual light response and external coincidence are the
often forgotten reports that photoperiodic response in some
plants can be completed following only a single light-off
signal (Fig. 1). A second, dawn signal is not required to
trigger the response. There is no essential requirement for
external coincidence.

If external coincidence is not an adequate explanation of
photoperiodic resonse what then are the timing mechanisms?
Pittendrigh's (e.g., 1972) model of internal coincidence
involving two rhythms provides an adequate explanation. Only
one of these oscillators is considered to be re-phased by
light and induction only occurs when the two rhythms harmo-
nize. On the other hand, only one rhythmic timer plus an
hourglass mechanism would produce the same response as also
would an hourglass alone but not a rhythm alone.

Some attempts have been made to separate responses involved
with these various internal coincidence models. In insects,
quasi photoperiodic response has been achieved using thermo-
periodic cycles (see Saunders, 1982). Thus, not only is there
no essential role for light signals (cf. internal coincidence)
but the timing of sensitivity to night interruptions shifts
with a temperature-induced phase shift. Similar experiments
have yet to be performed for flowering responses in plants but
would clearly be of great interest. Another approach is to
attempt to uncouple the various timers by prematurely
initiating dark period timing whilst plants remain in light.
This may occur for Pharbitis and Chenopodium when plants are
switched briefly from continuous R or white light into FR for
1-2 h and phytochrome is controlling as red/far-red photoreversibility is evident (King, 1974). Furthermore, such
premature initiation of dark timing has no effect on phasing
of the rhythm in Chenopodium (King, 1974). Thus, these
findings could indicate some dissociation of timing
mechanisms.

CONCLUSION

Until we have better understanding of mechanisms at the biochemical level debate about the nature of the biological
clocks controlling photoperiodism may be no more than a re-
statement of belief, not a critical examination of alternatives. However, some re-examination and a re-emphasis
appear essential at least for some beliefs relating to dual

light responses and external coincidence. For photoperiodic
timing to run to completion only a light-off signal is essential. Thus, the debate over the role of timers is about light
control of their phase and, possibly, about internal coincidence effects. This could involve either a two oscillator
model, action of an oscillator and hourglass, or action of all
three timers together.

ACKNOWLEDGEMENTS

Dr. L. T. Evans is thanked for his many valuable criticisms of
this manuscript. Support by the Underwood Foundation (U.K.)
is gratefully acknowledged.

REFERENCES
Blaney, L.T. and Hamner, K.C. (1957). *Bot. Gaz.* 119, 10–24
Bollig, I. (1975). *Z. Pflanzenphysiol.* 77,54–59.
Bollig, I., Chandrashekaran, M.K., Englemann, W. and Johnson,
   A. (1976). *Int. J. Chronobiol.* 4, 83–96
Brest, D.E., Hoshizaki, T. and Hamner, K.C. (1971). *Plant
   Physiol.* 47, 676–681
Bünning, E. (1973). "The Physiological Clock" Revised Third
   Edition, The English Universities Press Ltd., London
Cumming, B.G. and Wagner, E. (1968). *Annu. Rev. Plant
   Physiol.* 19, 381–415
Cumming, B.G., Hendricks, S.B. and Borthwick, H.A. (1965).
   Can. J. Bot. 43, 825–853
Daan, S. and Pittendrigh, C.S. (1976). *J. Comp. Physiol.* 106,
   253–266
Evans, L.T. (1976). *Aust. J. Plant Physiol.* 3, 207–217
Evans, L.T. and King, R.W. (1969). *Z. Pflanzenphysiol.* 60,
   272–288
Halaban, R. (1968). *Plant Physiol.* 43, 1894–1898
Hamner, K.C. and Bonner, J. (1938). *Bot. Gaz.* 100, 388–431
Harris, P.J.C. and Wilkins, M.B. (1978). *Planta* 143, 323–328
Hillman, W.S. (1964). *Am. Nat.* 98, 323–328
Hillman, W.S. (1976). *Annu. Rev. Plant Physiol.* 27, 159–179
Kato, A. (1979). *Plant Cell Physiol.* 20, 1285–1293
King, R.W. (1974). *Aust. J. Plant Physiol.* 1, 445–457
King, R.W. (1975). *Can. J. Bot.* 53, 2631–2638
King, R.W. and Cumming, B.G. (1972a). *Planta* 103, 281–301
King, R.W. and Cumming, B.G. (1972b). *Planta* 108, 39–57
King, R.W., Evans, L.T. and Wardlaw, I.F. (1968). *Z. Pflan-
   zenphysiol.* 59, 377–388
King, R.W., Vince-Prue, D. and Quail, P.H. (1978). *Planta*
   141, 15–22
King, R.W., Schäfer, E., Thomas, B. and Vince-Prue, D. (1982).
   Plant Cell Environ. 5, 395–404

Lumsden, P., Thomas, B. and Vince-Prue, D. (1982). *Plant Physiol.* 70, 277–282

Oda, Y. (1969). *Plant Cell Physiol.* 11, 417–425

Ogawa, Y. and King, R.W. (1979). *Plant Physiol.* 63, 643–649

Oota, Y. (1981). *Plant Cell Physiol.* 22, 99–113

Papenfuss, H.D. and Salisbury, F.B. (1967). *Plant Physiol.* 42, 1562–1568

Peterson, E.L. and Jones, M.D.R. (1979). *Nature (Lond.)* 280, 677–679

Pittendrigh, C.S. (1966). *Z. Pflanzenphysiol.* 54, 275–307

Pittendrigh, C.S. (1972). *Proc. Natl. Acad. Sci. USA* 69, 2734–2737

Saunders, D.S. (1982). "Insect Clocks" Second Edition. Pergamon Pess. Oxford, N.Y.

Satter, R.L., Guggino, S.E., Lonergan, T.A. and Galston, A.W. (1981). *Plant Physiol.* 67, 965–968

Schwabe, W.W. (1959). *J. Exp. Bot.* 10, 317–329

Searle, N.E. (1961). *Plant Physiol.* 36, 656–662

Takimoto, A. and Hamner, K.C. (1964). *Plant Physiol.* 39, 1024–1030

Vince-Prue, D. (1975). "Photoperiodism in Plants" McGraw Hill, London

Zeevaart, J.A.D. (1962). *Science* 137, 723–731

Zimmer, K. (1970). *Gartenbauwissenschaft* 35, 387–392

Chapter 8

PHOTORECEPTOR ACTION AND PHOTOPERIODIC INDUCTION
IN PHARBITIS NIL

B. THOMAS AND P. J. LUMSDEN

Glasshouse Crops Research Institute, Worthing Road,
Littlehampton, West Sussex, BN16 3PU, U.K.

INTRODUCTION

Photoperiodic regulation of floral induction is the consequence of an interaction between an endogenous timekeeper and
a light sensor (photoreceptor). The nature of photoperiodic
timekeeping has already been discussed in this volume by King
(see Chapter 7 in this volume). The aim of this chapter is to
consider the action of the photoreceptor in the photoperiodic
mechanism with particular emphasis on the light response of
single cycle SDP; photoreceptor action in LDP has been
discussed by Deitzer (Chapter 4 in this volume).
The photoreceptor involved in the sensing of daylength in
the vast majority of plants so far tested is phytochrome,
athough some evidence for a BAP or specific receptor for FR
can be found in the literature. It could be argued that the
identity of the photoreceptor for photoperiodism in plants is
of minor importance as animals show photoperiodic responses
without the benefit of phytochrome, adapting visual or other
pigments for use as necessary. Plants, however, differ from
animals in that their development is directly regulated by
light also acting through phytochrome. The possibility that
photomorphogenetic and photoperiodic effects of light are apt
to be confused must be appreciated by any experimenter attempting to elucidate the plants photoperiodic mechanism. In
essence the study of photoreceptor action in photoperiodism is
no different from the study of photoreceptor action in photomorphogenesis. The questions of which photoreceptor and how
does it act require the same types of experiment. In both

LIGHT AND THE FLOWERING PROCESS
ISBN 0.12.721960.9

cases it is desirable to identify the primary target for the
action of light and devise simple unambiguous assays for its
effect.

A major problem for both types of study, however, concerns
the uncertain nature of phytochrome action, especially in
light-grown plants (see Schäfer, Chapter 2 in this volume)
where responses can be a function of Pfr content (e.g. end-of
day responses) or photochemical turnover (e.g. irradiance-
dependent responses). Direct equivalents of these reactions
can be identified in photoperiodic systems and, in some cases
proof of phytochrome involvement remains circumstantial.

The complex and interactive nature of the plants photo-
responses make it necessary (at least initially) to seek the
least complicated experimental systems in which to study the
reactions of light which are exclusively associated with
photoperiodism. In our laboratory we have studied induction
in young initially dark-grown seedlings of *Pharbitis nil* cv
Violet. Some practical advantages of this system include the
relatively large numbers of uniform seedlings which can be
raised for experiments, their ability to respond to a single
inductive dark period without the prior provision of photosynthetic light, and the relatively short time-period of post-
inductive culture needed to develop a measurable flowering
response. Light-grown *Pharbitis nil* has been the subject of
vigorous investigation in several laboratories over many
years, enabling our studies to be carried out against a background of extensive characterization of the photoperiodic
responses of light-grown seedlings of this species.

INTERACTIONS BETWEEN LIGHT AND PHOTOPERIODIC TIMING

Dark-grown seedlings of *Pharbitis nil* will flower in response
to a single R pulse if Benzyl Adenine (BA) is given at the
same time and a subsequent long dark period is given prior to
transferring the plant to continuous (i.e. non-inductive)
light for flower development (Ogawa and King, 1979). The
flowering response can be modified by a R pulse given during
the inductive dark period; the sensitivity of the plant to
this treatment varying with the time in the form of a circadian rhythm (Fig. 1).

Replacing the initial R pulse with continuous light shows
that the phase of the rhythm is established by the beginning
of the light treatment as long as the duration of the light
treatment is less than 6 h. Following a light period longer
than 6 h the phase of the rhythm is determined by the transition to darkness. Two types of interaction between light
and an endogenous rhythm can therefore be postulated in this
system and analysed independently.

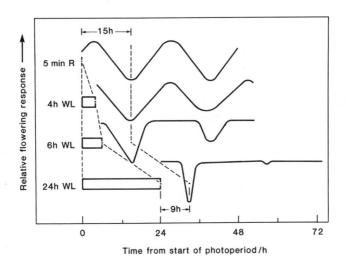

Fig. 1. *Schematic representation of how the circadian rhythm in sensitivity to a R interruption of an inductive dark period is modified by increasing photoperiod length in initially dark grown seedlings of* Pharbitis nil.

Rhythm Phasing

Light preceding an inductive dark period acts to entrain or phase the time measuring system. Photoperiodic time measurement is thought to be based on the operation of a circadian rhythm (see Chapter 7 in this volume), as manifested in the rhythmic flowering response of SDP to night length (Coulter and Hamner, 1964; Cumming et al., 1965), or to interruption of a long dark period by light pulses (Takimoto and Hamner, 1964; Cumming et al., 1965).

The responses of *Pharbitis nil* described in Fig. 1 resemble those of other SDP in that after short durations of light the phase of the subsequent response rhythm bears a fixed relationship to the beginning of the light period, but after longer durations the rhythm appears to become suspended and then has a fixed phase relationship with the end of the light period (Papenfuss and Salisbury, 1967; King and Cumming 1972; Lumsden et al., 1982). This is similar to the situation with overt rhythms where, under continuous light of high intensity, the rhythmic function disappears and is restored during subsequent darkness, with its phase bearing a fixed relationship to the end of the light period (Sweeney, 1969). Superficially therefore, light acts to suspend circadian rhythms although it is not certain how this is achieved. From observations on the overt rhythm of pupal eclosion in *Drosophila pseudoobscura*

Pittendrigh (1966) proposed that rhythmic functions are driven by an underlying pacemaker and that apparent phase-responses of the rhythm to light are actually responses of the pacemaker. Pavlidis (1968) proposed a "limit cycle model" for the hypothetical *Drosophila* pacemaker. In this model the path of the pacemaker is represented as a cycle which is variable in diameter and location. Light acts to alter the pacemaker dynamics by shrinking and displacing the limit cycle. Although the pacemaker continues to run in light the diameter of the light limit cycle is so reduced that its phase, and hence the phase of the rhythm, does not appear to change. If we apply the pacemaker limit cycle model to the control of induction in *Pharbitis*, the action of continuous light via the photoreceptor is considered as the maintenance of the pacemaker in the light limit-cycle. Although this model may not be fully correct, it provides a useful conceptual framework in which to consider the action of the photoreceptor.

As the photoreceptor is assumed to act on the pacemaker rather than on the flowering response *per se*, the assay for photoreceptor action must be to determine the effect of light on the progress of the pacemaker. In practice we have attempted to establish the underlying rhythm in light sensitivity during darkness by determining the time at which a R night-break is most effective at preventing induction (NBmax). Two lines of circumstantial evidence suggest that the light-dark transition is sensed by phytochrome. Normal night-break timing occurs in photobleached tissues which show no detectable photosynthesis (King *et al.*, 1978). Also, R is the most effective spectral region in preventing the onset of dark timing in green seedlings (Takimoto, 1967). The way in which the photoreversible photoreceptor, phytochrome, detects a light-dark transition is unclear, but some possibilities are outlined in Fig. 2. One way is that when Pfr is kept above a threshold level by light the pacemaker is maintained in the light limit cycle (Fig. 2c, d) and the end of the light period is signalled by a reduction of Pfr. However, in experiments where, at the end of the light period, the level of Pfr is reduced photochemically by exposing plants to FR, there is little advance in the onset of dark timing as compared with plants moved directly to darkness (Takimoto and Hamner, 1965; Vince-Prue, 1981).

Similar results from a more detailed experiment carried out in our laboratory are shown in Fig. 3. If the perception of the end of the light period is coupled to a reduction in Pfr, it follows that the thermal reactions which lower the level of Pfr must occur rapidly. Spectrophotometric measurements on

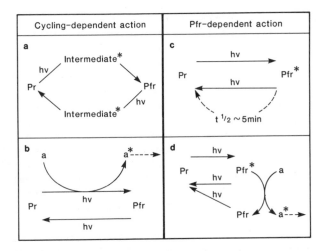

*Fig. 2.   Some ways in which phytochrome might detect con-
tinuous light enabling it to perceive light-dark transitions.
Continuous light could be sensed directly through photochemical turnover (cycling)-2a, b; or through the presence of
recently formed Pfr-2c, d.   In all cases light is detected
through the component marked *.*

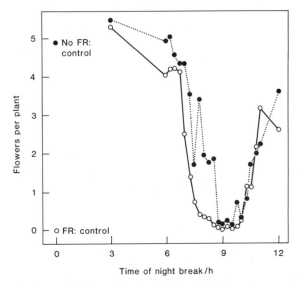

*Fig. 3.   The effect of FR at the beginning of a 48 h inductive
dark period on the timing of NB sensitivity in Pharbitis nil.
Plants were germinated in darkness and received one 24 h photoperiod prior to the FR treatment. O FR treated, ● FR omitted.
(After Lumsden and Vince-Prue, 1984).*

light-grown tissue, either photobleached at low temperature or
with Norflurazon, show that the amount of Pfr does decrease
rapidly on transfer to darkness, reaching a stable level after
about 1 h (Vince-Prue et al., 1978; Heim et al., 1981; Rombach
et al., 1982). The results of Rombach, using Pharbitis and of
Brockmann and Schäfer (1982), using Amaranthus caudatus,
suggest the existence of at least two kinetically distinct
pools of phytochrome, only one of which undergoes rapid decay.
The fact that photochemical lowering of Pfr accelerates the
onset of dark timing by much less than 1 h suggests that the
necessary changes must occur before the loss of Pfr is complete. Thus, the concept of a threshold level of Pfr being
the means of distinguishing between light and dark is supported only if a specific pool of phytochrome is involved and if
the threshold is high.

In an alternative approach to this problem, we have attempted to replace continuous light with intermittent pulses. In

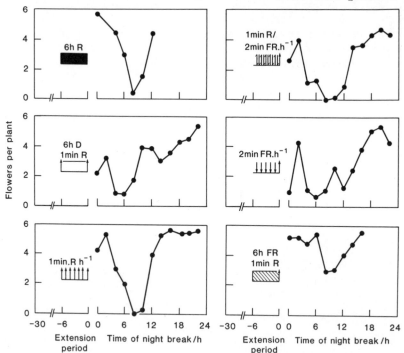

Fig. 4. Effect of various day extension treatments on the
response to R interruptions of an inductive dark period in
Pharbitis nil. Plants were germinated in darkness and received one 24 h photoperiod followed by a 6 h extension treatment as indicated (Adapted from Lumsden and Vince-Prue, 1984).

these experiments plants were exposed to a 6 h period of experimental light treatments immediately following a single 24
h photoperiod and NBmax was determined in a subsequent 48 h
dark period (Fig. 4). The rationale was that extension
periods perceived as continuous light would delay the initiation of dark timing giving NBmax after 8 h darkness. If, on
the other hand, the extension was percieved as darkness NBmax
would occur 8 h from the beginning of the extension period.
In such experiments 1-min pulses of R given every hour were as
effective as 6 h of continuous R in preventing the onset of
dark timing. Although this could have been due to their maintaining the level of Pfr above a threshold, previous data
(Fig. 3) suggest that any threshold must be passed well within
1 h. Treatments where the pulses of R were immediately
followed by 2 min FR or where continuous FR was given for 6 h,
both of which result in a low level of Pfr throughout the
extension period, were as effective as continuous R (Fig. 4).
The Pfr-threshold hypothesis is, therefore, not supported by
these results. The alternatives are that the presence of
continuous light is detected through some function of phytochrome photoconversion or cycling (Jose and Vince-Prue, 1978)
either directly (Fig. 2a, b) or by the continuous formation of
Pfr (Fig. 2d). Haupt and Reif (1979) suggested a similar
mechanism to that shown in Fig. 2d to explain phytochrome
control of chloroplast orientation in *Mesotaenium caldariorum*.
They suggested that, in darkness, Pfr rapidly lost its physiological activity which was restored by cycling the photoreceptor through Pr. Experiments to distinguish between mechanisms based on phytochrome cycling or phytochrome ageing for
end-of-day sensing remain to be carried out. Both, in theory,
could account for the observation that dusk sensing under
natural conditions is a consequence of decreasing irradiance
rather than spectral changes (Salisbury, 1981; Vince-Prue,
1981). Furthermore, both would enable the plant to detect a
light-dark transition independently of the prevailing R/FR
ratio which, under natural conditions, would vary with the
degree of shading. The sensing of continuous light by one of
these dynamic actions of phytochrome is then directly
analagous to the situation in photoperiodically sensitive
organisms which do not possess photoreversible sensors. In
these, an identifiable photoexcited state with a short half-
life ($\ll 1$ s) is the means by which photoreceptors allow the
discrimination between light and darkness.

Unless there is a delay of at least 1 h between the detection of darkness and the establishment of the dark limit cycle
an explanation of the effectiveness of hourly light pulses is
necessary as it does not conform to any of the schemes proposed for phytochrome action in Fig. 2. A possible mechanism

is suggested by the response to a single pulse of R after a
6 h dark treatment (Fig. 4), where NBmax occurred 3 h later
than would be predicted if the rhythm ran from the end of the
main light period. It is possible that this delay is due to a
phase shift elicited by the R pulse (Lumsden and Vince-Prue,
1984). The effect of hourly pulses can be attributed to the
same type of action. A phase shift produced by a pulse of
light after 1 h of darkness would effectively return the
pacemaker, and hence the rhythm, to the position occupied at
the end of the light period. Subsequent pulses would simply
repeat the sequence. The effect of R pulses was not reversed
by FR, but after pulses of FR alone the subsequent night-break
response was very similar to that after 6 h dark (Fig. 4).

A phase shift may, therefore, be a response to newly generated Pfr with an extremely rapid escape from reversibility by
FR. Phase shifting in response to Pfr input has also been
demonstrated for the overt leaf movement rhythm of *Samanea
saman* (Simon *et al.*, 1976). As the effects of R pulses and
continuous light are both consistent with response to the
input of 'new' Pfr, and both apparently involve phase adjust-
ments to the underlying pacemaker, it is tempting to suggest
that they are closely related in terms of biochemical or
biophysical mechanism.

Night-break Responses

In addition to the entraining effects of light acting on the
underlying pacemaker, a second action of light, involving an
interaction with the pacemaker, can be postulated. This is
the circadian rhythm in sensitivity to a R pulse during an inductive dark period, most commonly observed as the NB phenomenon. In seedlings of *Pharbitis nil* which have received at
least 6 h light, R is most inhibitory (NBmax) given 8 or 9 h
(depending on the seed batch) from the beginning of the dark
period, irrespective of total dark period duration (Lumsden *et
al.*, 1982). The inhibitory effect of a saturating R pulse at
NBmax cannot be reduced by manipulating the timing of subsequent light treatments suggesting that its action is on the
inductive process rather than on the pacemaker (but see
Chapter 7 in this volume). Two distinct features of photoreceptor action for these responses concern photoreceptor
identity and sensitivity changes. In contrast to entrainment
phenomena the classic criterion for phytochrome participation
can be demonstrated for NB inhibition in *Pharbitis nil*.
Reversibility of the R response by FR, with an escape time of
30 - 60 s, was demonstrated for light-grown *Pharbitis nil*
seedlings (Fredericq, 1964). Confirmation of the participation of phytochrome for NB response of several SDP including

Xanthium strumarium (Parker *et al.*, 1946) and LDP such as
Hyoscyamus niger (Parker *et al.*, 1950) has been afforded by
action spectra. There is to the knowledge of these authors,
no published action spectrum for the NB response of light-
grown *Pharbitis nil*. However, Saji *et al.*, (1983) recently
determined an action spectrum for the inhibition of flowering
by a R pulse in dark-grown seedlings which were potentiated to
flower by R and BA (i.e. Fig. 1, 15 h, top line). This was
entirely consistent with the absorption spectrum of Pr (Fig.
5).

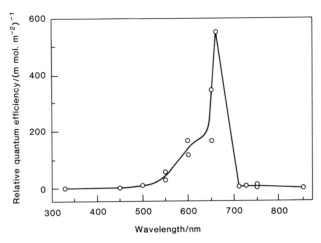

Fig. 5. Action spectrum for the inhibition of flowering in
Pharbitis nil. *Dark-grown seedlings were potentiated to*
flower with R and BA followed by a 48 h dark period. The
action spectrum for the inhibition of flowering was determined
15 h following the initial R pulse (Adapted from Saji et al.*,*
1983).

The rhythmic sensitivity to the light pulses suggests that the
system responds differently to Pfr input at different times.
This is supported by the observation that photoperiodic plants
show rhythmic changes in sensitivity to light, as first documented by König (1958) for *Chenopodium amaranticolor*. Similarly for *Pharbitis nil*, the rhythmic response is accompanied
by changes of up to two orders of magnitude in the sensitivity
of the response to light (King *et al.*, 1982). An alternative
interpretation of these results is, however, that the pacemaker acts to change the properties of phytochrome in the dark
period so that the rhythmic effect of light reflects the
transduction efficiency of the photoreceptor. King *et al.*
(1982) were, in fact, able to show that changes in sensitivity
were accompanied by changes in the quantum yield of photocon-

version from Pr --> Pfr and Pfr --> Pr. Superficially, these changes were much too small to account for the sensitivity changes but, as the kinetics of the dark reactions involved are not known, some doubt remains as to the correct interpretation of these observations.

Pfr Requirement for Flowering

It is interesting to note that the inhibitory effect of a R pulse given after 15 h darkness in the dark-grown *Pharbitis nil* system cannot be reversed by FR. To look at it in another way, at a time when Pfr formation is highly inhibitory for floral induction, Pfr removal, e.g. by a saturating 750 nm pulse, also inhibits flowering (Table 1). The most obvious explanation for these results is that there are two opposing

TABLE 1   *The effect of establishing various Pfr/Ptot ratios at 14 h following an initial R pulse and BA in dark-grown seedlings of* Pharbitis nil. *Seedlings were given a saturating exposure with the wavelength indicated after 14 h of a 48 h inductive dark period (Thomas and Vince-Prue, unpublished results).*

Wavelength	Pfr/Ptot	Flowers per plant	Control
750 nm	<0.01	0.1	1.0
730 nm	0.03	0	1.0
720 nm	0.04	0	2.5
708 nm	0.13	0	2.5
699 nm	0.24	0	2.5
688 nm	0.47	0	2.5
680 nm	0.58	0.2	2.5
660 nm	0.75	0	2.5

actions of Pfr at this time; 'new' Pfr inhibits flowering but 'old' Pfr is required for flowering. There is supporting evidence in the literature that, for the induction of flowering in SDP, Pfr is required at certain times in the daily cycle (Vince-Prue, 1975). In *Pharbitis nil* FR given at the end of short photoperiods suppresses the flowering response to an inductive dark period and this response shows full R/FR reversibility (Fredericq, 1964). Action spectra for the inhibition of flowering and its subsequent reversal by R

show maxima at ~720 nm and 600–700 nm respectively, consistent
with the involvement of phytochrome (Nakayama et al., 1960).
These and similar experiments with the SDP Xanthium, Kalanchoe
blossfeldiana and Lemna paucicostata show that phytochrome
action requires the persistence of Pfr for part of the inductive dark period (Vince–Prue, 1975). Takimoto and Hamner
(1965) showed that for plants grown in continuous light and
given a single 48 h inductive dark period, FR was fully
inhibitory immediately after the photoperiod but became
gradually less effective up to about 20 h of darkness, from
which time it had no effect. In a similar experiment for
dark-grown Pharbitis nil, FR pulses in a 72 h dark period
following a R + BA treatment indicated a requirement for Pfr,
even after 48 h in darkness, to achieve maximum flowering
(King et al. 1982). The conclusion that the Pfr requirement
can be satisfied in the light as well as in the darkness has
been tested by determining the effectiveness of FR pulses at
different times in a 60 h dark period following a 12 or 24 h
photoperiod in initially dark-grown Pharbitis nil seedlings
(Fig. 6). FR remained inhibitory for up to 55 h following

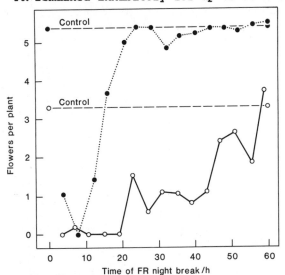

Fig. 6. Effect of photoperiod length on the requirement for
Pfr for flowering in Pharbitis nil. Dark-grown seedlings
received a 12 h (O) or 24 h (●) photoperiod followed by a 72 h
inductive dark period which was interrupted at various times
by a FR pulse (Lumsden, unpublished results).

the 12 h photoperiod and up to 20 h after the 24 h photoperiod. The difference greatly exceeds the difference in
photoperiod length, confirming that at least part of the Pfr

requirement is satisfied more rapidly in continuous light than in darkness.

One further feature of this particular action of phytochrome is that Pfr does not have to be present continuously in the dark period to be effective. Following an end—of—day FR treatment, R pulses show repromotion of flowering in light-grown *Pharbitis nil* for up to 20 h into the dark period (Takimoto and Hamner, 1965) and a comparable situation for dark—grown seedlings is shown in Fig. 3.

As discussed earlier, photochemically lowering Pfr at the end of the photoperiod dramatically reduces the flowering response, but has little effect on dark timing. This action of Pfr should, therefore, probably be considered as a photomorphogenetic response in which Pfr is required for floral induction to be established. As such it is directly comparable to the end—of—day growth response (Vince—Prue, 1977) first described by Downs *et al.* (1957).

INTERACTION OF LIGHT EFFECTS

In this chapter we have attempted to demonstrate that at least three distinct photoreactions are relevant to the photoperiodic regulation of flowering in both light—grown and dark-grown *Pharbitis nil*. These are the phasing effect of light to dark transitions, the inhibitory action of NB treatments and the requirement for Pfr for a strong flowering response as shown by end—of—day FR effects. Night—break responses and FR effects involve responses to Pfr which change independently with time during the inductive dark period. For NB responses there is a transient period of susceptibility to inhibition by Pfr whereas in the FR response Pfr promotion of flowering occurs progressively during the dark period. Inhibition of flowering by FR can be observed at times subsequent to NBmax indicating that Pfr has persisted through this period. Thus at NBmax, Pfr required for flowering is present yet newly formed Pfr inhibits flowering. The concept of two simultaneous actions of light, as outlined here, has particularly important consequences in the interpretation of null—point experiments. The null—point method is based on the assumption that if a light source establishes the same Pfr/Ptot ratio as is present in the tissues prior to illumination it will have no physiological effect. It was devised by Cumming *et al.* (1965) and subsequently used by several other workers to follow Pfr/Ptot ratios during inductive dark periods using flowering as the response (Evans and King, 1969; Evans, 1976; King *et al.*, 1978; Kato, 1979). However, if Pfr is having two separate and opposing effects the null test will be misleading. At NBmax when both Pfr input and removal inhibits

flowering one can predict that a null value would be unobtain-
able (e.g. Table 1). In their original paper, Cumming *et al.*
(1965) observed such points using *Chenopodium rubrum* but were
not able to explain why they should occur. In LDP where NB
(when effective) promote flowering, null points are unobtain-
able at certain times because all light treatments are promotive (e.g., Kato, 1979). Interpretation of null-point
experiments in terms of changes in the internal Pfr/Ptot ratio
should, therefore, be made with the greatest care.

The presence of more than one light-controlled component
also presents a problem in determining the identity of the
photoreceptor(s) for the first R pulse in the dark-grown
seedling system. The first R pulse synchronizes or initiates
the circadian rhythm in sensitivity to light (Lumsden *et al.*,
1982; King, Chapter 7 in this volume), and its effect is
apparently reversible by FR (King *et al.*, 1982). However,
reversibility occurs for up to 20 h after the initial R pulse
whereas the rhythm is clearly established at 15 h. It cannot
be assumed, therefore, that the participation of phytochrome
extends beyond the generation of the Pfr required for a
measurable flowering response. It has yet to be established
that setting the rhythm by R, equivalent to the 'light-on' or
dawn signal, involves phytochrome.

Sites of Photoreceptor Action

It is generally accepted that the leaves are the site of daylength perception with the response being expressed at the
apex. When leaves and apices on the same plant are treated
simultaneously with photoperiods of different length, the
flowering response is determined by the treatment received by
the leaves. One of the first experiments of this kind demonstrated that exposure of only the leaves of the LDP *Spinacia
oleracea* caused the initiation of floral primordia at the
terminal growing point (Knott, 1934). The question of where
perception occurs can also be asked with respect to the individual photoreactions. As daylength measurement must involve
the photoperiodic timer, actions of the photoreceptor which
alter timing, or are controlled by the pacemaker, presumably
occur in the leaf. There is some evidence, however, that in
Pharbitis nil seedlings, a NB can be perceived by vegetative
apical buds in which the leaves are not yet expanded allowing
the apex to override the signals from induced expanded cotyledons (Gressel *et al.*, 1980). Unlike the response to daylength or night length *per se*, the site of perception for the
end-of-day FR response has not been specifically determined.
If it could be shown that the requirement for Pfr for
flowering was restricted to the apex it would provide a

trivial explanation for the dual action of Pfr in the inductive dark period. Alternatively, if it is perceived in the
leaves or cotyledons other types of explanations for the dual
action of Pfr must be considered. It should be noted here
that there is no evidence as yet to rule out changes in the
availability of particular phytochrome receptors or the
kinetics of their action as the basis of the multiple phytochrome responses. However, an explanation favoured at present
by several workers is that dual action of Pfr involves
separate pools of phytochrome with different kinetics and
specificity of action. The spectrophotometric evidence for
such pools, which could possibly be separated at a tissue,
cellular or organellar level, was discussed earlier, and is
supported by immunochemical data (Thomas et al., 1984). It is
interesting to note that interactions with the circadian
rhythm are closely coupled to photochemical turnover of phytochrome whereas the end-of-day response is a persistent long-
term reaction to a stable fraction of Pfr. It is tempting to
ascribe these actions respectively to labile and stable pools
of phytochrome such as those which have been identified on the
basis of their Pfr destruction kinetics (see Chapter 2 in this
volume).

REFERENCES

Brockmann, J. and Schäfer, E. (1982). *Photochem. Photobiol.*
    35, 555-558
Coulter, M.W. and Hamner, K.C. (1964). *Plant Physiol.* 39,
    848-856
Cumming, B.G., Hendricks, S.B. and Borthwick, H.A. (1965).
    Can. J. Bot. 43, 825-853
Downs, R.J., Hendricks, S.B. and Borthwick, H.A. (1957). *Bot.
    Gaz.* 118, 199-208
Evans, L.T. (1976). *Aust. J. Plant Physiol.* 3, 207-217
Evans, L.T. and King, R.W. (1969). *Z. Pflanzenphysiol.* 60,
    277-288
Fredericq, H. (1964). *Plant Physiol.* 39, 812-816
Gressel, J., Zilberstein, A., Porath, D. and Arzee, T. (1980).
    In "Photoreceptors and Plant Development" (ed J. de Greef).
    pp. 525-530, Antwerpen University Press, Antwerp
Haupt, W. and Reif, G. (1979). *Z. Pflanzenphysiol.* 92,
    153-161
Heim, B., Jabben, M. and Schäfer, E. (1981). *Photochem.
    Photobiol.* 34, 89-93
Jose, A.M. and Vince-Prue, D. (1978). *Photochem. Photobiol.*
    27, 209-216
Kato, A. (1979). *Plant Cell Physiol.* 20, 1273-1283
King, R.W. and Cumming, B.G. (1972). *Planta* 103, 281-301

King, R.W., Vince-Prue, D. and Quail, P. (1978). *Planta* 141, 15-22

King, R.W., Schäfer, E., Thomas, B. and Vince-Prue, D. (1982). *Plant Cell Environ.* 5, 395-404

Knott, J.E. (1934). *Proc. Am. Soc. Hort. Sci.* 31, 152-154

Könitz, W. (1958). *Planta* 51, 1-29

Lumsden, P.J., Thomas, B. and Vince-Prue, D. (1982). *Plant Physiol.* 70, 277-282

Lumsden, P.J. and Vince-Prue, D. (1984). *Physiol. Plant.* 60, 427-432

Nakayama, S., Borthwick, H.A. and Hendricks, S.B. (1960). *Bot. Gaz.* 121, 237-243

Ogawa, Y. and King, R.W. (1979). *Plant Cell Physiol.* 20, 119-122

Papenfuss, H.D. and Salisbury, F.D. (1967). *Plant Physiol.* 42, 1562-1568

Parker, M.W., Hendricks, S.B., Borthwick, H.A. and Scully, N.J. (1946). *Bot. Gaz.* 108, 1-26

Parker, M.W., Hendricks, S.B. and Borthwick, H.A. (1950). *Bot. Gaz.* 111, 242-252

Pavlidis, T. (1968). *In* "Lectures on Mathematics in the Life Sciences" (ed M. Gerstenhabeer). Vol. I, pp. 88-112. American Mathematical Society, Providence, Rhode Island

Pittendrigh, C.S. (1966). *Z. Pflanzenphysiol.* 54, 275-307

Rombach, J., Benzink, J. and Katsura, N. (1982). *Physiol. Plant.* 56, 251-258

Saji, H., Vince-Prue, D. and Furuya, M. (1983). *Plant Cell Physiol.* 24, 1183-1189

Salisbury, F.B. (1981). *Plant Physiol.* 67, 1230-1238

Simon, E., Satter, R.L. and Galston, A.W. (1976). *Plant Physiol.* 58, 421-425

Sweeney, B.M. (1969). "Rhythmic Phenomena in Plants" Academic Press, London

Takimoto, A. (1967). *Bot. Mag. Tokyo* 80, 241-247

Takimoto, A. and Hamner, K.C. (1964). *Plant Physiol.* 39, 1024-1030

Takimoto, A. and Hamner, K.C. (1965). *Plant Physiol.* 40, 859-864

Thomas, B., Crook, N.E. and Penn, S.E. (1984). *Physiol. Plant.* 60, 409-415

Vince-Prue, D. (1975). "Photoperiodism in Plants". McGraw-Hill, Maidenhead, England

Vince-Prue, D. (1981). *In* "Plants and the Daylight Spectrum" (ed H. Smith). pp. 223-242. Academic Press, London

Vince-Prue, D. (1977). *Planta* 133, 149-156

Vince-Prue, D., King, R.W. and Quail, P.H. (1978). *Planta* 141, 9-14

Chapter 9

BIOCHEMISTRY OF INDUCTION - THE IMMEDIATE ACTION OF LIGHT

CHARLES F. CLELAND

Smithsonian Environmental Research Center
12441 Parklawn Drive, Rockville, Maryland, 20852, U.S.A.

INTRODUCTION

The photoperiodic stimulation of flowering involves events
both in the leaves and the meristems. Flower induction takes
place in the leaves in response to photoinductive light/dark
cycles, while evocation occurs in the meristems in response to
the arrival of the flowering stimulus and leads to floral
morphogenesis. The present paper will deal only with events
taking place in the leaf and thus with flower induction.

TIME OF FLOWER INDUCTION

With only a few exceptions flower induction requires some
exposure to light (Vince-Prue, 1975). The time when flower
induction actually occurs, however, is difficult to determine
precisely. This is particularly true for plants that require
multiple cycles to achieve flower induction, but even in
plants that flower in response to a single inductive light/
dark cycle, it is difficult to determine the precise time. In
long-day plants flower induction occurs during the extended
light period, but efforts to grow plants on short days and
induce flowering with a single brief light treatment during
the dark period have usually failed (Vince-Prue, 1975).
    In short-day plants the induced state develops in the dark
period, and in the absence of sufficient darkness flowering
will never occur. Nevertheless, light is essential if flower
induction is to occur. When *Pharbitis nil* was grown in the
dark it required two brief red light treatments 24 hours apart

LIGHT AND THE FLOWERING PROCESS
ISBN 0.12.721960.9

in order to make a subsequent 24-h dark period inductive
(Friend, 1975). In the absence of either of these light
treatments the dark period was ineffective. Thus, light is
crucial for flower induction in all photoperiodic plants, but
the actual transition to the induced state need not take place
in the light nor in response to a specific light stimulus.

PHYTOCHROME INVOLVEMENT IN FLOWER INDUCTION

In many short-day plants, red/far-red reversibility has been
demonstrated for night-break treatments and end-of-day light
treatments (Vince-Prue, 1975). In the work of Friend (1975)
the two red light treatments necessary to permit *Pharbitis nil*
to flower in response to a subsequent dark period were both
reversible by far-red light. Clearly in this case the only
light needed for flower induction is red light and the effect
is mediated by phytochrome. Thus, in short-day plants it is
clear that phytochrome is the photoreceptor for flower induction.

In long-day plants, red/far-red reversibility for night-
break treatments has only been shown in Wintex barley (*Hordeum
vulgare*) and *Hyoscyamus niger* (Downs, 1965) and only if the
plants were grown on dark periods about 12 h long. When 16 h
dark periods were used instead, brief red light night-breaks
were ineffective and flowering was only obtained if 4-h night-
breaks or 8-h daylength extensions were used (Lane *et al.*,
1965).

Most long-day plants need night-break or daylength extension treatments much longer than would be required for conversion of Pr to Pfr. Furthermore, the action maximum for
such light treatments is often in the 700-720 nm region
(Schneider *et al.*, 1967; Blondon and Jacques, 1970; Imhoff *et
al.*, 1979). These results raise the question of whether the
photoreceptor for these light effects is phytochrome or some
other pigment system such as photosystem I activity mediated
by chlorophyll or the activity of another, as yet undiscovered
pigment system. There is no direct evidence for the existence
of a new pigment system, and the involvement of chlorophyll
seems unlikely based on work in *Arabidopsis thaliana* where
stimulation of flowering by addition of far-red light to a
background of white light occurred equally well in green
plants and in white plants that had been bleached by treatment
with the herbicide Norflurazon (4-chloro-5-(methylamino)-2-
(α,α,α-trifluoro-m-tolyl)-3(2H)-pyridazinone) (Deitzer, 1982).
On the assumption that the Norflurazon-treated plants were
completely bleached and contained no chlorophyll, this work
strongly argues against the involvement of chlorophyll, at
least in this plant. Models have been developed that invoke

phytochrome as the photoreceptor and account for the shift in the action maximum to the 700–720 nm region (Mancinelli and Rabino, 1978), but there is no direct evidence to support any of the models. Nevertheless, it is generally accepted that phytochrome is involved in the flowering of long–day plants (perhaps in combination with other photoreceptors), and thus that phytochrome acts as the primary photoreceptor for flower induction in all photoperiodic flowering plants.

PHYTOCHROME ACTION IN THE CONTROL OF FLOWER INDUCTION

There are two main models on the mode of action of phyto–chrome. The first proposes that phytochrome exerts its effect at the level of differential gene activation and repression (Mohr, 1972). Phytochrome clearly has effects at this level as shown by recent work in barley (Gollmer and Apel, 1983) and *Lemna gibba* G3 (Stiekema *et al.*, 1983) where molecular hybrid–ization probes were used to demonstrate that the steady–state level of mRNA sequences encoding for both the light–harvesting chlorophyll a/b protein and the small subunit of ribulose–1,5–bisphosphate carboxylase (only in *Lemna*) are under phytochrome control. This evidence, however, does not indicate whether or not the primary effect of phytochrome is at the gene level.

The second theory proposes that phytochrome acts at the membrane level to alter membrane properties and only in–directly acts elsewhere such as at the gene level (Marme, 1977). In the case of leaflet movements in *Albizzia juli–brissin* and *Samanea saman*, direct effects of phytochrome on membrane permeability have been well documented (Satter and Galston, 1981), and in several other systems the response to red light is so fast that the effect almost certainly is at the membrane level (Marme, 1977). Thus, this model has generally received the most support in recent years.

There is virtually no information on the immediate conse–quence of phytochrome action with regard to flower induction. The ultimate consequence is the formation of a flowering stimulus, but at present nothing is known about the identity of the flowering stimulus or even whether it consists of one, or more than one substance. Even if the flowering stimulus were identified, its formation is probably many steps removed from the primary action of phytochrome in flower induction. Phytochrome could be acting to stimulate formation of the mRNA for a crucial enzyme needed for the biosynthesis of the flowering stimulus, or it could be acting to alter membrane permeability and thereby set in motion a series of events that eventually leads to the formation of the flowering stimulus. In the absence of any information on the identity of the flowering stimulus, one can only probe the flower induction

process through indirect approaches and hope that such efforts
will provide insights on how phytochrome controls this
process.

Control of Flower Induction at the Level of Gene Expression

Relatively little attention has been given to the possibility
that flower induction involves changes in protein and/or
nucleic acid metabolism in the leaves. Efforts to compare
proteins from vegetative and induced leaves with gel electrophoresis failed to detect any reproducible differences in
Xanthium strumarium (Sherwood *et al.*, 1971), *Pharbitis nil*
(Oota and Umemura, 1970) and *Impatiens balsamina* (Sawhney *et
al.*, 1976). In contrast, when leaf extracts from three different cultivars of *Amaranthus* were examined by gel electrophoresis, two new protein bands appeared in every case after
3-5 short days (sufficient to induce flowering) but the new
bands were different in each cultivar (Kohli *et al.*, 1980).
     Treatment of *Xanthium strumarium* leaves with cycloheximide
strongly inhibited flowering, but the minimum concentration
needed to suppress flowering completely was nearly 10-fold
less than the minimum concentration that had any inhibitory
effect on protein synthesis (Ross, 1970). Thus, it seems
doubtful that the cycloheximide effect was mediated through an
inhibition of protein synthesis.
     In studies on *Perilla crispa*, plants were given 14-18 short
days and in one set of plants the leaves were treated with
5-fluorouracil, 2-thiouracil or ethionine. Both treated and
untreated leaves were grafted on to long-day receptor plants
and flowering resulted in every case. Therefore, it was
concluded that synthesis of nucleic acids and proteins is not
directly involved in flower induction (Zeevaart, 1969).
Similar studies with *Lolium temulentum* failed to show any
significant inhibition of flowering when various inhibitors of
protein and nucleic acid synthesis were applied to the leaves
at different times during the single long-day treatment
(Evans, 1969). In contrast, application of actinomycin D to
cotyledons of *Pharbitis nil* led to inhibition of flowering
(Arzee *et al.*, 1970). In addition, the base ratios of RNA
extracted from cotyledons exposed to one short day were
different from the base ratios of RNA from cotyledons exposed
to long days or one short day plus night-break treatment (Oota
and Umemura, 1970).
     The above results taken together provide little evidence
that synthesis of proteins and nucleic acids in the leaves is
important for flower induction. Only a few plants have been
examined, however, and thus this question needs to be examined
more carefully using the better methods that are now available

before a final conclusion can be made.

Control of Flower Induction Through Alteration of Membrane Properties

Considerable attention has been given to the hypothesis that the phytochrome control of flower induction occurs at the level of interaction with membranes (Vince-Prue, 1975). One line of evidence is that escape from photoreversibility for night-break treatments occurs within only 2–3 minutes in *Pharbitis nil* (Fredericq, 1964) and *Chenopodium album* (Borthwick, 1964). For other plants escape from photoreversibility often takes much longer (Vince-Prue, 1975), but at least in the above cases it could be argued that Pfr action is completed very quickly which supports action at the membrane level.

Two other lines of evidence for membrane involvement in the phytochrome control of flower induction are the interaction of phytochrome with circadian rhythms and chemical studies on flowering in *Lemna*.

Involvement of Phytochrome with Circadian Rhythms of Flowering
There is considerable support for the hypothesis that changes in membrane properties are an integral part of the circadian system (Engelmann and Schrempf, 1980). In green plants, phytochrome is usually the photoreceptor that interacts with the circadian clock and this action sometimes involves a change in membrane properties (Gorton and Satter, 1983).

In *Chenopodium rubrum* the effect of red light on flowering when given as a night-break varies in a circadian fashion (Cumming *et al.*, 1965). This rhythm of sensitivity to red light is affected by ethanol which is thought to influence circadian rhythms by altering membrane properties (Cumming, 1969). Thus, based on work in *Chenopodium rubrum* and other plants it can be postulated that flower induction in some way involves a circadian clock and that circadian changes in membrane properties alter the effectiveness of phytochrome and its ability to control flower induction.

Studies with Lemna Most work on the effect of light on flowering in *Lemna* has been carried out with different strains of the short-day plant *Lemna paucicostata* and the long-day plant *Lemna gibba*, both of which show typical photoperiodic flowering responses. The morphology of a *Lemna* plant, however, is quite unusual (Hillman, 1961). Recognizable leaves and stems do not exist and the apices are located within the reproductive pockets where they are in close proximity to the photosynthetic tissue of the frond.

The photosynthetic tissue of the frond can be thought of as the physiological equivalent of a leaf and undoubtedly serves as the site of flower induction. Because of the small size of *Lemna* (3–10 mm long) and its aquatic habit, chemical substances in the medium are only a few cell layers away from any part of the frond. This means it is much easier to treat *Lemna* "leaves" with chemical substances on a continuous basis than is true for leaves on a more typical flowering plant. Virtually all light effects on flowering in photoperiodic plants are perceived by the leaves (Vince—Prue, 1975), and thus it seems reasonable to assume that studies dealing with light effects on flowering in *Lemna* are directed at events occurring in the "leaves" and not the apex. Therefore, *Lemna* is an ideal plant to study the interaction of different chemical substances with light in the control of flower induction.

In *Lemna paucicostata* 6746 daily transfers of the plants to distilled water for 2–4 h during each dark period resulted in a substantial inhibition of flowering (Halaban and Hillman, 1970). The time of maximum effectiveness coincided very closely with the time when a night—break was most effective for inhibiting flowering. In *Lemna gibba* G3 a 12 h exposure to distilled water was inhibitory for flowering if given during the subjective night, but not when given during the subjective day (Oota and Kondo, 1974). In *Lemna paucicostata* 6746 the inhibitory effect of water transfer could be partially reversed by 1 mM $Ca(No_3)_2$ (Halaban and Hillman, 1971). In addition, water in which plants were incubated during any part of the dark period could largely reverse the inhibition caused by water transfer treatment during the sensitive part of the dark period (Halaban and Hillman, 1971). This suggests that what changes is not the degree of leakage, but rather the extent to which the plants are sensitive to this leakage. Thus, one interpretation would be that both water transfer and red light night—break treatments induce some change in membrane permeability, but this change leads to flower inhibition only during the sensitive phase, 6–10 h after the start of the dark period.

Under long—day conditions 1 mM LiCl inhibited flowering in the long—day plant *Lemna gibba* G1 but stimulated flowering in the short—day plant *Lemna paucicostata* 6746 (Kandeler, 1970). ADP had an antagonistic action to lithium by promoting flowering in *Lemna gibba* G1 and inhibiting flowering in *Lemna paucicostata* 6746. Lithium is an antagonist of potassium and both potassium and ADP are required as cofactors for the red light—induced adhesion of root tips to negatively charged glass surfaces (Tanada, 1968). Therefore, these results could be interpreted as supporting the idea that alteration of membrane properties may be important in the control of flower induction by phytochrome.

Oota and co-workers have carried out extensive investigations of the chemical control of flowering in *Lemna gibba* G3 through the use of the minimum long-day (min-LD) method (Oota and Nakashima, 1978). In this method the plants receive only a single experimental 24-h photoperiod and according to Oota, this 24-h cycle functions as a long day only if both the L1 phase (initial 5-10 minutes of the light period) and the L2 phase (5-10 minute interval starting approximately 12 hours later) are illuminated (Oota and Nakashima, 1978). The L1 phase showed a peak sensitivity in the red region and was far-red reversible, while the L2 phase showed maximum sensitivity in the blue and far-red regions (Oota and Hoshino, 1979). Clearly the L1 phase is mediated by phytochrome, and by analogy with other long-day plants the L2 phase is also probably mediated by phytochrome, at least in the far-red region.

The light requirement for the L1 phase could be replaced by the ionophores valinomycin and gramicidin, which are known to enhance potassium transport, and various other substances such as isoproterenol and cyclic AMP. The light requirement for the L2 phase could be substituted for by propranolol and salicylic acid (SA), both of which are known to interact with membrane binding or membrane permeability in certain systems. A combination of cyclic AMP and SA was able to substitute for both the L1 and L2 phase and render a completely dark day physiologically equivalent to a long day, but actual flower formation in complete darkness was not possible (Oota and Nakashima, 1978). This work provides additional evidence that phytochrome action in controlling flower induction may involve changes in membrane properties.

Another line of study that supports this hypothesis involves SA which is known to influence membrane properties in many systems. It has been shown to increase permeability to potassium and decrease permeability to chloride in human erythrocytes (Wieth, 1969) and molluscan neurons (Barker and Levitan, 1971) with a resulting increase in membrane potential and decrease in membrane resistance. In yeast, SA also stimulates potassium permeability leading to increased leakage of potassium (Scharff and Perry, 1976).

In higher plants SA inhibits potassium and phosphate uptake in barley (Glass, 1973, 1974) and potassium uptake in oats (*Avena sativa*) (Harper and Balke, 1981). In barley, SA also causes a very rapid depolarization of membrane potential (Glass and Dunlop, 1974). Other analogues of SA were also tested and their effectiveness for influencing changes in membrane potential or ion uptake was positively correlated

with their lipid solubility. Therefore, it was concluded that
these effects were caused by a generalized increase in membrane permeability to inorganic ions.

In recent years considerable attention has been focused on
the flower-inducing ability of SA in a number of different
Lemnaceae (Cleland et al., 1982). The mechanism by which SA
exerts its effect on flowering is unknown, but based on the
fact that SA must be present continuously in the medium to be
effective and is quickly inactivated once it is taken up, it
was concluded that it must act either during the uptake
process or very soon thereafter, and that it may be affecting
membrane permeability (Ben-Tal and Cleland, 1982).

A number of Lemnaceae can be grown in the dark on a simple
salts medium containing 1% sucrose as the energy source if
given periodic exposures to low irradiance red light (0.1 to
1.0 W m^{-2}) (Hillman, 1957; Rombach, 1976). This effect was
shown to be far-red reversible and thus under phytochrome
control (Rombach, 1976).

A similar red/far-red reversible control of growth has been
demonstrated for Lemna gibba G3 (Cleland, unpublished
results). The plants are grown on E medium (Cleland, 1979)
with 1% sucrose and given periodic 15 min exposures to red

TABLE 1. *Influence of 10 μM salicylic acid (SA) on flowering
and growth in* Lemna gibba *G3 when grown under 15 min of red
light every four hours (R/4 h), every two hours (R/2 h), or
every hour (R/h).*

Light treatment	SA	FL%	No. VF	TF No.
R/4 h	−	0	25.3 ± 1.2	25.3 ± 1.2
R/4 h	+	2.2 ± 2.2	14.3 ± 0.3	14.7 ± 0.3
R/2 h	−	0	31.7 ± 0.7	31.7 ± 0.7
R/2 h	+	6.9 ± 0.4	13.7 ± 0.9	14.7 ± 0.9
R/h	−	0	37.7 ± 1.8	37.7 ± 1.8
R/h	+	11.7 ± 2.7	14.7 ± 0.7	16.7 ± 1.2

Plants were grown for 3 weeks at 28 ± 1°C on E medium
containing 1% sucrose under periodic red light of 360 mW m^{-2}.
Results are expressed as flowering percent (FL%), number of
vegetative fronds (No. VF), and total frond number (TF No.),
and they are presented as mean ± standard error. For more
experimental details see Cleland (1979).

light. The extent of the growth response depends on the
frequency of the red light treatments (Table 1). The growth
response increases as the frequency of the red light is increased from 15 min every 4 h (R/4 h) to 15 min every hour
(R/h). Under these conditions flowering is zero despite the
fact that the critical night length for *Lemna gibba* G3 is
about 14 h (Cleland and Briggs, 1967) and the longest dark
period in the case of R/h is only 45 min. Clearly flowering
in *Lemna gibba* G3 requires more than just maintaining Pfr over
long periods of time. Preliminary experiments (Cleland and
Deitzer, unpublished results) indicate that giving R + FR/h
results in significant flowering, and thus flowering in *Lemna
gibba* G3 is similar to that in other long-day plants in that
it is often promoted better by mixtures of red and far-red
light than by red light alone (Vince-Prue, 1975).

In the absence of far-red light treatment, a small
flowering response can be obtained with these periodic red
light treatments by giving 10 μM SA (Table 1). These
flowering responses are very small because there is so little
growth and in *Lemna* a certain amount of growth is required
before flowering can be observed (Cleland *et al.*, 1982). One
way to increase growth is to give the herbicide Norflurazon
which prevents carotenoid and chlorophyll accumulation and
normal chloroplast development (Bartels and McCullough, 1972).
The original four fronds are green but the rest of the plants
are completely white. Both growth and flowering are stimulated (Table 2), possibly because the plants are effectively
receiving a higher red light dose due to the absence of
chlorophyll and carotenoids that normally act as screening
pigments.

TABLE 2. *Influence of Norflurazon on flowering and growth in*
Lemna gibba *G3 when grown under 15 min red light every hour.*

Norflurazon conc.(μM)	FL%	No. VF	TF No.
0	0	48.3 ± 1.8	48.3 ± 1.8
1.0	0	61.0 ± 3.6	61.0 ± 3.6
1.8	1.8 ± 1.3	82.7 ± 3.5	84.3 ± 4.7
3.2	27.8 ± 5.2	83.3 ± 2.3	116.3 ± 6.8
5.6	24.8 ± 1.8	86.7 ± 3.4	115.3 ± 4.5
10.0	20.8 ± 0.5	88.7 ± 2.4	112.0 ± 3.0

Experiment lasted 3 weeks. Other experimental details were as
in Table 1.

With 3.2 μM Norflurazon in the medium, SA becomes much more
effective for flower induction under R/h (Table 3). Of particular interest is the fact that a definite stimulation of
flowering was obtained with as little as 0.1 μM SA and the

TABLE 3. *Influence of salicylic acid (SA) on flowering and
growth in* Lemna gibba *G3 when grown in the presence of 3.2 μM
Norflurazon under 15 min of red light every hour.*

SA conc.(μM)	Norflurazon	FL%	No. VF	TF No.
0	–	0	36.0 ± 1.5	36.0 ± 1.5
0	+	2.8 ± 2.2	69.0 ± 7.1	71.3 ± 8.6
0.10	+	16.2 ± 2.8	63.7 ± 3.9	76.0 ± 4.2
0.32	+	25.1 ± 5.1	42.3 ± 3.3	56.7 ± 3.3
1.00	+	50.0 ± 1.2	22.7 ± 1.2	45.3 ± 1.8
3.20	+	30.4 ± 2.6	19.7 ± 0.9	28.3 ± 1.8
10.00	+	15.7 ± 1.0	19.7 ± 0.3	23.3 ± 0.7

Experiment lasted 3 weeks. Other experimental details were as
in Table 1.

optimal SA concentration was only 1 μM. The effectiveness of
SA for stimulating flowering with periodic red light is increased with increasing frequency of the red light. In Fig.1,
10 μM Norflurazon was used and the threshold concentration of
SA that gave definite flower promotion decreased from 0.32 μM
with R/4 h to 0.1 μM under R/2 h to between 0.01 and 0.032 μM
under R/h. This is definitely the lowest concentration at
which SA has ever been reported to promote flowering. In
contrast, when Lemna gibba G3 is grown under white light the
threshold concentration at which SA stimulates flowering in
short days or reverses the inhibition of flowering in long
days caused by ammonium-free half-strength Hutner's medium is
about 1 μM (Cleland and Ajami, 1974; Tanaka et al., 1979).
    SA has definite effects on membrane permeability and the
fact that the interaction of SA and red light has such a
pronounced effect on promoting flowering in Lemna gibba G3
raises the possibility that red light also has an effect on
membrane permeability. SA and red light may influence ion
uptake, sucrose uptake or some metabolic process(es) that
leads to a stimulation of flowering. The membrane effects of
SA discussed earlier were all obtained at 10-50 μM and thus at
a much higher concentration than was found to be optimal for
flowering in Table 3 and Fig. 1. This means either that in
the present system SA is able to stimulate uptake of ions or

sucrose at a much lower concentration than in other systems or
that it has some other effect. Either way, it seems reasonable to propose that the SA effect in some way involves action
at the membrane level, and that these results provide another

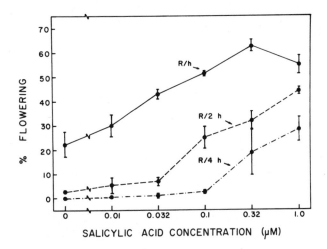

Fig. 1. *Influence of salicylic acid on flowering and growth
in Lemna gibba G3 when grown in the presence of 10 μM Norflurazon under 15 min of red light every 4 hours (R/4 h),
every 2 hours (R/2 h), or every hour (R/h). Experiment lasted
3 weeks. Other experimental details were as in Table 1.*

line of evidence that is compatible with the suggestion that
the primary action of phytochrome in the control of flower
induction is to alter membrane properties which then ultimately leads to the synthesis of the flowering stimulus.

CONCLUSIONS

Photoperiodic flower induction takes place in the leaf in
response to photoinductive light/dark cycles and the light
effect is mediated by phytochrome. Very little is known about
the immediate biochemical consequences of phytochrome action
in controlling flower induction. While the possibility that
phytochrome action may involve gene activation and repression
cannot be ruled out, most evidence suggests that the primary
mode of action of phytochrome in flower induction is at the
membrane level to alter membrane properties. There may be an
effect on membrane permeability and thus one of the earliest
biochemical effects could be changes in transport of critical

ions or organic compounds. Unfortunately, we have almost no idea which ions and/or organic compounds may be critical and nothing is known about the chemical identity of the flowering stimulus. Hopefully, in the near future a breakthrough in understanding the primary effect of phytochrome or the chemical nature of the flowering stimulus will lead to a clearer idea of how the process of flower induction is controlled in photoperiodic plants.

REFERENCES

Arzee, T., Gressel, J. and Galun, E. (1970). *In* "Cellular and Molecular Aspects of Floral Induction" (ed G. Bernier). pp. 93–107. Longman, London

Barker, J.L. and Levitan, H. (1971). *Science* 172, 1245–1247

Bartels, P.G. and McCullough, C. (1972). *Biochem. Biophys. Res. Commun.* 48, 16–22

Ben-Tal, Y. and Cleland, C.F. (1982). *Plant Physiol.* 70, 291–296

Blondon, F. and Jacques, R. (1970). *C.R. Hebd. Seances Acad. Sci. Paris, Ser. D.* 270, 947–950

Borthwick, H.A. (1964). *Am. Nat.* 95, 347–355

Borthwick, H.A., Hendricks, S.B. and Parker, M.W. (1948). *Bot. Gaz.* 110, 103–118

Cleland, C.F. (1979). *Plant Cell Physiol.* 20, 1263–1271

Cleland, C.F. and Ajami, A. (1974). *Plant Physiol.* 54, 904–906

Cleland, C.F. and Briggs, W.R. (1967). *Plant Physiol.* 42, 1553–1561

Cleland, C.F., Tanaka, O. and Feldman, L.J. (1982). *Aquat. Bot.* 13, 3–20

Cumming, B.G. (1969). *In* "The Induction of Flowering" (ed L.T. Evans). pp. 156–185. Cornell Univ. Press, Ithaca, New York

Cumming, B.G., Hendricks, S.B. and Borthwick, H.A. (1965). *Can. J. Bot.* 43, 825–853

Deitzer, G.F. (1982). *Plant Physiol.* 69 Supp., 81

Downs, R.J. (1956). *Plant Physiol.* 31, 279–284

Engelmann, W. and Schrempf, M. (1980). *Photochem. Photobiol. Rev.* 5, 49–86

Evans, L.T. (1969). *In* "The Induction of Flowering" (ed L.T. Evans). pp. 328–349. Cornell Univ. Press, Ithaca, New York

Fredericq, H. (1964). *Plant Physiol.* 39, 812–816

Friend, D.J.C. (1975). *Physiol. Plant.* 35, 286–296

Glass, A.D.M. (1973). *Plant Physiol.* 51, 1037–1041

Glass, A.D.M. (1974). *J. Exp. Bot.* 25, 1104–1113

Glass, A.D.M. and Dunlop, J. (1974). *Plant Physiol.* 54, 855–858

Gollmer, I. and Apel, K. (1983). *Eur. J. Biochem.* 133, 309–313

Gorton, H.L. and Satter, R.L. (1983). *Bioscience* 33, 451–457

Halaban, R. and Hillman, W.S. (1970). *Plant Physiol.* 46, 641–644

Halaban, R. and Hillman, W.S. (1971). *Plant Physiol.* 48, 760–764

Harper, J.R. and Balke, N.E. (1981). *Plant Physiol.* 68, 1349–1353

Hillman, W.S. (1957). *Science* 126, 165–166

Hillman, W.S. (1961). *Bot. Rev.* 27, 221–287

Imhoff, C.H., Lecharny, A., Jacques, R. and Brulfett, J. (1979). *Plant Cell Environ.* 2, 67–72

Kandeler, R. (1970). *Planta* 90, 203–207

Kohli, R.K., Sawhney, N. and Sawhney, S. (1980). *Plant Cell Physiol.* 21, 1483–1490

Lane, H.C., Cathey, H.M. and Evans, L.T. (1965). *Am. J. Bot.* 52, 1006–1014

Mancinelli, A.L. and Rabino, I. (1978). *Bot. Rev.* 44, 129–180

Marmé, D. (1977). *Annu. Rev. Plant Physiol.* 28, 173–198

Mohr, H. (1972). "Lectures on Photomorphogenesis". Springer-Verlag, Berlin

Oota, Y. and Kondo, T. (1974). *Plant Cell Physiol.* 15, 403–411

Oota, Y. and Hoshino, T. (1979). *Plant Cell Physiol.* 20, 1531–1536

Oota, Y. and Nakashima, H. (1978). *Bot. Mag. Tokyo Spec. Issue 1*, 177–198

Oota, Y. and Umemura, K. (1970). In "Cellular and Molecular Aspects of Floral Induction" (ed G. Bernier). pp. 224–240. Longman, London

Rombach, J. (1976). *Meded. Landbouwhogesch. Wageningen* 76, 1–114

Ross, C. (1970). In "Cellular and Molecular Aspects of Floral Induction" (ed G. Bernier). pp. 139–151. Longman, London

Satter, R.L. and Galston, A.W. (1981). *Annu. Rev. Plant Physiol.* 32, 83–110

Sawhney, S., Sawhney, N. and Nanda, K.K. (1976). *Plant Cell Physiol.* 17, 751–755

Scharff, T.G. and Perry, A.C. (1976). *Proc. Soc. Exp. Biol. Med.* 151, 72–77

Schneider, M.J., Borthwick, H.A. and Hendricks, S.B. (1967). *Am. J. Bot.* 54, 1241–1249

Sherwood, S.B., Evans, J.O. and Ross, C. (1971). *Plant Cell Physiol.* 12, 111–116

Stiekema, W.J., Wimpee, C.F., Silverthorne, J. and Tobin, E.M. (1983). *Plant Physiol.* 72, 717–724

Tanada, T. (1968). *Plant Physiol.* 43, 2070–2071

Tanaka, O., Cleland, C.F. and Hillman, W.S. (1979). *Plant Cell Physiol*. 20, 839–846

Vince–Prue, D. (1975). "Photoperiodism in Plants". McGraw–Hill, London

Wieth, J.O. (1970). *J. Physiol. (Lond.)* 207, 563

Zeevaart, J.A.D. (1969). *In* "The Induction of Flowering" (ed L.T. Evans). pp. 116–155. Cornell Univ. Press, Ithaca, New York

Chapter 10

PHOTOPERIODIC INDUCTION, THE FLORAL STIMULUS AND
FLOWER-PROMOTING SUBSTANCES

JAN A. D. ZEEVAART

MSU-DOE Plant Research Laboratory,
Michigan State University, East Lansing, MI 48824, U.S.A.

INTRODUCTION

A transmissible flower-inducing stimulus can be most readily
demonstrated in photoperiodically sensitive plants. For this
reason, the following discussion will be restricted to work
carried out with plants in which flowering is under photoperiodic control.

THE FLORAL STIMULUS

Evidence for the Floral Stimulus

There are basically three kinds of experiments that have given
rise to the concept of a floral stimulus (flower hormone,
florigen; Lang, 1965). For historical reasons, these will be
reviewed here briefly. All three have in common that photoperiodic induction acts over a certain distance which implies
the movement of a signal, the floral stimulus, from the site
of production to the site of action. (a) When differential
photoperiodic treatments are given to the leaves and shoot
tips, it turns out that only the leaves have to be exposed to
the inductive daylength in order to obtain flowering. As a
further extension of this type of experiment, leaves of
Perilla crispa can be detached and induced without any buds or
roots, as can be shown by grafting the leaves on vegetative
plants under non-inductive conditions (Zeevaart, 1958). Thus,

LIGHT AND THE FLOWERING PROCESS
ISBN 0.12.721960.9

the leaves perceive the inductive daylength, and the formation
of flower buds occurs in the shoot apex. (b) In species which
require only one inductive cycle for floral induction, formation of the stimulus in the leaves and its subsequent movement to the shoot tips can be demonstrated by removal of the
leaves at intervals during and after the inductive treatment.
For example, in seedlings of *Pharbitis nil*, it took approximately 14 hours of darkness for production of the floral
stimulus, but when the cotyledons were removed at that time,
no flower formation took place. An additional 4 hours were
necessary for the stimulus (or its slowest component) to be
translocated from the cotyledons to the shoot tips (Zeevaart,
1962). (c) The flowering condition can be transmitted via a
graft union from an induced shoot or leaf (donor) to a non-
induced partner (receptor), while the entire graft combination
is kept under non-inductive conditions. It is essential for
the success of grafting experiments that a functional phloem
connection is established between the donor and receptor, and
that assimilates move from the donor to the receptor. This
latter condition usually requires defoliation of the receptor
shoots.

Transmission of the floral stimulus by grafting has not
only been demonstrated within various photoperiodic response
types, but also between different photoperiodic response types
in interspecific and intergeneric grafts (Lang, 1965;
Zeevaart, 1976). There is even a report describing transmission of the flowering condition between species of different families, viz. from the SDP *Xanthium strumarium* and
Perilla to the LDP *Silene armeria*, but it now appears more
likely that flowering in *Silene* was due to removal of the
roots which, in this LDP, results in flowering under SD (see
Zeevaart, 1979a). In the Crassulaceae, all photoperiodic
response types are available, and it has been possible to
transmit the floral stimulus in various graft combinations
between the SDP *Kalanchoe blossfeldiana*, the LDP *Sedum specta-
bile*, the LSDP *Bryophyllum daigremontianum* and the SLDP
Echeveria harmsii (Zeevaart, 1979b, 1982). These results
suggest that the final outcome of photoperiodic induction in
all four response types is the production of transmissible
stimuli which are similar, if not identical.

Persistence of Photoperiodic Induction

When photoperiodic induction is discontinued, some plants
revert to vegetative growth quickly, but many others continue
to flower under non-inductive conditions. The underlying
mechanisms have been studied in only a few species. At
present, two types of plants can be distinguished with respect

to the after-effect of induction. (a) *Xanthium*, *Silene*, *Bryophyllum* and green perilla, *Perilla ocymoides*, are capable of indirect induction which means that receptor shoots brought into flowering under non-inductive conditions by grafting can themselves function as donors in the next grafting experiment (Zeevaart, 1976). Thus in these species the floral stimulus appears to have self-perpetuating properties. This should not necessarily be taken as evidence that the stimulus is virus-like in nature, because the presence of stimulus in young leaves and buds may cause the synthesis of more stimulus (positive feedback). Such a phenomenon is well established for ethylene in ripening fruits. (b) In red perilla, *P. crispa* an induced leaf continues to produce floral stimulus indefinitely when no longer under inductive conditions. However, flowering receptor shoots do not function as donors (Zeevaart, 1958). Although it appears that the stimuli in these two types of plants have different physiological properties, the stimulus is readily transmitted from *P. ocymoides* to *P. crispa* and *vice versa*. In addition, *P. crispa* donor leaves bring about the phenomenon of indirect induction in *P. ocymoides* (Allot-Deronne, 1983; Zeevaart, unpublished results). So, different mechanisms to preserve the flowering state in these two species are not due to different stimuli, but are presumably the result of different internal conditions.

The Nature of the Floral Stimulus

So far, the floral stimulus is strictly a physiological concept. The proof for a flower hormone would be extraction of induced plants and subsequent induction of flowering by application of the extract to vegetative plants. It must be emphasized that the crucial test for a flower hormone is that an extract is active in the same species or variety from which it was obtained, while a similar extract from vegetative material should not be active (Zeevaart, 1979a). Although there have been a number of reports with active extracts (see Zeevaart, 1976, 1979a), none of these were reproducible in other laboratories. A recent report (Chailakhyan *et al.*, 1977) looks promising, but it does not contain sufficient experimental details for reproducing the experiments elsewhere.

Thus, the floral stimulus has remained a physiological concept, and has not (yet) become a chemical reality. Failure to isolate a flower-inducing substance has resulted in a number of different proposals concerning the nature of the floral stimulus. These have been discussed at some length (Zeevaart, 1979a) and will not be repeated here. Suffice it to say that none of these ideas have so far furthered our knowledge of the floral stimulus.

Since the floral stimulus moves in the phloem with the assimilates, one possible approach is to collect phloem exudate by means of the EDTA technique (King and Zeevaart, 1974) and either test this material for flower-promoting activity, or analyse its chemical composition. We (Boyer and Zeevaart, unpublished results) have analysed the neutral, acidic, and basic fractions of exudates from *Perilla* by gas-liquid chromatography, and have found no significant differences in fractions obtained from induced and non-induced plants. The possibility of differences in minor components, presumably of a hormonal nature, that were beyond the limits of detection, cannot be ruled out.

FLOWER-PROMOTING SUBSTANCES

General

Various chemicals, in particular plant growth substances, have been applied to plants under non-inductive conditions to see if they can induce flower formation. So far, there is no evidence that any of the known plant growth substances, or a combination of them, can replace the floral stimulus and induce flowering in vegetative plants. This does not mean that these substances do not play a role in the over-all flowering process, but they are probably non-limiting for flowering in most plants.

Although plant growth substances cannot replace the floral stimulus, they can have a dramatic effect on flowering in some plants. Gibberellins are the most interesting, since they are the first group of chemicals that can cause flower formation in many plants under non-inductive conditions. Since GAs are present in higher plants, it would appear that the effects of GAs are not merely pharmacological, but reflect the role of native GAs.

Role of Gibberellins in Flower Formation

GAs can induce flowering when applied to many rosette LDP, and also to LSDP under SD. However, GAs cannot substitute for photoinduction in SDP. Since it was concluded above from grafting experiments that the floral stimuli in LDP and SDP are the same, it follows immediately that GAs are not identical with the floral stimulus.

Not all rosette LDP can be induced to flower with GAs under non-inductive conditions. In some species, only stem elongation without any flowering takes place. GAs appear, therefore, to be primarily stem growth factors, and as a secondary effect, flowering may also take place.

For those plants in which applied GAs (usually GA_1, GA_3, GA_4, or GA_7) do not cause flowering, it has often been suggested that the "wrong" GA was applied. However, there is not much evidence to support this suggestion. The current view is that the various GAs native in a particular plant form a biosynthetic pathway from C20-GAs to C19-GAs with only one C19-GA being active, and the others functioning as precursors or degradation products (Hedden et al., 1978). In many higher plants a number of C-13 hydroxylated GAs have been identified which are related as precursor-product in the following pathway: GA_{53} --> GA_{44} --> GA_{19} --> GA_{20} --> GA_1 --> GA_8. In this series, GA_1 is the active form of the hormone, while the earlier ones in the sequence are precursors, and GA_8 is an inactive degradation product. Minor modifications of this pathway have been found. For example, in spinach, GA_{20} is the active form which is converted to the inactive GA_{29}. In this plant, the photoperiod is a controlling factor in the conversion of GA_{19} to GA_{20} (Gianfagna et al., 1983). In spinach plants under SD, GA_{19} accumulates and little GA_{20} is present. Upon transfer of the plants to LD the level of GA_{19} decreases rapidly with a concomitant rise in GA_{20}. These considerations make it improbable that there are GAs that will specifically induce flowering in those plants in which the more common GAs, such as GA_3 and GA_7, cause only stem elongation and no flowering. Nevertheless, it would be of interest to identify the native GAs in such plants and then apply each GA separately to see if any could induce flowering. At present, however, it appears more likely that in such plants factors other than GAs are limiting for flowering (see Zeevaart, 1983).

Grafting of GA-induced donors to vegetative receptors has been carried out with only three species, but in each case it was found that the GA-induced plants could transmit the floral stimulus to non-induced plants (see Zeevaart, 1983). This implies that applied GAs act in the leaves to cause production of the floral stimulus. This has indeed been demonstrated with Bryophyllum (see Zeevaart, 1983). Warm (1980) working with annual Hyoscyamus niger suggested that applied GA has two separate effects: (a) it causes production of the floral stimulus in the leaves which results in flowering, and (b) it acts in the shoot apex and causes stem elongation. It may be worth while to take these two separate effects of GA into account in future work.

CONCLUSIONS

It is clear from the foregoing discussion that determination of the nature of the floral stimulus remains as a challenge to

plant physiologists. Once this problem has been solved,
important questions can be tackled, such as: Is the same
stimulus necessary for flowering in all plants? How is its
biosynthesis controlled by daylength? How does it cause
flower formation? With respect to the role of GAs in
flowering, the techniques are now available to investigate the
effect of daylength on GA metabolism in leaves.

ACKNOWLEDGEMENT

My research since 1965, which is discussed in this review, was
supported by AEC/ERDA/DOE. The preparation of this chapter
was supported by Contract DE-ACO2-76ERO-1338.

REFERENCES
Allot-Deronne, M. (1983). Thesis, L'Universite Pierre et
    Marie Curie (Paris VI)
Chailakhyan, M.Kh., Grigoryeva, N.Y. and Lozhnikova, V.N.
    (1977). Dokl. Akad. Nauk. SSSR 236, 773-776
Gianfagna, T., Zeevaart, J.A.D. and Lusk, W.J. (1983). Plant
    Physiol. 72, 86-89
Hedden, P., MacMillan, J. and Phinney, B.O. (1978). Annu.
    Rev. Plant Physiol. 29, 149-192
King, R.W. and Zeevaart, J.A.D. (1974). Plant Physiol. 53,
    96-103
Lang, A. (1965). In "Encyclopedia of Plant Physiology" (ed W.
    Ruhland). Vol. XV/1, pp. 1380-1536. Springer-Verlag,
    Berlin
Warm, E. (1980). Z. Pflanzenphysiol. 99, 325-330
Zeevaart, J.A.D. (1958). Meded. Landbouwhogesch. Wageningen
    58(3), 1-88
Zeevaart, J.A.D. (1962). Science 137, 723-731
Zeevaart, J.A.D. (1976). Annu. Rev. Plant Physiol. 27,
    321-348
Zeevaart, J.A.D. (1978). In "Phytohormones and Related
    Compounds" (eds. D.S. Letham, P.B. Goodwin and T.J.V.
    Higgins). Vol.II, pp. 291-327. Elsevier/North-Holland,
    Amsterdam
Zeevaart, J.A.D. (1979a). In "La Physiologie de la Floraison"
    (eds P. Champagnat and R. Jacques). pp. 59-90. C.N.R.S.,
    Paris
Zeevaart, J.A.D. (1979b). Plant Physiol. 615, 14
Zeevaart, J.A.D. (1982). Ann. Bot. (Lond.) 49, 549-552
Zeevaart, J.A.D. (1983). In "The Biochemistry and Physiology
    of Gibberellins" (ed A. Crozier) Vol. II, pp. 333-374.
    Praeger Scientific, New York

Chapter 11

PHOTOPERIODIC INDUCTION - FLOWER INHIBITING SUBSTANCES

W. W. SCHWABE

Dept. of Horticulture, Wye College, University of London,
Nr. Ashford, Kent, TN25 5AH, U.K.

INTRODUCTION

Ever since the original hypothesis of the flowering stimulus
being a specific substance was formulated in the papers by
Chailakhyan and Moshkov in 1936, the search for a flower-
promoting substance, florigen, or anthesin, has concentrated
on a specific hormone-like material. The work on grafting and
graft-transmission, starting with Kuijper and Wiersum (1936),
and followed up by so many other workers, particularly
Zeevaart (e.g., 1957a, b; 1958), has given almost overwhelming
support for the existence of such a translocatable promotive
substance. Interestingly, the idea of flowering inhibitors
has almost as long an ancestry beginning with Lang and
Melchers (1943), Withrow et al. (1943) and Harder et al.
(1949). The most recent reviews of the topic are by Jacobs
(1980) and Lang (1980).
    Chemical inhibition could involve (a) a direct reaction
with a promoter, (b) competition for a crucial site of action,
or (c) interference with the intracellular membrane transport
of one of the reactants, as well as (d) some indirect effects;
(a) and (b) at least could be reversible.
    Assuming that normal perception of the photoperiodic stimu-
lus for flowering occurs in the leaf, and that the original
light-dark based changes themselves are not specifically
interfered with, where in the reaction chain leading to
flowering could such inhibition operate?
(1) it could interfere in the production of the promoter;

(2) it could interfere in the export of the promoter (or its

precursor) from the leaf itself, but without preventing the
actual production. For both 1) and 2) there would be no need
for the inhibitor itself to be mobile and its action would be
restricted to the leaf itself.

(3) the inhibitor could itself be transported to the meristem
target and could then interfere with the transport of the
promoting stimulus and its arrival at the target site, as has
been shown for general metabolic inhibitors (Kinet et al.,
1971) and for ABA applied to the apical buds of Chenopodium
rubrum (Seidlova et al., 1981).

(4) it could interfere at the receptor site with the action of
the promoter in the meristem cells.
All those effects which generally interfere with the tissue's
metabolism and which must be considered non-specific will be
disregarded in this context.

In attempting to summarise briefly what is known about
these four possible effects of the inhibitor itself, one must
conclude that this is not very much. There is little possibility of distinguishing from available experimental evidence
between possibilities 1) and 2), both of which will occur in
the leaf. Equally, it would be very difficult at the present
time to distinguish between effects of a mobile inhibitor
acting during transport or acting after transport at the
target site itself, possibly as a competitive inhibitor.

Thus we may restrict consideration to those aspects which
involve any transport at all and those which may be confined
to the perceiving leaf.

INHIBITION INVOLVING TRANSPORT

There are two possible situations:- (a) where the inhibitor is
produced at a different site from that of the promoter, and
hence both must be transported, interacting during transport
or at the target site, and (b) where the promoter must travel
through a zone of inhibition. The inhibitory effect on
flowering of daughter plants of exposing strawberry mother
plants to LD (Guttridge 1959; Thompson and Guttridge, 1960;
Vince-Prue and Guttridge, 1973) is a prime example of inhibition involving transport, and there can be no doubt about
the mobility of the inhibitor. The interesting demonstration
by Lang et al. (1977) and Lang (1980), that a day-neutral
Nicotiana tabacum variety (Trapezond) can be inhibited in its
flowering when a LD-requiring species of tobacco (N. silves-
tris), held in non-inductive SD, is grafted with it, is
clearly another case where a mobile inhibitor has been demonstrated almost incontrovertibly. Searle's (1965) experiment

with split donor leaves of *Xanthium strumarium* with different
proportions subjected to long day also suggested the action of
a mobile inhibitor. The evidence from Bhargava's (1963, 1964,
1965) experiments, where the inhibitory effects were apparently derived from leaves below those induced, is less cogent
and possibly an explanation other than a mobile inhibitor
could apply.

When the promoter must move more through what might be
called a zone of inhibition, there are two types of situation.
There is the 'half leaf' effect, shown so strikingly by
Chailakhyan (1945), where, in *Perilla* (red), the promoter
fails to pass through a LD-treated proximal zone (base of
leaf). Gibby and Salisbury's (1971) further analysis of this
effect in *Xanthium* is also very instructive. It indicated
that the distal part of the leaf in SD can produce the
promoter which reaches the meristem if the basal part of the
leaf lamina is cut away, even after the end of the 16 h inductive dark period. The effect of the basal leaf part in LD
was similar to that of an entire leaf above the induced one,
i.e. between it and the terminal apex. Although the authors
did not reach a very firm conclusion, they indicated that "...
inhibitory substances did move at least as far as the veins to
destroy or inactivate the promoter".

Their experiments also made it unlikely that what might be
described as the 'carbohydrate diversion' theory of transport
was applicable here.

A recent series of experiments by Kulkarni and Schwabe
(1984) with *Kleinia articulata* and *K. repens*, the former being
an obligate SDP and the latter being a LSDP, also indicates
that this theory is not tenable in these species and that a LD
inhibitor functions, probably along the pathway of the transmission of the flowering stimulus to the target meristem.
When an entire plant of *K. articulata* (previously held in LD
conditions, which also make it dormant) is given a short-day
stimulus by grafting on to the stem a series of SD-induced
leaves of the same species, no flowering results. Yet, with
the same technique, grafting leaves of *K. articulata* on to
another species of *Kleinia*, *K. repens*, graft transmission from
leaves is easily demonstrable, even when *K. repens* is held in
non-inductive LD conditions throughout (Table 1). Why can *K.
articulata* not be induced to flower by its own leaves when
these demonstrably export and transmit the flowering stimulus?
The answer almost certainly lies in the fact that in LD the
few young and unexpanded leaves (less than 0.5 cm in length)
at the terminal apex must prevent the flowering stimulus from
reaching the apex itself. These leaf primordia are themselves
highly sensitive to daylength, even when the plant is quite
dormant, and if given only a few SD will induce the apex to

TABLE 1. *Graft transmission of flowering stimulus between* Kleinia articulata, *an obligate SDP and* K. repens, *a LSDP (always exposed to 24 h days before transfer to 8 h or 16 h days). Graft combination was held in 16 h photoperiods except where indicated.*

Donor (from 8h days)	Receptor (from 24h days or ungrafted control)	Proportion of receptors flowering	Days to flowering
K. repens	ungrafted (in 16 h)	0/15	veg.
K. repens	ungrafted (in 8 h)	15/15	33.0
K. repens	K. articulata	0/10	veg.
K. articulata	K. repens	15/15	22.0
K. articulata (shoot)	K. articulata	0/15	veg.
K. articulata (freshly detached leaf)	K. articulata	0/10	veg.
K. articulata (rooted leaf)	K. articulata	0/10	veg.
K. articulata	ungrafted (in 16h)	0/10	veg.
K. articulata	ungrafted (in 8h)	10/10	21.0

resume growth (Schwabe, 1970). Clearly the non-induced leaves between the induced leaf and the terminal bud cannot, in this case, be acting as an alternative and more powerful source of photosynthate supply, and the only possible explanation is that these young leaves exert an inhibitory influence, either by preventing the stimulus from reaching the target site, or by preventing it from acting at this point. This situation closely resembles that found in *Perilla ocymoides* (green) by Raghavan and Jacobs (1961), where young unexpanded leaves effectively prevented flowering of apical buds in tissue culture.

The effect of an intervening inhibitory LD leaf was tested in another experiment by Brackpool and Schwabe (unpublished) in which the transport of labelled carbohydrate to the growing point from the induced SD leaf was tested in several treatments. The results indicated that the association between carbohydrate transport and flowering stimulus transmission is perhaps not as strong and universal as is generally assumed (Fig. 1). The log of the number of flowers is shown at the foot of each treatment diagram and the amount of radioactivity

h

Tip	16	6.65	6.69	6.74	7.13	6.75	6.05
	24	6.77	5.92	6.90	6.85	6.50	6.36
	40	6.77	6.41	6.96	6.90	6.71	5.61
Leaf	16	–	4.32	4.32	4.77	5.14	6.00
	24	–	4.10	4.51	4.73	5.68	5.78
	40	–	4.46	4.92	4.84	4.47	4.70

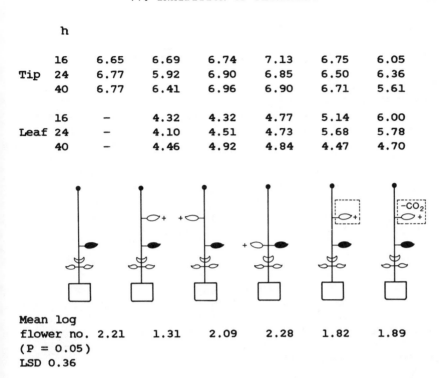

Mean log
flower no.   2.21   1.31   2.09   2.28   1.82   1.89
(P = 0.05)
LSD 0.36

Fig. 1. Flowering and ^{14}C activity exported from SD-induced
leaf to shoot tip and intervening LD leaf (+) after 16, 24 and
40 h. Mean log flower number, and log DPM g dry wt^{-1}.
(Induced leaf shown in black).

transported to the apex after different times is shown above
it, as is also the amount that has gone to the non-induced
intervening leaf.

Another possibility which should not be overlooked is that
the final leaf product may, in some instances, not be the
complete stimulus and may have to undergo further reactions at
the meristem site itself. This might be inferred from the
different ways induction can occur in Perilla and in Xanthium.
Whereas Perilla can be induced by a grafted, SD-treated leaf
even if induced after detachment (Zeevaart, 1958), a plant
made to flower in this way will not itself have the capacity
to donate the floral stimulus from its own leaves to a further
non-induced plant in LD. Yet in Xanthium (Lona, 1946, 1959) a
secondarily-induced plant can yield leaves capable of producing the transferable flowering stimulus. This difference
may, of course, be merely a quantitative one, or one determined by the within-plant distribution of the stimulus (see
also Chapter 10 in this volume).

INHIBITION WITHIN THE INDUCED LEAF

The effects of differential photoperiodic treatments applied
to different parts of the same leaf has already been discussed, since they must involve some transport even if only
over very short distances.

What can be said about the process going on in the leaf
which involves hypothetical inhibitors? Here the evidence is
mainly derived from experiments with the SDP *Kalanchoe blossfeldiana*, *Perilla*, and soybean *Glycine max* (Schwabe, 1959).
It is perhaps less definite to regard the experiments with
fronds of *Lemna* strains as strictly within leaf tissue and,
since this genus shows so many features which seem specific
(e.g., Kandeler, 1969; Cleland, 1974 and Tanaka *et al.*, 1979),
they have been omitted from this discussion.

1. Where more than one inductive cycle is required these must
be received in the same leaf or leaves; for instance, 12 SD to
a single *Kalanchoe* leaf is strongly promotive of flowering,
while 1 SD given each to 12 different leaves, simultaneously
or successively, is virtually non-inductive, i.e. the *factory*
making the promoter has to be created in the leaf. *Xanthium*,
with its rapid response, is perhaps an exception, or more
likely the extreme case.

2. Intercalating non-inductive LD cycles (or SD with light
breaks) is inhibitory – each such cycle preventing the next
two normal SD cycles from having any effect.

3. Both promoter and inhibitor production are reduced by
lowering the temperature.

4. There is no accumulation of the inhibitor beyond the equivalent of one or two LD cycles, i.e. no counter induction.

5. A leaf, whether partially induced or not, is capable of
producing the inhibitor if the photoperiod is greater than the
critical, but the critical length of the dark period decreases
with progressive induction.

6. In *Kalanchoe*, crude extracts from LD leaves can be injected
into leaves undergoing periods of SD and are inhibitory in the
same manner as LD treatment. SD leaf extracts are not inhibitory. This represents positive evidence for the existence
of an inhibitory substance. The basic data for these conclusions have been published by Schwabe in 1959, 1972 and 1981.

More recently, very similar results have been obtained by
Zen *et al.*, (1982) with the SDP *Hibiscus cannabinus* cv South

Selected. However, in this species the inhibitory LD effect
accumulated to a greater maximum, so that subsequent SD induction became considerably slower. These authors also succeeded in transmitting the inhibitory effect by injection into
the cotyledons of *Pharbitis nil*. Their studies with known
hormones also indicated that the inhibitory effect could not
be simulated or modified by IAA, NAA, ABA, Ethrel, GA, BA,
kinetin or TIBA.

Thus the evidence for a flowering inhibitor operating in
the leaf and antagonising the process of establishing a
factory for the promoter is strong and, in view of the fact
that an inhibitory component has been extracted and transferred to leaves of other plants, is stronger than the present
evidence for florigen, which appears to move only across graft
junctions.

THE IDENTITY OF THE INHIBITOR

It would be very attractive if the inhibitor of flowering were
both as specific and as universal as has been postulated for
florigen or anthesin. The difficulties in establishing this
are considerable, the main reason being that other and sometimes several substances may have similar effects, perhaps in
co-existence with a specific *antiflorigen*. There are indeed
several reports of known substances acting as flowering
inhibitors, among the earliest being those of Bonner and
Thurlow (1949) and Van Senden (1951) showing that auxin can
inhibit flowering in the SDP *Xanthium* and *Kalanchoe blossfeldiana* respectively. However, in the latter species it has
also been shown that GA_3 can be inhibitory (Harder and Bünsow,
1958) as well as ABA and xanthoxin, which are inhibitory to
flowering if injected into the leaf receiving the inductive SD
treatment (Schwabe, 1972). Quite recently, Dr. Bongi (unpublished results) working with me, has shown that oleuropein
(Fig. 2) is also inhibitory to flowering in *Kalanchoe*, without
general toxicity.

In a number of other situations, although no clear-cut
attempts have been made to identify the stimulus, the response
that was obtained could be due to one or other of the known
plant growth regulators. Thus, the mobile LD inhibitor preventing induction of flowering in the strawberry (Guttridge,
1969) could perhaps be one of the many gibberellins, although
probably not GA_3 according to the author. The detailed work
by Murfet and Reid (1973) on the transmissible inhibitor in
Pisum sativum, using selected lines, has led Proebsting *et
al.*, (1978) to suggest a particular gibberellin as the factor
associated with the *Sn* gene.

In the case of LDP, Evans (1969) summarising the experi-

mental work on *Lolium temulentum* discussed the inhibitory and
transmissible SD effect and suggested that this could well be
equated with ABA. However, the content of ABA in leaves and
apices was not found to change in any consistent way with
daylength (King and Evans, 1977). The striking effects
demonstrated in the experiments of Lang et al., (1977), could
perhaps also be interpreted as due to the transmission of
abscisic acid. In grafting experiments there is, moreover,
the possibility that an ABA effect could have been reinforced
if one of the graft partners had wilted during the actual
grafting procedures.

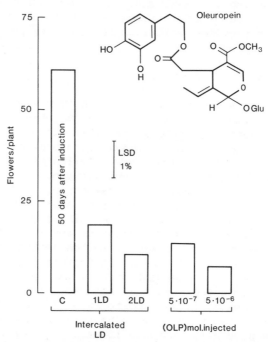

Fig. 2. Effect of injecting oleuropein on two occasions into
Kalanchoe *leaves undergoing SD induction in comparison with*
the intercalation of LD into a 14-SD induction period.

   In woody perennials, and in particular in fruit trees, it
is well-known that gibberellins tend to be inhibitory to the
formation of fruit buds. This applies to apples, pears, plums
and cherries, etc. (e.g. Luckwill, 1970), to the citrus family
(Monselise and Halevy, 1964, Guardiola et al., 1982) and also
to such plants as *Bougainvillea* cv. San Diego Red (Hackett and
Sachs, 1967). Moreover, such a generalised reduction in
flowering can be counteracted by application of substances
with anti-gibberellin activity, e.g., daminozide is known to

increase fruit bud numbers in apple.

The results of studies on juvenility in the blackcurrant
(Schwabe and Al-Doori, 1973) suggest that here also prevention
of flower initiation in the lateral buds in short (or pseudo-
juvenile) shoots is due to endogenous gibberellins emanating
from the root system.

In all these cases, it would seem that the inhibitor concerned is mobile and may therefore be one which interferes
with either the transport of the flower-promoting stimulus to
the meristem or, alternatively, prevents its action at the
meristem site.

However, the inhibitor that we have tried to identify in
Kalanchoe is probably of a different kind, namely one that
prevents the establishment of the florigen 'factory'. This
anti-florigen may therefore be an enzyme inhibitor which
prevents the production of the flowering stimulus, rather than
its action at the meristem. Whether this inhibitor will turn
out to be universal in the same way as florigen seems to be
universal is, as yet, entirely uncertain.

As far as the *Kalanchoe* inhibitor is concerned, work on its
identification and characterization is still in progress
(Brackpool and Schwabe, unpublished). It seems that there is
a diffusible, relatively heat-stable, phenolic moiety involved, which is found in LD treated leaves and which is
absent from SD leaves; these may be 2 flavan-3-ol fractions of
relatively low molecular weight, which have strongly inhibitory effects (Brackpool, 1982). For all such work a bioassay
is essential and the one evolved (Schwabe, 1972) clearly
allows such tests to be made. Although the bioassay is somewhat slow and tedious, it is reliable and would not lead to
erroneous identifications, such as that by Pryce (1972), who
mistakenly claimed that gallic acid was the flowering inhibitor in *Kalanchoe*.

A UNIFYING HYPOTHESIS

Some years ago, a model scheme for the reaction sequence
leading to flowering, which fitted long- and short-day plants
as well as other types, was put forward and, while it is not
my intention to go over all the ground which led to the particular biochemical scheme and its computer-based test
(Schwabe and Wimble, 1976), it is perhaps again worth drawing
attention to this scheme as the various facts discussed in
terms of inhibitors can still be accounted for by the series
of hypotheses made. The basic assumptions are that a flower-
promoting substance is produced from a substrate and a photosynthetic product through the action of an enzyme, which
increases in amount during induction and can be inhibited

reversibly by an inhibitor. The flavan–3–ols found in LD–treated leaves would fit this description well and may thus serve in the regulation of the formation of the florigen factory in the leaf.

REFERENCES

Bhargava, S.C. (1964). *Meded. Landbouwhogesch. Wageningen* 64–12, 1–70

Bhargava, S.C. (1965). *Proc. K. Ned. Akad. Wet. Ser. C.* 68, 63–68

Bhargava, S.C. (1983). *Proc. K. Ned. Akad. Wet. Ser. C.* 66, 371–376

Bonner, J. and Thurlow, J. (1949). *Bot. Gaz.* 110, 613–624

Brackpool, A.L. (1982). Ph.D. Thesis, University of London

Chailakhyan, M.Kh. (1936). *Dokl. Acad. Nauk. SSSR* 13, 79–83

Chailakhyan, M.Kh. (1945). *Dokl. Acad. Nauk. SSSR* 47, 220–224

Cleland, C.F. (1974). *Plant Physiol.* 54, 889–903

Evans, L.T. (1969). In "The Induction of Flowering" (ed L.T. Evans). Macmillan, Canberra

Gibby, D.D. and Salisbury, F.B. (1971). *Plant Physiol.* 47, 784–789

Guardiola, J.L., Monerri, C. and Agusti, M. (1982). *Physiol. Plant.* 55, 136–142

Guttridge, C.G. (1959). *Ann. Bot. (Lond.)* 23, 351–360

Guttridge, C.G. (1969). In "The Induction of Flowering" (ed L.T. Evans). pp. 247–267. Macmillan, Canberra

Hackett, W.P. and Sachs, R.M. (1967). *Proc. Am. Soc. Hortic. Sci.* 90, 361–364

Harder, R. and Bünsow, R. (1958). *Planta* 51, 201–222

Harder, R., Westphal, M. and Behrens, G. (1949). *Planta* 51, 424–438

Jacobs, W.P. (1980). In "Plant Growth Substances 1979" (ed F. Skoog). pp 301–309. Springer–Verlag, Berlin

Kandeler, B. (1969). *Planta* 84, 279–291

Kinet, J.M., Bodson, M., Alvinia, A.M. and Bernier, G. (1971). *Z. Pflanzenphysiol.* 66, 49–63

King, R.W. and Evans, L.T. (1977). *Aust. J. Plant Physiol.* 225–233

Kuijper, J. and Wiersum, L.K. (1936). *Proc. K. Ned. Akad. Wet. Ser. C.* 39, 1114–1122

Kulkarni, V.J. and Schwabe, W.W. (1984) *J. Exp. Bot.* 35, 422–430

Lang, A. (1980). In "Plant Growth Substances 1979" (ed F. Skoog). pp. 310–322. Springer–Verlag, Berlin

Lang, A., Chailakhyan, M.Kh., Frolova, I.A. (1977). *Proc. Natl. Acad. Sci. USA.* 74, 2412–2416

Lang, A. and Melchers, G. (1943). *Planta* 33, 653–702

Lona, F. (1946). *Nuovo G. Bot. Ital.* 53, 548–575

Lona, F. (1959). *Proc. K. Ned. Akad. Wet. Ser. C.* 62, 204–210

Luckwill, L.C. (1970). *In* "Physiology of Tree Crops" (ed L.C. Luckwill). pp. 237–254. Academic Press, London

Monselise, S.P. and Halevy, A.H. (1964). *Proc. Am. Soc. Hortic. Sci.* 84, 141–146

Moshkov, B.S. (1936). *Bull. Appl. Bot. Gen. Plant Breed. Ser. A.* 17, 25–30

Murfet, I.C. and Reid, J.B. (1973). *Aust. J. Biol. Sci.* 26, 675–677

Proebsting, W.M., Davies, I.P. and Marx, G.A. (1978). *Planta* 141, 231–238

Pryce, R.J. (1972). *Phytochemistry* 11, 1911–1918

Raghavan, V. and Jacobs, W.P. (1961). *Am. J. Bot.* 48, 751–760

Searle, N.E. (1965). *Plant Physiol.* 40, 261–267

Seidlova, F., Kohli, R.K. and Pavlova, L. (1981). *Ann. Bot. (Lond.)* 48, 777–785

Senden, H. van (1951). *Biol. Zentralbl.* 70, 537–565

Schwabe, W.W. (1959). *J. Exp. Bot.* 10, 317–329

Schwabe, W.W. (1970). *Ann. Bot. (Lond.)* 34, 29–41

Schwabe, W.W. (1972). *Planta* 103, 18–23

Schwabe, W.W. (1981). *In* "Biological Clocks in Seasonal Reproductive Cycles" (eds B.K. Follett and D.E. Follett). pp. 45–55. Wright, Bristol

Schwabe, W.W. and Al-Doori, A.H. (1973). *J. Exp. Bot.* 24, 969–981

Schwabe, W.W. and Wimble, R.H. (1976). *In* "Perspectives in Experimental Biology" (ed N. Sunderland) Vol. 2, pp. 41–57. Pergamon Press, Oxford

Tanaka, O., Cleland, C.F. and Hillman, W.S. (1979). *Plant Cell Physiol.* 20, 839–846

Thompson, P.A. and Guttridge, C.G. (1960). *Ann. Bot. (Lond.)* 24, 482–490

Vince-Prue, D. and Guttridge, C.G. (1973). *Planta* 110, 165–172

Withrow, A.P., Withrow, R.B. and Biebel, J.P. (1943). *Plant Physiol.* 18, 294–298

Zeevaart, J.A.D. (1957a). *Proc. K. Ned. Akad. Wet. Ser. C.* 60, 325–331

Zeevaart, J.A.D. (1957b). *Proc. K. Ned. Akad. Wet. Ser. C.* 60, 332–337

Zeevaart, J.A.D. (1958). *Meded. Landbouwhogesch. Wageningen.* 58(3), 1–88

Zen, X–C., Zhang, J–Y., Luo, W–H. and Jin, S–P. (1982). *Acta Phytophysiol. Sin.* 8, 214–221

LIGHT–DEPENDENT CHANGES AT THE APEX – EVOCATION

Chapter 12

ASSIMILATES AND EVOCATION

MONIQUE BODSON

Centre de Physiologie Vegetale Appliquee (I.R.S.I.A.)
Departement de Botanique, Universite de Liege, Sart Tilman,
B-4000 Liege, Belgium.

The aim of this paper is to review information related to the
role of assimilates during evocation but first it is necessary
to define these terms. In its broadest sense, the term
assimilate signifies any organic molecule metabolized or
assimilated by the leaves. In this paper, however, its use
will be restricted to signify molecules resulting from the
photosynthetic assimilation of CO_2 in the leaf tissue and
translocatable within the plant. Evocation, as proposed by
Evans (1969), is a term used for the processes occurring at
the shoot apex in response to the arrival of the floral
stimulus and committing it irreversibly to the formation of
flower primordia. The problem of the possible relationships
between assimilates and evocation is mainly related, therefore, to changes in concentration or in metabolism of assimilates at the apex after the arrival of the floral stimulus and
before the initiation of flower primordia.

This problem has never received much attention although
modifications of assimilate partitioning within the plant and
of assimilate levels in the aerial parts have for long been
suspected of being associated with flowering. The beneficial
effects on flowering of horticultural practices such as gird-
ling, partial defoliation, and root restriction led to the
idea that better flowering occurred when more assimilates were
made available for forming reproductive structures. Much
physiological evidence has emphasized the importance of photosynthetic assimilation for the floral transition. This will
not be included here as it has been reviewed recently (Sachs,
1979; Bernier et al., 1981a, b).

Early studies by Klebs (1913), and Kraus and Kraybill
(1918) established a positive relationship between the transition to flowering and the carbohydrate content of the leaves
and stems of several species and Klebs postulated that flower
initiation was controlled by an increase in the carbon/nitro-
gen ratio in the plant. This hypothesis was soon rejected,
however, because such changes were not observed in several
other species (Murneek, 1937, 1948). Nevertheless, most of
the studies which either supported or refuted Klebs's hypothesis suffered from two shortcomings: 1) the physiological
stage (partially or fully induced, transitional or reproductive) of the plant was not properly defined and 2) the
samples analysed were far larger than the target tissue, the
shoot meristem.

Experimentation with photoperiodically sensitive plants has
made it possible to distinguish four major steps in the floral
transition (Lang, 1965):-
1. the induction of the leaf leading to the synthesis of the
   floral stimulus;
2. the migration of the floral stimulus from the induced leaf
   to the shoot apex;
3. the evocation of the apex;
4. the initiation and differentiation of floral primordia by
   the meristem.

The duration of these different phases, however, cannot
always be fixed with certainty. This is particularly true for
evocation since it commences with the arrival of the floral
stimulus at the meristem, but the nature of this stimulus is
still unknown and the time of its export from the leaves can
only be studied by indirect methods based on sequential defoliation of induced leaves. This method provides information
about the time when a quantity of floral stimulus sufficient
to allow flower primordium initiation has migrated out of the
leaf tissue but does not tell us the time of arrival of this
stimulus at the apex. In the case of a multicomponent floral
stimulus, a hypothesis discussed by Bernier et al. (1981b),
defoliation experiments are an assay of the migration out of
the leaves of the slowest moving component. Whatever the
nature of the floral stimulus, whether it be simple or complex, it is clear that evocation may begin well before the
time defoliation experiments suggest the transport of the
floral stimulus starts (Bernier, 1979). The floral stimulus
appears to migrate in the phloem with the bulk of assimilates
(Lang, 1965) and has been shown to co-migrate with the assimilates from the induced leaves in many species (Evans, 1971;
Zeevaart, 1976, 1979).

Precise information concerning the problem of assimilate
level and metabolism during evocation is scarce and even broad

generalizations are not possible at present. The nutrient diversion hypothesis formulated by Sachs (1977) and Sachs and Hackett (1969, 1983) is the only hypothesis related to that question. I will, therefore, first review it and, thereafter, present results for two species where assimilate or carbohydrate level of the apical bud has been analysed with regard to the sequence of other evocational events.

THE NUTRIENT DIVERSION HYPOTHESIS

A variety of physical and chemical treatments have a florigenic effect in some species. In an attempt to integrate the flower-promotive effect of these various unrelated treatments into a unifying hypothesis, Sachs (1977), and Sachs and Hackett (1969, 1983) formulated the nutrient diversion hypothesis. Basically, it proposes that induction of flowering is a means of modifying source and sink relationships within the plant in such a way that the shoot apex receives a higher concentration of assimilates than under non-inductive conditions. This can be achieved either by increasing the competitive ability of the receptive apex, by reducing the strength of competing sinks or by increasing the source strength. This hypothesis, therefore, assigns a non-specific role to the many chemical and environmental factors known to promote flowering and explains their effects through their influence on assimilate distribution. In the nutrient diversion hypothesis, the increase in assimilate level at the bud is of paramount importance for floral transition and it suggests that reproductive development is controlled essentially by the nutrient level at the shoot apex.

This hypothesis, however, fails to account for the precise timing of action observed when promotive treatments are applied to the leaf or to the bud of plants kept under suboptimal inductive conditions (Bernier et al., 1981b). Such precise timing could be explained, however, within the framework of the nutrient diversion hypothesis, if the floral transition requires an interaction at the apex between an increased assimilate supply and some other rhythmic processes. Rhythmicity of shoot apex activities has indeed been suggested as a possible control point for the floral transition of *Chenopodium rubrum* (King, 1975).

As originally stated, carbohydrates play a central role in the nutrient diversion hypothesis since an increase in carbohydrate at the shoot apex is assumed to be the critical requirement for the transition from leaf to flower initiation (Sachs and Hackett, 1969). Basic to this reasoning is the assumption that the assimilates transported from the leaf to the apex are principally carbohydrates. Although sucrose is

likely to represent the bulk of the molecules transported in
the phloem, a wide variety of other molecules (organic acids,
amino acids, and cofactors) are also transported in the sieve
tubes.

CARBOHYDRATE LEVEL AND EVOCATION

Several studies with photoperiodically induced plants and
cold-requiring plants established a positive relationship
between increases in the carbohydrate level of the shoot tip
and flower initiation (Biddulph, 1935; Rodrigues Pereira,
1962; Shvedskaya and Kruzhilin, 1964; Sadik and Ozbun, 1968;
Babenko and Inkina, 1970; Fontes and Ozbun, 1972). In most of
these cases, however, flower transition extended over days or
weeks and the relationship between the observed changes and
floral evocation was not always very clear. This problem is
more readily approached by using plants which require only one
inductive cycle, since the floral transition usually extends
over shorter periods of time and can be more conveniently
timed in these plants. For these reasons, the carbohydrate
content and other related aspects have been analysed in apical
buds (3-mm long) of the LDP *Sinapis alba* and the SDP *Xanthium
strumarium* after exposure to a single inductive cycle.

The *LDP* Sinapis alba

Sinapis belongs to the group of LDP, including *Brassica campestris* (Friend, 1969) and *Anagallis arvensis* (Brulfert,
1965), which requires a moderately high but constant irradiance during the inductive treatment. The floral response of
this plant to one LD can also be modified by treatments which
influence photosynthetic assimilation, such as a change in the

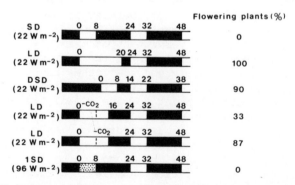

*Fig. 1. Diagramatic representation of some environmental
treatments which affect the floral response of* Sinapis. *The
irradiance is given within brackets.*

CO_2 concentration (Kinet *et al.*, 1973; Bodson, 1984),
variation in irradiance (Bodson *et al.*, 1977) or sucrose
application (Bodson *et al.*, 1979). Some of these environmental treatments are illustrated in Fig. 1. Treatments
inducing a high floral response include a LD, a displaced SD
(DSD) which is an 8-h SD displaced by 10 h in the 24-h cycle
(Kinet *et al.*, 1973), and a LD with CO_2 removed from the air
during the supplementary lighting period. It must be emphasized that all these inductive treatments differ markedly with
regard to the duration of photosynthetic assimilation which
makes this plant most valuable for studying the carbohydrate
level of the bud during evocation. As shown in Figs. 2 and 3,

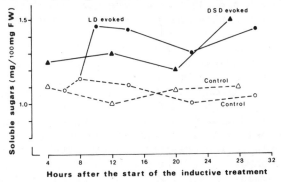

*Fig. 2. Soluble carbohydrate content of the apical bud of
Sinapis induced by one 20-h long day (LD) or by one 8-h displaced short day (DSD) (adapted from Bodson, 1977). Zero time
is arbitrarily placed at the beginning of the LD or at the
beginning of the DSD.*

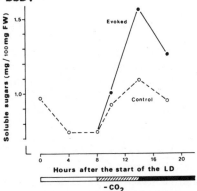

*Fig. 3. Soluble carbohydrate content of the apical bud of
Sinapis induced to flower by one 14-h long day but deprived of
CO_2 during the supplementary lighting period (Bodson and
Havelange, unpublished). Zero time is arbitrarily placed at
the beginning of the LD.*

the soluble carbohydrate content of the bud increased from 10
– 12 h after the beginning of induction in all three highly
inductive treatments.

This change is observed despite the large differences in
the duration of photosynthetic assimilation and, in each case,
occurs early in floral evocation. Thus, it is very likely
that an increase in the soluble carbohydrate content of the
apex is a critical event associated with evocation and this
observation provides support for the nutritional hypothesis of
Sachs and Hackett. Note, also, that the increase in the
carbohydrate content of the bud of LD–induced plants deprived
of CO_2 during the period of supplementary light, supports the
conclusion of Evans (1975) that the apex continues to be
steadily supplied with assimilates, even under stress conditions.

The increase in the carbohydrate content of the apical bud
could, however, result from a slowing down of the metabolic
pathways that use carbohydrates as substrates. To assess the
utilisation of carbohydrates by the apical tissues during
floral evocation, total acid invertase activity was measured,
as this enzyme releases carbohydrates that can more readily be
used by the cell. A rise in invertase activity in the bud of
LD–induced plants was observed shortly after the increase in
soluble carbohydrates (Pryke and Bernier, 1978), which indicates an increased metabolism of carbohydrates at the time of
the floral transition. This point is further substantiated by
an increase in the ATP and ADP content of the apical bud which
is observed to occur about 16 h after the start of the LD
(Bodson, in preparation). Clearly, profound modifications of
the adenylate balance occur in the bud within the first 20 h
from the beginning of the LD.

These changes in the soluble carbohydrate level and related
events may actually be required to support the stimulation of
the diverse cellular activities occurring during evocation.
However, the earliness of these events in the sequence of
floral evocation (Bernier et al., 1981b) and their repeated
occurrence, whatever the conditions used to induce floral
evocation, may indicate that they are more directly involved
in floral evocation.

In the nutrient diversion hypothesis, increased nutrient
level at the shoot apex is assumed to be the only critical
event for the floral transition. This possibility has been
considered in Sinapis alba by submitting the plant to one SD
cycle at a high irradiance. This treatment, which does not
induce flowering (Bodson et al., 1977), nevertheless produces
an increase in the soluble sugar content of the apical bud
(Havelange and Bernier, 1983) as well as in invertase activity
(Pryke and Bernier, 1978), both rises being of almost the same

magnitude as those observed in the bud of LD-induced plants. It is clear, therefore, that the increase in the soluble sugar level of the apical bud cannot be the only requirement for the transition of the meristem of *Sinapis alba* from leaf to flower initiation.

There is some evidence, described in detail by Bernier *et al.* (1981b), that cytokinins should be considered part of the floral stimulus in *Sinapis*. It has been suggested that the cytokinin content of the meristem increases about 16 h after the start of the LD and is responsible for the release into mitosis of cells in the G_2 phase of the cell cycle which occurs 26 h after the start of the inductive treatment. It must be emphasized, however, that application of cytokinin to the buds of vegetative plants does not induce flowering (Bernier *et al*, 1977). Changes in the cytokinin status of the bud associated with induction might also be responsible for the increase in the carbohydrate content of the bud. Hormone directed transport is considered to be a possible control mechanism in the nutrient diversion hypothesis as proposed by Sachs and Hackett (1983).

For this reason, the effect of a BA application on the ^{14}C-assimilate and carbohydrate content of the apical bud has been studied in SD. As shown in Table 1, 5 h after application of BA to the apical bud of vegetative plants, the mobilizing ability of the bud for ^{14}C-assimilates exported by an adult leaf was stimulated; the starch content of the bud

TABLE 1 *Import of ^{14}C-assimilates, soluble sugar and starch content, and acid invertase activity in the apical bud of* Sinapis alba *grown continuously in SD and treated with a single dose of benzyladenine. BA (4.3×10^{-5} M) was applied to the bud of vegetative plants and bud samples were collected 5 h later. ^{14}CO$_2$ was provided to a young adult leaf for 10 min, 1 h after the BA treatment. The means are shown $\pm$ SE.*

	Treated	Control
^{14}C-assimilates (as % of exported ^{14}C)	0.95 ± 0.18	0.41 ± 0.06
Soluble sugars (mg/100 mg fresh weight)	1.33 ± 0.09	1.17 ± 0.1
Starch (mg/100 mg fresh weight)	0.54 ± 0.02	0.25 ± 0.01
Acid invertase activity (µM sucrose hydrolysed/ h/100 mg fresh weight)	11.90 ± 0.91	10.41 ± 1.90

also increased while the soluble sugar content and the acid invertase activity remained unchanged. Thus the two latter changes, which are observed in the buds of plants induced to flower by a LD, do not result from a cytokinin-induced mobilization of assimilates associated with the increased cytokinin level of the transitional bud.

Since there is no change in the rate of CO_2 fixation during the inductive LD (Bodson, unpublished) the rise in carbohydrate content of the apical bud does not come from an increased source strength but is likely to result from the steady supply of ^{14}C-assimilates to the apex during the extension of the light period (Bodson et al., 1977).

The SDP Xanthium strumarium

If an increase in the carbohydrate level at the apex participates in the floral transition in LD-induced plants which require moderately high irradiances for induction, such as Sinapis, it seems a priori more doubtful in the case of SDP, since these require a shortening of the daylength and therefore a reduction in the period of photosynthetic assimilation. Work on this problem was recently initiated with unifoliated Xanthium plants which can be induced to flower at the age of seven weeks by a single long night of 16 h (Salisbury, 1963).

The soluble carbohydrate content of the apical bud of induced plants remained close to the control level during the first 12 h after the end of the long night, it then dropped below the level in the vegetative bud from 20 to 44 h but rose back to the control level by 110 h after the end of the inductive night (Fig. 4). To determine whether this decrease

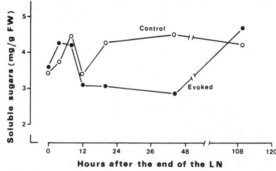

Fig. 4. Soluble carbohydrate content in the apical bud of Xanthium strumarium induced to flower by one 16-h long night (Havelange and Bodson, unpublished).

in the soluble carbohydrate content resulted from reduced import of assimilates into the apical bud, the export of ^{14}C-

assimilates from the induced leaf was studied during the
transition to flowering (Table 2). The data show that there
was an increase in ^{14}C-assimilates at the apex within 42 h
from the end of the long night, i.e., at a time when the
proliferation of the meristematic cell population is known to
occur (Jacqmard et al., 1976).

TABLE 2 ^{14}C-activity in the apex of Xanthium induced by one
16-h long night. The induced leaf was labelled with ^{14}CO$_2$ for
10 min and the apices were collected 3 h later.

Time of leaf labelling (h after the end of the long night)	Transitional events	cpm mg^{-1} DW	
		Evoked	Control
15	Transport of the floral stimulus	895.8 ± 188.5	987.2 ± 230.4
39	Stimulation of the meristematic cell population growth rate	1074.4 ± 203.5	491.2 ± 131.0
111	Initiation of in-volucral bracts	1307.0 ± 266.2	1016.3 ± 136.9

Further work is needed to know the precise timing of the
changes between 18 and 42 h but, since the soluble carbohydrate level of the bud decreases below the control level at a
time when an increased ^{14}C import into the apex is recorded,
an increased capacity of the apical tissue to metabolize
carbohydrate is likely to occur between 20 and 42 h after the
end of the long night. This may be due to a stimulation of
the respiratory pathways since the number of mitochondria per
cell increases in the meristem 44 h after the end of induction
(Havelange, 1980), and a stimulation of dehydrogenase activity
has also been related to the floral transition in the Xanthium
meristem (Thein, 1957).

The consumption of the soluble carbohydrates of the bud
through other metabolic pathways cannot be disregarded and, in
this connection, it is interesting to note that it has been
suggested that a stimulation of glucose-6-phosphate-dehydro-
genase activity is associated with floral evocation in the
Spinacia meristem (Auderset et al., 1980).

CONCLUSIONS

Observations related to the carbohydrate or assimilate level
in the buds of *Sinapis* and *Xanthium*, induced to flower by a
single LD or SD cycle respectively are summarized in Fig. 5.
The times of occurrence of mitotic stimulation and of the
initiation of reproductive structures have also been noted.

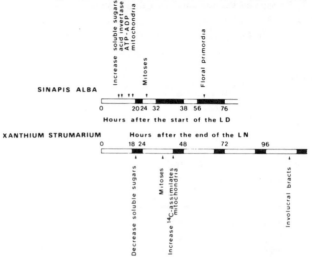

*Fig. 5. Summary of the observations related to the soluble
carbohydrate level and metabolism in the apical bud of* Sinapis
and Xanthium *induced to flower by a LD or long night (LN)
respectively.*

The available information points to there being an increase
in carbohydrate concentration or a stimulation of carbohydrate
metabolism at the time of evocation in plants of both photoperiodic response types. In *Sinapis*, an increase in the
soluble carbohydrate level is observed within 10 h from the
beginning of the LD. In *Xanthium*, changes in the metabolism
of soluble carbohydrates occur between 20 and 42 h after the
end of the long night.

In both species, changes in the carbohydrate concentration
and related events occur early in the sequence of evocational
events, well before the initiation of the reproductive structures (i.e. bracts or flowers), which suggests that they form
part of the signal for the transition to reproductive development.

Most of these studies, however, were conducted with apical
buds i.e., samples including, besides the meristem, a large
amount of stem and leaf tissue which makes it more difficult
to interpret this information in relation to the evocation of

the meristem itself. Clearly, the study of the biochemistry of evocation requires methods adapted to the handling and quantitative analysis of the meristem. This is now possible with the micromethods developed by Lowry (Lowry and Passonneau, 1972) and adapted to plant material by Outlaw (1980), which use cycling enzymes. These techniques make it possible to study the meristem, or even parts of it, isolated from the leaves and other contaminating tissues.

Recently, sucrose concentration has been analysed in the meristem of *Sinapis* by these methods. It has been shown to rise from 91.2 nmol mg^{-1} dry weight in the meristem of vegetative plants to 153.0 nmol mg^{-1} dry weight in the evoked meristem by 10 h after the start of the LD (Bodson and Outlaw, unpublished). A similar increase has been observed in the meristem of plants induced by a single DSD, 8 h after the start of this SD. These results show unequivocally that the sucrose concentration in the meristem of *Sinapis* increases within the first 10 h after the start of the inductive light period. The carbohydrate content of the meristem of *Xanthium* should be similarly studied to determine whether the changes reported for the bud also occur in the meristem.

Changes in sucrose concentration may indicate modifications of the energy status of the meristematic cells which in turn may affect a number of cell properties such as enzyme and membrane activities, and osmotic regulation. The problem of the significance of changes in carbohydrate concentration for floral evocation will only be solved by a quantitative study of the activities of key enzymes as well as of intermediate metabolites in biochemical pathways using carbohydrates as substrates. Although the available information emphasizes the importance of the carbohydrate concentration at the meristem for floral evocation, the possible participation of other assimilates, such as organic acids, amino acids, and cofactors should also be considered.

ACKNOWLEDGEMENTS

Financial support from the Belgian Government through the programme of "Action de Recherche Concertee" (No. 80/85-18) is gratefully acknowledged.

REFERENCES
Auderset, G., Gahan, P.B., Dawson, A.L. and Greppin, H. (1980). *Plant Sci. Lett.* 20, 109-113
Babenko, V.I. and Inkina, A.G. (1970). *Fiziol. Rast.* 17, 515-523

Bernier, G. (1979). *In* "Physiologie de la Floraison" (eds P. Champagnat and R. Jacques). pp. 129–168. C.N.R.S. No. 285, Paris

Bernier, G., Kinet, J.M., Jacqmard, A., Havelange, A. and Bodson, M. (1977). *Plant Physiol.* 60, 282–285

Bernier, G., Sachs, R.M. and Kinet, J.M. (1981a). *In* "The Physiology of Flowering" Vol. 1, CRC Press, Boca Raton, Florida

Bernier, G., Sachs, R.M. and Kinet, J.M. (1981b). *In* "The Physiology of Flowering" Vol. 2, CRC Press, Boca Raton, Florida

Biddulph, O. (1935). *Bot. Gaz.* 97, 139–155

Bodson, M. (1977). *Planta* 135, 19–23

Bodson, M. (1984). *In* "Handbook on Flowering" (ed A.H. Halevy). CRC Press, Boca Raton, Florida

Bodson, M., Bernier, G., Kinet, J.M., Jacqmard, A. and Havelange, A. (1979). *In* "Photosynthesis and Plant Development" (eds R. Marcelle, R. Clijsters and M. Van Poucke). pp. 37–82. W. Junk, The Hague

Bodson, M., King, R.W., Evans, L.T. and Bernier, G. (1977). *Aust. J. Plant Physiol.* 4, 467–478

Brulfert, J. (1965). *Rev. Gen. Bot.* 72, 641–694

Evans, L.T. (1969). *In* "The Induction of Flowering" (ed L.T. Evans). pp. 457–480. MacMillan, Melbourne

Evans, L.T. (1971). *Annu. Rev. Plant Physiol.* 22, 365–394

Evans, L.T. (1975). *In* "Photosynthesis and Plant Productivity in Different Environments" (ed J.P. Cooper). pp. 501–507. Cambridge University Press, Cambridge

Fontes, M.R. and Ozbun, J.L. (1972). *J. Am. Soc. Hortic. Sci.* 97, 346–348

Friend, D.J.C. (1969). *In* "The Induction of Flowering" (ed L.T. Evans). pp. 364–375. MacMillan, Melbourne

Havelange, A. (1980). *Am. J. Bot.* 67, 1171–1178

Havelange, A. and Bernier, G. (1983). *Physiol. Plant.* 59, 545–550

Jacqmard, A., Raju, M.V.S., Kinet, J.M. and Bernier, G. (1976). *Am. J. Bot.* 63, 166–174

Kinet, J.M., Bernier, G., Bodson, M. and Jacqmard, A. (1973). *Plant Physiol.* 51, 598–600

King, R.W. (1975). *Can. J. Bot.* 53, 2631–2638

Klebs, G. (1913). *Sitzungsber. Acad. Wiss. Heidelb. Ser. B.* 5, 3–47

Kraus, E.J. and Kraybill, H.R. (1918). *Oreg. Agric. Exp. Stn. Bull.* No. 149

Lang, A. (1965). *In* "Encyclopedia of Plant Physiology" (ed W. Ruhland). Vol 15, pp. 1380–1536. Springer-Verlag, Berlin

Lowry, O.H. and Passonneau, J.V. (1972). "A Flexible System of Enzymatic Analysis" Academic Press, New York

Murneek, A.E. (1937). *Mo. Agric. Exp. Stn. Res. Bull.* 268, 1–84

Murneek, A.E. (1948). *In* "Vernalization and Photoperiodism" (eds A.E. Murneek and R.O. Whyte). pp. 83–90, Waltham, Mass.

Outlaw, W.H. (1980). *Annu. Rev. Plant Physiol.* 31, 299–311

Pryke, J.A. and Bernier, G. (1978). *Ann. Bot. (Lond.)* 42, 747–749

Rodrigues Pereira, A.S. (1962). *Acta Bot. Neerl.* 11, 92–138

Sachs, R.M. (1977). *Hortscience* 12, 220–222

Sachs, R.M. (1979). *In* "Physiologie de la Floraison" (eds P. Champagnat and R. Jacques). pp. 169–208. C.N.R.S. No. 285, Paris

Sachs, R.M. and Hackett, W.P. (1969). *Hortscience* 4, 103–107

Sachs, R.M. and Hackett, W.P. (1983). *In* "Strategies of Plant Reproduction. BARC Symposium 6" (ed W.J. Meudt). pp. 263–272. Allanheld Osmun, Totowa

Sadik, S. and Ozbun, J.L. (1968). *Plant Physiol.* 43, 1696–1698

Salisbury, F.B. (1963). "The Flowering Process". Pergamon Press Inc., New York

Shvedskaya, Z.M. and Kruzhilin, A.S. (1964). *Fiziol. Rast.* 11, 279–286

Thein, M.M. (1957). *Am. J. Bot.* 44, 514–522

Zeevaart, J.A.D. (1976). *Annu. Rev. Plant Physiol.* 27, 321–348

Zeevaart, J.A.D. (1979). *In* "Physiologie de la Floraison" (eds P. Champagnat and R. Jacques). pp. 59–90. C.N.R.S. No. 285, Paris

Chapter 13

THE RESPONSE OF THE SHOOT APEX TO LIGHT-GENERATED SIGNALS FROM THE LEAVES

R. F. LYNDON[1] and D. FRANCIS[2]

[1]Department of Botany, University of Edinburgh,
    Mayfield Road, Edinburgh, EH9 3JH, U.K.
[2]Department of Plant Science, University College,
    P.O. Box 78, Cardiff, CF1 1XL, U.K.

INTRODUCTION

Evocation has been defined as the initial events at the shoot apex in response to the arrival of the photoperiodic stimulus, which commit the plant to the subsequent formation of flower primordia (Evans, 1971). We shall address ourselves to three questions concerning evocation. First, what are the events in the apex which occur in response to light-generated signals from the leaves? Second, are all of the associated events in the apex concerned with committing it to flower and if not, which are associated, but non-essential events? Third, what do the events of evocation achieve and how do they result in the formation of flowers?

THE EVENTS OF EVOCATION

Since the earliest time of arrival of the floral stimulus at the apex is difficult to measure, any events occurring after the beginning of induction may be considered as part of evocation. The end of evocation is when the apex is committed to flower, and can be determined as the time at which inhibitors applied to the apex during or after induction can no longer prevent flowering (Kinet et al., 1971). For plants in which this point is not known, the end of evocation is taken as the time at which the first morphologically distinct signs of flowering occur (Vince-Prue, 1975).

LIGHT AND THE FLOWERING PROCESS
ISBN 0.12.721960.9

Morphological Changes

The morphological changes preceding flower initiation (Table 1) are common, but not inevitable, concomitants of flowering in most plants, whether or not they need a stimulus to flower.

TABLE 1. *Common morphological changes preceding flower initiation.*

---

1. Precocious axillary bud growth
2. Change in branching pattern
3. Internode extension
4. Change in leaf form (bract formation)
5. Change in phyllotaxis to more complex system
6. Enlargement of apical dome

An increase in the rate of initiation of leaf primordia (Langer and Bussell, 1964) is often associated with a change to a higher order of phyllotaxis, as in *Xanthium strumarium* (Erickson and Meicenheimer, 1977). In plants in which flowering follows very rapidly after a single inductive photoperiod, such as *Pharbitis nil* (King and Evans, 1969) and *Anagallis arvensis* (Brulfert, 1965), such changes may not occur. The most obvious increase in the rate of primordial initiation occurs later, during the initiation of the floral organs.

Often, axillary buds form precociously and closer to the apex in prefloral shoot apices as compared with vegetative ones (Thomas, 1961). This is associated with loss of apical dominance so that lateral branches grow out forming flowers or inflorescences, although buds from the base of the plant may grow out but remain vegetative. Exceptions are mineral-starved *Silene coeli-rosa* in which the axillary buds do not grow, and a *Silene* mutant in which axillary bud outgrowth was suppressed, yet the plants flowered (Lyndon, unpublished results). The growth of axillary buds (tillers) is also suppressed in uniculm varieties of cereals (Kirby, 1973).

Rapid internode extension is often a characteristic of the prefloral phase, but not in plants such as daisies (*Bellis perennis*) and dandelions (*Taraxacum officinale*), which remain rosettes on flowering, elongation being restricted to the peduncle.

In most plants the size of the apical dome increases just before flower initiation, usually in diameter, but mainly in length in the grasses and cereals (Evans, 1960). In *Chrysanthemum morifolium*, the initiation of the first bract always occurs when the apical dome reaches a diameter of 0.23—0.26mm (Horridge and Cockshull, 1979). However, in a few plants, such as *Perilla nankinensis* (Nougarede *et al.*, 1964) and *Humulus lupulus* (Thomas and Schwabe, 1970), the apical dome clearly becomes smaller just before flowering.

Some of these prefloral morphological changes may be essential in some plants, such as the increase in apical dome volume seems to be in *Chrysanthemum*, or the outgrowth of axillary buds which always accompanies flowering in *Kalanchoe blossfeldiana* (Harder, 1948). In other plants these changes may be incidental and may be responses to changes in internal concentrations of metabolites or growth substances necessary for flowering, and may perhaps be symptoms of flowering rather than essential to it.

Cytological Changes

The cytohistological zonate pattern is usually lost on flowering (Nougarede, 1967). The distinction between the central and peripheral zones of the apical meristem tends to disappear as RNA and ribosome density increases throughout the apex (Nougarede and Bronchart, 1965; Lin and Gifford, 1976) and the distribution of enzyme activity also becomes more uniform (Jacqmard, 1978). In *Impatiens balsamina*, in which reversion of the flower to vegetative growth can occur, the zonation persists (Simon, 1972) as it also does in some species in which the meristem continues a plastochronic—like functioning by forming lateral flowers (Bernier *et al.*, 1981). An example is *Sinapis alba*, in which the meristem can also be made to revert to vegetative growth (Bagnard *et al.*, 1972). A gradual loss of the zonate pattern and an increase in meristem size are also characteristic of ageing vegetative (inter-mediate) meristems. Thus some features associated with the transition to flowering may also occur during vegetative growth, independently of floral evocation.

Changes in the size and numbers of starch grains in the apical meristem are also characteristic of the transition to flowering (Bernier, 1971) and presumably indicate changes in carbohydrate metabolism perhaps associated with increased growth and cell division. Other cytological changes are an increase in nucleolar volume, which may be linked to the synthesis of rRNA, and an increase in dictyosome number, which is probably linked to changes in carbohydrate metabolism and the increased synthesis of cell wall material associated with increased rates of cell division and growth (Havelange, 1980).

Changes in Growth Rates

The rate of growth and cell division in the apex increases
just before or at flower initiation (Table 2). In *Silene*
apices induced at 13°C, although an increase in size of the
apical dome was accomplished without an increase in growth
rate, there was still an increase in growth rate after the
sepals had begun to be initiated (Lyndon, 1977).

TABLE 2. *Cell doubling times (h) in vegetative and early
floral shoot apices.*

	Vegetative	Floral	
Lupinus	48	34	Sunderland, 1961
Secale	50	31	Sunderland, 1961
Datura	36	26	Corson, 1969
Sinapis	157	25	Bodson, 1975
Silene	20	10	Miller and Lyndon, 1975
Triticum	41	22	Griffiths, 1981

The increase in the rate of cell division is in both the
peripheral and central regions of the meristem although the
differential between these regions, which is most marked in
the vegetative apex, is retained in the reproductive apex in
Datura stramonium, (Corson, 1969) and *Sinapis* (Bodson, 1975).
In both of these species the cytohistological zonation persists. The growth rate of the apex therefore increases before
or at flower initiation in all the plants that have so far
been examined, whether photoperiodic or day—neutral.

Cellular Events

A number of events are apparently common to a variety of
photoperiodically—sensitive plants and occur in a similar
sequence in all of them (Bernier, 1971). The events are best
documented for *Sinapis* (Table 3). Ten hours after the beginning of the inductive LD there is an increase in the rate of
RNA synthesis. From 12 – 18 h there is an increase in the
activity of several enzymes – invertase, phosphatase, and
ribonuclease. At 18 h there is an increase in the number of
mitochondria, soon followed by an increase in the activity of
succinic dehydrogenase, suggesting an increase or changes in
respiratory metabolism. There is a first peak in mitotic
index at 26 h, when RNA synthesis is at a minimum. This is

followed by an accumulation of cells in the G_1 phase of the
cell cycle at about 30 h, then a peak of DNA synthesis at
38 h, a G_2 maximum at 44 h — "the point of no return" (Kinet
et al., 1971) — and a second peak of mitotic index at 62 h,
when the first flower buds begin to become visible. Throughout, nucleolus volume gradually increases to a maximum about
the time of the second mitotic peak, when the number of dicty-
osomes also reaches a peak (Bernier *et al.*, 1967; Havelange
and Bernier, 1974; Havelange *et al.*, 1974; Pryke and Bernier,
1978a,b; Jacqmard, 1978; Jacqmard *et al.*, 1972).

TABLE 3. *Sequence of events during evocation in* Sinapis alba.

Hours after beginning of inductive LD		
0		Most cells in G_2
10	Increase in RNA synthesis	
12	Increase of invertase activity	
14	Increase of phosphatase activity	
18	Increase of ribonuclease activity	
	Increase in mitochondria	
22	Increase of succinic dehydroge-nase activity	
26	1st ribosome maximum	1st mitotic peak
27	RNA synthesis at minimum	
30		Most cells in G_1
36	RNA synthesis increased	
38		Peak of DNA synthesis
44	Point of no return	
46		Most cells in G_2
54	ER maximum	
	2nd ribosome maximum	
62	Nucleolar volume maximum	2nd mitotic peak
	Dictyosome number maximum	
	Mitochondria number maximum	
	Flower buds begin to differentiate	

All these events are consistent with a synchronized cell
cycle of about 34 h. The variations in the rate of RNA synthesis are what would be expected in the course of a cell
cycle, with minima at the times of mitosis (Mitchison, 1971).
The increases in the cytoplasmic matrix (probably indicative
of an increase in ribosome number) to maxima just before the

two mitotic peaks (Havelange *et al*., 1974) are consistent with
the release of ribosomes from the nucleolus when it is dispersed at mitosis. The increases in ER and dictyosome number
about the time of the second mitotic peak are probably linked
to the formation of the cell plate and the new cell wall
during cytokinesis.

A similar sequence of events, though not known in such
detail, and with minor modifications, is also found in the SD
Xanthium, *Pharbitis*, and *Chenopodium rubrum*, and in the LDP
Lolium temulentum (Bernier, 1971).

Synchronization of cell division also occurs in apices of
Silene but as a final event of evocation, on the 8th and 9th
days after the beginning of induction, immediately before
sepal appearance (Francis and Lyndon, 1979). The occurrence
of two mitotic peaks during evocation in all the photoperiodic
plants examined, irrespective of the number of inductive
cycles required, implies that synchronization is an important
event of floral evocation.

In *Silene* there is also a smaller increase in mitotic index
in the apical dome at the very beginning of induction (Francis
and Lyndon, 1978a). This is associated with a reduction in
the length of the cell cycle from 20 to 13 h during the first
LD (Francis and Lyndon, 1978b), and an increase in the proportion of cells in the G_2 phase of the cell cycle, measurable
only 1 h after the beginning of induction (Francis, 1981a).
This is a phytochrome effect, as shown by its R/FR reversibility, although FR does not simply reverse the effect of R
but itself causes changes to the cell cycle (Francis, 1981b).
This initial effect does not result in synchrony and is
clearly separated in time and in its effects from synchrony,
which occurs 7 days later. Since changes in the Pfr/Ptot
ratio during the first few hours of induction are characteristic features of photoperiodically sensitive plants
(Vince—Prue, 1975) they could be associated with very early
changes in the cell cycle. If so, these would be difficult to
distinguish from the events of synchronization in plants which
require only a single inductive photoperiod.

Increases in the rate of RNA synthesis are not related only
to a synchronous cell cycle. In *Silene*, the RNA concentration
increases from the 4th day of induction (Miller and Lyndon,
1977) whereas synchronous cell division does not occur until
the 8th day (Francis and Lyndon, 1979). A universal observation is that the concentration of RNA increases in prefloral
apices and is most marked in the outer layers of the apex,
corresponding to the meristematic mantle which develops in the
reproductive apex (Nougarede, 1967), and in the target tissues
e.g. where spikelets will develop in *Lolium* (Knox and Evans,
1966). It is less marked and may be ephemeral in the pith and

the pith rib meristem (Miller, 1976). The bulk of this new
RNA is undoubtedly rRNA, as shown by the increase in density
of ribosomes in the peripheral regions of the apex on evo-
-cation (Nougarede, 1967) and by the amplification of rRNA
cistrons (Jacqmard *et al.*, 1981). Protein concentration also
shows a sustained increase in parallel with RNA (Jacqmard *et
al.*, 1972; Miller, 1976).

The events of evocation are similar in plants which show
the ability to flower at the seedling stage (e.g. *Pharbitis*
and *Chenopodium*) and in those requiring a period of ageing
before they flower (e.g. *Xanthium*) and therefore occur regardless of developmental age of the meristem at the time of induction.

NECESSITY OF THE EVENTS OF EVOCATION FOR SUBSEQUENT FLOWERING

The events of evocation follow as a result of induction, but
changes in photoperiod produce a plethora of morphogenetic
changes in plants in addition to flowering (Vince-Prue, 1975).
Which of the events of evocation are important or necessary
for commitment to flowering? Do some events occur as a result
of changes of photoperiod, regardless of flowering? Strong
evidence for the essentiality of particular events would be
their constant occurrence in plants induced to flower, their
inhibition thereby inhibiting flowering, and their promotion
in a vegetative apex thereby inducing subsequent flower
formation.

RNA Synthesis

Pharbitis nil can be induced to flower by a single dark
period. The incorporation of [^{3}H] uridine into RNA increased,
immediately at the end of the critical dark period of 11 h, to
twice that in the vegetative plants kept in LD (Gressel *et
al.*, 1978). Plants subject to the dark period but given three
15 min light breaks at 4, 8, and 12 h did not flower and did
not show an increased rate of RNA synthesis. Particular care
was taken during extraction to minimize the effects of the
very active ribonuclease in these plants. Lack of such pre-
cautions may account for the different results of Stiles and
Davies (1976). Although the tissue taken for these experiments was the whole plumule, the results probably represent
what was happening in the apex because the increase in the
rate of RNA synthesis occurs not only within the apical dome
but also in the young leaves (Arzee *et al.*, 1975). The very
early increase in *Pharbitis* therefore occurs only when the
apex goes on to flower.

In *Sinapis* the increase in the rate of RNA synthesis also

occurred only in plants which went on to flower, whether
induced by a LD or by a displaced SD (Pryke and Bernier,
1978a). The first increase in the rate of RNA synthesis was
also immediately at the end of the critical day. Treatment
with cytokinin can mimic some aspects of the synchronised cell
division but cannot induce flowering (Bernier et al., 1977)
and does not result in an increased rate of RNA synthesis
(Pryke and Bernier, 1978a).

In *Silene* plants induced with 7 LD, the RNA concentration
in the apex increased by about 25% and remained higher than in
vegetative plants (Miller and Lyndon, 1977). In fractional
induction treatments which resulted in flowering, the RNA
concentration always increased and remained higher than in the
SD vegetative controls, whereas in those which did not induce
most of the plants (3 LD and 3 LD/6 SD/3 LD), the RNA concentration increased only temporarily before falling again to the
value in the controls. The conclusion was that a sustained
RNA increase was a necessary precursor to flowering, although
RNA increase alone is not sufficient for flowering in *Silene*.
Application of GA_3 to shoot apices resulted in a significant
increase in RNA concentration in the apex but did not result
in flowering or an increase in the growth rate of the apex
unless inductive LD were given simultaneously (Miller and
Lyndon, 1977).

The relationship between RNA content, growth rate and
flowering was examined in *Silene* by comparing plants induced
by LD at 13°C with non-induced plants in SD at 20°C (Miller
and Lyndon, 1977). Both treatments resulted in almost the
same concentration of RNA and the same growth rate at the
apex, showing that whether or not the plants flowered did
not depend on either the absolute RNA concentration or apical
growth rate. However, the non-induced plants in SD at 13°C
had a lower RNA concentration and a lower growth rate than
those in LD at this temperature. These results are consistent
with a higher growth rate and RNA content being necessary for
flowering under strictly comparable inductive and non-
inductive conditions. They are also consistent with an increased growth rate of the apex being associated with an
increased RNA content.

In *Chenopodium* (SDP) an increase in the growth rate and the
RNA content of the apex do not seem to be essential for evocation. During the first inductive dark period there is a
decrease in RNA and DNA synthesis in the apex and apical
growth is inhibited. The increase in RNA after induction is
attributed to enhanced growth in the course of floral differentiation (Seidlova, 1980a,b; Seidlova and Sadlikova, 1983).
An inhibition of growth before or during induction may
actually promote flowering. When 6-azauridine, an inhibitor

of RNA synthesis, was applied (via the roots) for 1–2 days
before induction, the RNA content of the apex decreased and
the leaves each appeared about one day later than in the
untreated controls, consistent with an inhibition of apical
growth, but flowering was promoted (Seidlova and Krekule,
1973).

Increase in RNA content and increase in growth rate of the
apex are general events of evocation, except perhaps in *Chenopodium*. Events in non–flowering apices stimulated into growth
may closely resemble some of the changes at the beginning of
evocation. When axillary buds of *Cicer arietinum* were stimulated into vegetative growth by cytokinin there was a trebling
of the mitotic index within an hour and an increased rate of
synthesis of RNA within 1.5 h. An increase in growth rate was
detectable after 2 h (Usciati *et al.*, 1972). These observations show that an increase in growth rate, whether or not
part of evocation, may be preceded by an increase in synthesis
of RNA and by changes in mitotic index, indicating perturba-
tions of the cell cycle. At least some of the increase in RNA
and protein and some of the changes in mitotic frequency may
be expected to be linked to increases in growth rate rather
than being involved more directly in flowering.

Protein Synthesis

Obviously, different genes are expressed in the flower and in
the vegetative shoot, but does this change in gene expression
occur during evocation? Is evocation perhaps a general activation of the apex as Evans (1969, 1971) suggests, with major
changes in gene expression occurring only during flower development? Certainly there is no overriding reason to invoke
changes in gene expression for the early stages of flower
initiation, which do not seem to differ qualitatively from the
sort of changes which can be observed in changing phyllotaxis
in vegetative apices (Lyndon, 1979b).

If evocation does involve the expression of new genes then
this should be detectable as the synthesis of novel proteins
during evocation. Early changes in gene expression could
therefore be looked for either as new proteins or new mRNAs.
In *Sinapis* apices there was an increase in synthesis of rRNA
and sRNA during evocation but not of poly(A)–containing RNA
(mRNA) (Pryke and Bernier, 1978a) although increases have been
found in evoked buds of *Pharbitis* (Stiles and Davies, 1976).
Qualitative changes, and especially small ones, would not,
however, be detected by the methods used.

Apical meristems of *Sinapis* were labelled with [^{35}S]methio-
nine and the complements of newly synthesized proteins in
vegetative and evoked meristems (51–53 h after the beginning

of induction) were compared using the technique of isoelectri
focussing and polyacrylamide gel electrophoresis (Lyndon *et
al.*, 1983). Most of the differences in the patterns of proteins synthesized were quantitative and most of the proteins
were common to both evoked and vegetative meristems. However
there were some possible qualitative differences. In particular a few of the proteins synthesised in the evoked apices
but not (or to a much lesser extent) in the vegetative apices
occupied the same positions on the gels as proteins which were
characteristic of floral buds, although in the evoked apices
the flower primordia had not yet begun to be initiated.
Whether such changes would be found in the earlier stages of
evocation is not known.

Another approach to investigating changes in protein com-
plement during evocation is to examine changes in amounts of
antigenic proteins characteristic of vegetative or flowering
apices. On evocation the apical meristem of *Sinapis* shows the
appearance of two antigens not present in the vegetative apex
and the disappearance of one characteristic of the vegetative
apex. Neither of the new proteins was specific to flowering,
however, since they could both be found in other parts of the
vegetative plant (Pierard *et al.*, 1977, 1980). When antisera
were raised to the floral organs, two antigens were found
specific to the stamens and one to the pistil, but none of
them could be detected in the apical meristem; they were
restricted to the almost mature stamens and pistil respectively and appeared to be proteins concerned with the male-
female recognition system (Jacqmard *et al.*, 1984).

Changes in protein composition and enzyme activity have
been shown to precede the morphological changes of flower
initiation. The major problem is, what enzymes would be
expected to change in activity in order to bring about the
morphological changes? Changes in the shoot apex that can be
predicted are a decrease in the activity of enzymes of photosynthesis and an increase for enzymes involved in pigment
synthesis in the petals, and for synthesis of characteristic
constituents of the stamens (e.g. sporopollenin) and the
pistil. These changes could be fairly late in flower formation, just as the appearance of the antigens specific to the
stamens and pistil was late in the development of these
organs. The evidence so far is consistent with qualitative
changes in gene expression occurring late in floral realization rather than in evocation. Some of the earliest changes
in evocation may involve synthesis of enzymes of respiratory
metabolism but again these are likely to be quantitative
rather than qualitative changes.

Synchronization of Cell Division

Conspicuous features of evocation are the characteristic increases in the mitotic index which have been observed in prefloral apices of a whole range of different species (Bernier, 1971; Bernier *et al.*, 1981). Experiments with *Sinapis* have shown that it has not been possible to dissociate flowering from the early increase in mitotic index (Bernier *et al.*, 1974). No matter whether flowering was induced by a LD of 13 or more hours, by a displaced 18-h LD, or a displaced 8-h SD, there was an increase of mitotic index 16-28 h after the start of induction. In each case this was followed by a second mitotic peak about 36 h later, consistent with a synchronous cell cycle. When the plants were induced with a 16-h day but were deprived of CO_2 for the last 8 h, the initial mitotic wave was delayed and so was flower initiation. In these experiments there was therefore a consistent temporal link between the rises in mitotic index, indicative of a synchronous cell cycle, and subsequent flowering.

A good test of the importance of synchrony would be specifically to inhibit it and subsequently examine the plants for evidence of effects on flower initiation. Recently, *Silene* plants were given 7 LD and then kept in darkness for 48 h before placing them in SD (Grose and Lyndon, unpublished results). The synchronous divisions were suppressed but the plants went on to flower, although flower initiation was delayed by approximately 48 h. The conclusion drawn was that synchronization itself was not an essential process for subsequent flower initiation but that it was a secondary effect of some stimulus required for an as yet unidentified aspect of flower initiation.

In *Sinapis*, the synchronized cell cycle occupies most of the period of evocation. In *Silene*, which has a much shorter cell cycle than *Sinapis* and a requirement for at least 4 cycles for induction, the synchronized cell cycles occur at the end of evocation, just before sepal initiation. In *Silene*, many events of evocation must already have occurred by the time the cells become synchronized. During synchronization the cells become more physiologically isolated from each other (Goodwin and Lyndon, 1983) and it could be that this is the important feature and still occurs even when the growth of the apex and synchronization are inhibited by darkness.

Early Changes in Cell Cycle

In *Silene*, early changes in the cell cycle occur during the first LD. Since even 3 LD are not inductive for most *Silene*

plants, are these early changes relevant to flowering? It was
shown that if *Silene* plants were given 6 LD but with the first
20 min of the low light intensity extension of each LD replaced by darkness, then flowering was inhibited (Taylor,
1975). These experiments have been repeated and confirmed
(Ormrod and Francis, 1983). Exposure to this 20 min dark
treatment for only the first 3 LD was still sufficient to
inhibit flowering by 90%. The change in the cell cycle,
measured as an increase in the proportion of cells in the G_2
phase of the cell cycle each evening at 20.00 in plants given
3 LD, was not found in the plants given 20 min darkness at the
beginning of each extended light period. The suppression of
the G_2 increase and the suppression of subsequent flowering
are therefore correlated. The initial change in the cell
cycle resulting from the first few minutes of the first LD may
therefore be an important part of evocation in *Silene*.
Whether this is because the changes in the cell cycle are
essential or whether these are simply side effects of phytochrome changes which are achieving something else for evocation is not yet known. Light must also be required later in
each LD, since the critical daylength for *Silene* is about 16 h
(Lyndon, 1984).

Another LDP, *Sinapis*, differs in that the first 20 min of
the extended day are not critical because *Sinapis* will flower
when given a displaced SD (Kinet, 1972). This necessarily
means that instead of the normal LD there is darkness from the
8th to the 16th h of the inductive cycle.

Which are the Essential Events of Evocation?

The general occurrence of many events of evocation suggests
that they are necessary for flowering although it has been
possible to inhibit some of them without inhibition of
flowering in some plants. However, the inability to separate
events of evocation from subsequent flowering may not mean
that they are essential, but only that the appropriate experimental treatment to divorce them from flowering has not yet
been found. Alternatively, it is possible that an event may
be obligatory in one species but not in another; for example,
synchrony may be necessary for *Sinapis* but not for *Silene*,
while events triggered by the first 20 min of light during
each extended day seem essential in *Silene* but not in *Sinapis*.
Perhaps the early cell cycle changes in *Silene* accomplish the
same as synchronization in *Sinapis*. If, for instance, it is
an increase in growth rate which is essential it may be unim-
portant exactly how it is achieved.

Some events of evocation are clearly linked. The occurrence of a synchronous cell cycle will necessarily result in

changes in mitotic index, rates of RNA synthesis, rates of protein synthesis, and nucleolar volume. The importance of some individual events may therefore be not in themselves but in some other aspect of the process of which they are an obligatory part. Other sets of events, perhaps like synchronization in *Silene*, may be by-products of the action of a stimulus whose principal effect is to alter an as yet unrecognized aspect of cellular functioning.

THE SIGNIFICANCE OF EVOCATION

What does Evocation lead to?

One way to try to understand the nature of evocation is to ask what it leads to and what type of changes would therefore have to occur in the shoot apex on flowering. For the early stages of flower initiation it is difficult to visualize what types of genes would have to be activated in order to change the form of the apex and the arrangement of the primordia on it. However, a consideration of these early morphological changes can perhaps give some clue to the type of cellular change which evocation may bring about.

On flowering the rate of initiation of primordia increases markedly, as exemplified by *Chrysanthemum* (Schwabe, 1959), *Triticum* (Kirby, 1974) and *Silene* (Lyndon, 1979a). This is despite a reduction in relative growth rate at this time which has also been shown for *Chrysanthemum* (Jeffcoat and Cockshull, 1972), *Triticum* (Williams, 1966) and *Silene* (Lyndon, 1979a). This is possible because the phyllotaxis also usually changes so that the plastochron ratio decreases. The implication is that the reduction of the size of the primordia at initiation, relative to the apical dome, which is a characteristic of flower initiation in *Silene* (Lyndon, 1978), is probably universal. In *Silene*, sepals are smaller than leaves at initiation, both relative to the apical dome and in absolute terms, and there is a further decrease in primordial size on initiation of the petals and stamens.

Probably then, one of the changes that occurs at flower initiation is in whatever controls the size of primordia at initiation relative to the apical dome. Substances which consistently affect the positioning and number of primordia at a node and the fusion of primordia, are auxins and auxin antagonists (Soma, 1968; Schwabe, 1971; Meicenheimer, 1981). Gibberellic acid may speed up the rate of primordium initiation and alter phyllotaxis (Bernier *et al.*, 1981) and it may do so by altering primordial or apical size since it resulted in a reduction in the plastochron ratio in *Xanthium* which mimicked the reduction occurring on floral induction

(Maksymowych and Erickson, 1977). If, on flowering, there are relatively major changes in the rates of synthesis of growth substances in the shoot apex and young primordia, they might be difficult to duplicate by exogenous application and large reductions in the rate of synthesis would be almost impossible to mimic experimentally.

Does Evocation lead to Changes in Growth Substance Synthesis?

The initiation of shoots or roots from callus can be manipulated by altering the relative concentrations of growth substances in the media. If the formation of flowers is analogous then we would expect alterations in the relative rates of synthesis or availability to the apex of growth substances to be a feature of flower initiation. Such changes have been brought about in callus by altering the concentrations of auxin (Cheng, 1972) or cytokinin (Meins and Lutz, 1980) in the medium, causing the callus to habituate or to revert to dependence on an exogenous supply of the growth substance. If apical tissues were at all to resemble such callus, then changes in the rates of synthesis of one or more growth substance at evocation might be brought about by a short pulse of increased or decreased amounts coming from elsewhere in the plant. If evocation were to involve changes in the ability to synthesize some growth substances in the apical meristem, this might allow the expression of genetic information in a way not possible in the vegetative apex. Changes in gene expression during evocation could then be limited to a very few genes concerned with the regulation of growth substance metabolism and could be quantitative rather than qualitative.

The Nature of the Commitment to Flower

The ending of the juvenile stage in trees means that meristems have become competent to flower under the appropriate circumstances of environment and position on the plant although not every meristem does so. In the herbaceous plant *Silene* which, once induced, continues to flower until it dies, each newly formed axillary bud bears two or more leaves below each flower, suggesting that each meristem is unable to flower until it has produced two leaves. Conversely, in induced *Pharbitis*, the apices of the lateral buds are not able to form flowers if they have more than two primordia, although at the same time other buds on the plant are forming flowers (King and Evans, 1969). The difference, therefore, between a vegetative and a flowering plant is that in the flowering plant the meristems now have the competence to form flowers although they may not necessarily do so.

This is also shown by experiments with cultures of epi-
dermal thin layers from flowering tobacco plants. These can
be made to develop to form roots, leaves or flowers according
to the environment in which they are grown (Tran Thanh Van,
1980). Similarly, callus from flowering tobacco could be made
to develop reproductive shoots or only vegetative ones, according to whether or not glucose was present in the medium
(Chailakhyan *et al.*, 1975) but callus from vegetative plants
with or without glucose always produced only vegetative
shoots. The competence of the parent plant to flower was
transmitted through culture i.e. in the cellular state. This
argues for a stable difference at the cellular level between
the vegetative and the reproductive states. Stable differences have been shown in the ability of callus to habituate to
growth substances in the culture media (Meins and Binns,
1979), but differences between callus from vegetative and
flowering plants have not yet been looked for.

Is Evocation the Same in all Plants?

The transition to flowering is a 2-step process - commitment
and realization. Clearly, to recognize a meristem as being
evoked it is necessary for it to be subject to conditions
which will allow the commitment to flower to be expressed.
The action of a stimulus from the leaves could be at either
step. Inhibitors can be used to prevent flowering and so
identify the time of commitment. But in some plants the apex
may already be committed and the effect of signals from the
leaves would be to cause realization. There may also be
plants in which specific stimuli are required for commitment
and realization. Both steps could perhaps result from a
single stimulus, or separate stimuli may be required, either
simultaneously or sequentially. If signals from the leaves
achieve different steps in different plants then the events in
the apex leading to flowering would be expected to be different in plants requiring evocation from those requiring only
realization.

Changes in Gene Expression

Even if changes in gene expression to bring about differentiation of the floral organs occur relatively late in flower
development, the initial morphological changes might require
early changes in the regulation of the expression of a few
genes. This suggests a possible significance of the initial
cell cycle events in *Silene* in which the proportion of cells
in G_2 is enhanced for 6 or more hours (Francis and Lyndon,
1978a; Francis, 1981a). It is known that chromatin undergoes

successive cycles of condensation and decondensation during a normal cell cycle (Nagl, 1977). In *Sinapis*, the ratio of dispersed to condensed chromatin increased when the nuclei were in G_2 and reached maxima at or just before the peaks of mitosis (Havelange and Bernier, 1974; Havelange and Jeanny, 1984). At the first peak of RNA synthesis, 18 h after the start of induction (Pryke and Bernier, 1978a), there was a marked shift of RNA synthesis from the nucleolus to the chromatin (Bronchart *et al.*, 1970). If this were to result in a change in the degree of transcription of a few key genes, then an increase in the proportion of cells in G_2 as one of the first events in evocation might result in a quantitative shift in gene expression. If these genes were concerned with the synthesis of regulatory metabolites then changes in apical development could conceivably result. If evocation is a change in cellular state (commitment) then there might be a critical event common to all evoked apices. The problem is to know what sort of cellular changes might be expected in order to bring about changes in metabolism to produce flowers.

ACKNOWLEDGEMENTS

We are grateful to the A.R.C. for supporting work as yet unpublished through grants AG72/43 to D.Francis and AG15/166 to R. F. Lyndon.

REFERENCES

Arzee, T., Zilberstein, A. and Gressel, J. (1975). *Plant Cell Physiol.* 16, 505–511

Bagnard, C., Bernier, G. and Arnal, C. (1972). *Physiol. Veg.* 10, 237–254

Bernier, G. (1971). *Can. J. Bot.* 49, 803–819

Bernier, G., Kinet, J.-M. and Bronchart, R. (1967). *Physiol. Veg.* 5, 311–324

Bernier, G., Kinet, J.-M., Bodson, M., Rouma, Y. and Jacqmard, A. (1974). *Bot. Gaz.* 135, 345–352

Bernier, G., Kinet, J.-M., Jacqmard, A., Havelange, A. and Bodson, M. (1977). *Plant Physiol.* 60, 282–285

Bernier, G., Kinet, J.-M. and Sachs, R.M. (1981). In "The Physiology of Flowering" Vol. II. CRC Press, Boca Raton, Florida

Bodson, M. (1975). *Ann. Bot. (Lond.)* 39, 547–554

Bronchart, R., Bernier, G., Kinet, J.-M. and Havelange, A. (1970). *Planta* 91, 255–269

Brulfert, J. (1965). *Rev. Gen. Bot.* 72, 641–694

Chailakhyan, M. Kh., Aksenova, N.P., Konstantinova, T.N. and Bavrina, T.V. (1975). *Proc. R. Soc. Lond. B.*, 190, 333–340

Cheng, T.-Y. (1972). *Plant Physiol.* 50, 723–727

Corson, G.E. (1969). *Am. J. Bot.* 56, 1127–1134
Erickson, R.O. and Meicenheimer, R.D. (1977). *Am. J. Bot.* 64, 981–988
Evans, L.T. (1960). *New Phytol.* 59, 163–174
Evans, L.T. (1969). In "The Induction of Flowering" (ed L.T. Evans). pp. 457–480. MacMillan, Melbourne
Evans, L.T. (1971). *Annu. Rev. Plant Physiol.* 22, 365–394
Francis, D. (1981a). *Ann. Bot. (Lond.)* 48, 391–394
Francis, D. (1981b). *Protoplasma* 104, 285–291
Francis, D. and Lyndon, R.F. (1978a). *Planta* 139, 273–279
Francis, D. and Lyndon, R.F. (1978b). *Protoplasma* 96, 81–88
Francis, D. and Lyndon, R.F. (1979). *Planta* 145, 151–157
Goodwin, P.B. and Lyndon, R.F. (1983). *Protoplasma* 116, 219–222
Gressel, J., Zilberstein, A., Strausbauch, L. and Arzee, T. (1978). *Photochem. Photobiol.* 27, 237–240
Griffiths, F.E.W. (1981). M.Phil. Thesis, University of Edinburgh
Harder, R. (1948). *Symp. Soc. Exp. Biol.* 2, 117–138
Havelange, A. (1980). *Am. J. Bot.* 67, 1171–1178
Havelange, A. and Bernier, G. (1974). *J. Cell Sci.* 15, 633–644
Havelange, A. and Jeanny, J.-C. (1984). *Protoplasma* (In press)
Havelange, A., Bernier, G. and Jacqmard, A. (1974). *J. Cell Sci.* 16, 421–432
Horridge, J.S. and Cockshull, K.E. (1979). *Ann. Bot. (Lond.)* 44, 547–556
Jacqmard, A. (1978). *Protoplasma* 94, 315–324
Jacqmard, A., Miksche, J.P. and Bernier, G. (1972). *Am. J. Bot.* 59, 714–721
Jacqmard, A., Kettmann, R., Pryke, J.A., Thiry, M. and Sachs, R.M. (1981). *Ann. Bot. (Lond.).* 47, 415–417
Jacqmard, A., Lyndon, R.F. and Salmon, J. (1984) *J. Cell Sci.* (In press)
Jeffcoat, B. and Cockshull, K.E. (1972). *J. Exp. Bot.* 23, 722–732
Kinet, J.-M. (1972). *Nature (Lond.)* 236, 406.
Kinet, J.-M., Bodson, M., Alvinia, A.M. and Bernier, G. (1971). *Z.Pflanzenphysiol.* 66, 49–63
King, R.W. and Evans, L.T. (1969). *Aust. J. Biol. Sci.* 22, 559–572
Kirby, E.J.M. (1973). *J. Exp. Bot.* 24, 567–578
Kirby, E.J.M. (1974). *J. Agric. Sci.* 82, 437–447
Knox, R.B. and Evans, L.T. (1966). *Aust. J. Biol. Sci.* 19, 233–245
Langer, R.H.M. and Bussell, W.T. (1964), *Ann. Bot. (Lond.)* 28, 163–167

Lin, J. and Gifford, E.M. (1976). *Can. J. Bot.* 54, 2478–2483

Lyndon, R.F. (1977). *Symp. Soc. Exp. Biol.* 31, 221–250

Lyndon, R.F. (1978). *Ann. Bot. (Lond.)* 42, 1349–1360

Lyndon, R.F. (1979a). *Ann. Bot. (Lond.)* 43, 539–552

Lyndon, R.F. (1979b). *Ann. Bot. (Lond.)* 43, 553–558

Lyndon, R.F. (1984). *In* "Handbook of Flowering" (ed A. H. Halevy). CRC Press Inc., Boca Raton, Florida (In press)

Lyndon, R.F., Jacqmard, A. and Bernier, G. (1983). *Physiol. Plant.* 59, 476–480

Maksymowych, R. and Erickson, R.O. (1977). *Am. J. Bot.* 64, 33–44

Meicenheimer, R.D. (1981). *Am. J. Bot.* 68, 1139–1154

Meins, F. and Binns, A.N. (1979). *Bioscience* 29, 221–225

Meins, F. and Lutz, J. (1980). *Planta* 149, 402–407

Miller, M.B. (1976). Ph.D. Thesis, University of Edinburgh

Miller, M.B. and Lyndon, R.F. (1975). *Planta* 126, 37–43

Miller, M.B. and Lyndon, R.F. (1976). *J. Exp. Bot.* 27, 1142–1153

Miller, M.B. and Lyndon, R.F. (1977). *Planta* 136, 167–172

Mitchison, J.M. (1971). *In* "The Biology of the Cell Cycle" Cambridge University Press, Cambridge

Nagl, W. (1977). *Protoplasma* 91, 389–407

Nougarede, A. (1967). *Int. Rev. Cytol.* 21, 203–351

Nougarede, A. and Bronchart, R. (1965). *C.R. Hebd. Seances Acad. Sci.*, 260, 3140–3143

Nougarede, A., Bronchart, R., Bernier, G. and Rondet, P. (1964). *Rev. Gen. Bot.* 71, 205–238

Ormrod, J.C. and Francis, D. (1983). *Protoplasma* (In press)

Pierard, D., Jacqmard, A. and Bernier, G. (1977). *Physiol. Plant.* 41, 254–258

Pierard, D., Jacqmard, A., Bernier, G. and Salmon, J. (1980). *Planta* 150, 397–405

Pryke, J.A. and Bernier, G. (1978a). *J. Exp. Bot.* 29, 953–961

Pryke, J.A. and Bernier, G. (1978b). *Ann. Bot. (Lond.)* 42, 747–749

Schwabe, W.W. (1959). *J. Linn. Soc. Lond. Bot.* 56, 254–261

Schwabe, W.W. (1971). *Symp. Soc. Exp. Biol.* 25, 301–322

Seidlova, F. (1980a). *Biol. Plant.* 22, 428–433

Seidlova, F. (1980b). *Physiol. Veg.* 18, 477–481

Seidlova, F. and Krekule, J. (1973). *Ann. Bot. (Lond.)* 37, 605–614

Seidlova, F. and Sadlikova, H. (1983). *Biol. Plant.* 25, 50–62

Simon, J. (1972). *C.R. Hebd. Seances Acad. Sci.*, 274, 1485–1492

Soma, K. (1968). *Phytomorphology* 18, 305–324

Stiles, J.I. and Davies, P.J. (1976). *Plant Cell Physiol.* 17, 825–833

Sunderland, N. (1961). *J. Exp. Bot.* 12, 446–457

Taylor, S.J. (1975). Ph.D. Thesis, University of London
Thomas, R.G. (1961) *Ann. Bot. (Lond.)* 25, 138-151
Thomas, G.G. and Schwabe, W.W. (1970). *Ann. Bot. (Lond.)* 34, 849-859
Tran Thanh Van, K.M. (1980). *Adv. Biochem. Eng.*, 18, 151-171
Usciati, M., Codaccioni, M. and Guern, J.C. (1972). *J. Exp. Bot.* 23, 1009-1020
Vince-Prue, D. (1975). "Photoperiodism in Plants" McGraw-Hill, London.
Williams, R.F. (1966). *Aust. J. Biol. Sci.* 19, 949-966

GENETIC STUDIES

Chapter 14

GENETICS AND ITS POTENTIAL FOR UNDERSTANDING THE
ACTION OF LIGHT IN FLOWERING

C. N. LAW AND RACHEL SCARTH

Plant Breeding Institute, Maris Lane, Trumpington,
Cambridge, CB2 2LQ, U.K.

INTRODUCTION

In a recent review of the physiology of flowering, the opening
sentence states that "flower initiation is best investigated
in the minority of species or varieties in which this process
is under relatively strict control of the environment"
(Bernier et al., 1981). Whilst it is difficult to fault this
statement, it nevertheless typifies an attitude towards
physiological research which emphasizes the environment as the
principal controlling mechanism in plant development and tends
to ignore an equally important aspect of control which is
exercised by the plant itself through its genes.

It is evident that genes are primarily responsible for the
major differences that exist between LDP and SDP, or between
plants that need several inductive cycles and those that only
need one before flowering. If such genes could be isolated
and their structure and products described in detail this
would increase the understanding of the flowering process
immeasurably. In the same way, the genetic variation in
flowering that exists within a species can also be exploited.
Frequently, environmental agencies are used as probes to study
the processes leading to flowering. This approach has disad-
vantages since environmental probes are likely to affect many
plant processes. It is, therefore, difficult to establish
amongst a range of correlated responses those which are
causally related to flowering. This is not the case with
genetic variation, where a comparison between lines with and
without a gene for flowering provides an unequivocal test of

LIGHT AND THE FLOWERING PROCESS
ISBN 0.12.721960.9

the functional relationships between characters correlated
with flowering.

This paper, therefore, sets out to describe briefly the
recent advances that have been made in the genetics of
flowering in one of the most important crop plants, the bread
wheat of agriculture. Although this species cannot be considered as fitting the requirements of a species that is under
the strict control of the environment, it nevertheless has
certain features which make it ideal for genetic studies. At
the same time, the possibilities of isolating genes affecting
flowering by exploiting new developments in molecular biology
will be considered.

CHROMOSOME ORGANIZATION OF WHEAT

Wheat, *Triticum aestivum*, is an allohexaploid composed of 21
pairs of homologous chromosomes (2n=6x=42) which can be
grouped into three genomes, A, B and D, each comprising seven
pairs of chromosomes and each having been derived from a
separate ancestral diploid species. Within each genome,
chromosomes have been identified which are genetically similar
to chromosomes in each of the other genomes. These genetically similar groups of three chromosomes are referred to as
homoeologous and seven groups of homoeologues have been identified. Each homologous pair of chromosomes can thus be
uniquely designated as belonging to a particular homoeologous
group and genome, for example chromosome 1A belongs to homoeologous group 1 and the A genome.

Because of the triplication of genes that can occur within
a homoeologous group, wheat will tolerate the loss of or
increased dosage of whole chromosomes. These aneuploid lines
have been systematically collected, principally by Professor
E. R. Sears of the University of Missouri, U.S.A. (Sears,
1954), and aneuploid lines for each of the 21 homologous pairs
of chromosomes have been obtained. The different types of
aneuploids that exist are illustrated in Fig. 1 and indicate
that through the use of aneuploids chromosome dosage can be
varied between 0 and 4. This can also apply to chromosome
arms as well as to whole chromosomes, since some aneuploids
lack only a chromosome arm. The influence of chromosome
dosage on a character can thus be studied.

Aneuploid lines are used by wheat geneticists to transfer
chromosomes from one variety of wheat into another or from a
relative of wheat such as rye. Frequently such transfers are
made as substitutions where a particular chromosome in a
recipient variety is replaced by a homologue or homoeologue
from a donor wheat variety or related species. These substitution lines allow a particular varietal difference to be

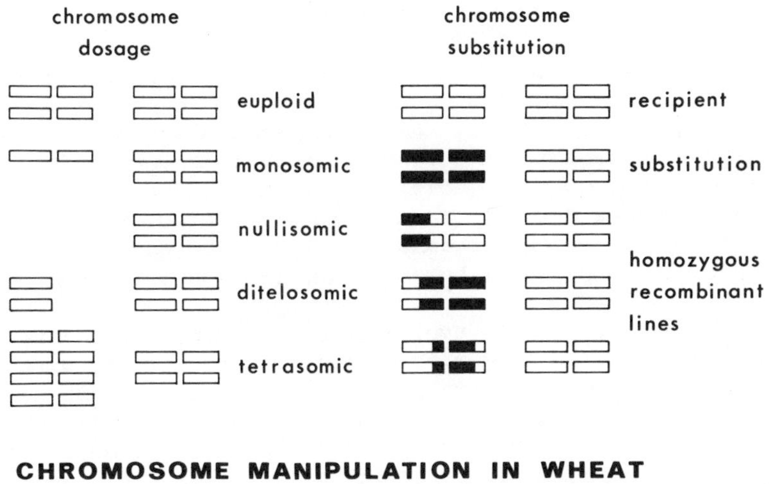

CHROMOSOME MANIPULATION IN WHEAT

*Fig. 1. Simplified diagram of the different types of chromo-
somal lines available in wheat for carrying out genetical and
physiological studies. Variation resulting from different
chromosome dosages or from different chromosome substitutions
are depicted for one homologous chromosome.*

dissected, chromosome by chromosome, so that the chromosomes
responsible for the difference can be identified. In the same
way, the chromosomal differences between wheat and its rela-
tives can also be established.

Once a chromosomal difference has been detected then the
numbers of genes responsible for this difference can be determined by crossing the critical substitution line with its
recipient variety to give a single chromosome heterozygote and
observing the segregation that occurs between the resulting
lines. In effect, this allows the study of a single chromosome difference on a constant genetical background so that the
potentially obscuring effects of segregating background genes
are removed. Moreover, by using cytogenetic and genetic techniques, homozygous recombinant lines can be produced from such
a single—chromosome heterozygous hybrid. Because such lines
are true—breeding, this enables them to be replicated extensively within and between different environments, so that the
effects of the environment can be estimated accurately.

Using these methods a wide range of maintainable aneuploid
and chromosome substitution lines have been produced in wheat.
These provide one of the best sources of plant material available for studying the genetics of complex characters such as
flowering, which may be under the control of many genes and
subject to considerable environmental variation.

THE CHROMOSOMAL CONTROL OF DAYLENGTH RESPONSE IN WHEAT

As already mentioned, the first step in studying the genes responsible for controlling the interaction of flowering with daylength, is to identify the chromosomal differences affecting this character. A good example of this comes from the study of a set of *alien* chromosome substitution lines in the variety Chinese Spring (CS) in which the chromosomes of homoeologous group 2 (chromosomes 2A, 2B and 2D) have been separately replaced by their homoeologues from the wild goat grasses, *Aegilops umbellulata* (chromosome 2U), Ae. *comosa* (chromosome 2M) and perennial rye, *Secale montanum* (chromosome $2R^m$). These nine lines, along with Chinese Spring itself, were grown under controlled environment conditions of LD and SD, using vernalized and unvernalized seedlings, and their days to ear-emergence scored (Law et al., 1978). Analysis showed that vernalization had no differential effect upon the lines, whereas the interaction between the lines and daylength was significant. This interaction is evident in Table 1, where the ear-emergence times averaged over the vernalization treatments are given for each of the lines. Under LD, variation between the lines was negligible, whereas under SD, the variation was considerable.

TABLE 1. *Mean ear-emergence times (days) under SD and LD for Chinese Spring (CS) and nine* alien *chromosome substitution lines in which chromosome 2M of* Aegilops comosa, *2U of* Aegilops umbellulata *and $2R^m$ of* Secale montanum *have been separately substituted for their homoeologues 2A, 2B and 2D in CS.*

Chromosome constitution			SD	LD
Chinese Spring (CS)	2A	2B	2D	100	51
CS 2A (2M)	2M	2B	2D	107	53
CS 2A (2U)	2U	2B	2D	126	52
CS 2A ($2R^m$)	$2R^m$	2B	2D	116	49
CS 2B (2M)	2A	2M	2D	127	54
CS 2B (2U)	2A	2U	2D	130	53
CS 2B ($2R^m$)	2A	$2R^m$	2D	170	52
CS 2D (2M)	2A	2B	2M	93	51
CS 2D (2U)	2A	2B	2U	98	52
CS 2D ($2R^m$)	2A	2B	$2R^m$	107	51

The greatest delays in ear emergence under SD were found

when chromosome 2B of CS was replaced by each of the *alien*
chromosomes, indicating that this chromosome carried genes for
greater insensitivity to daylength than those present on the
other chromosomes. The substitutions for chromosome 2A were,
on average, later than those for chromosome 2D, thus indicating that 2A carried genes for insensitivity which were more
potent than those on 2D. Using a similar reasoning, comparisons between 2M, 2U and $2R^m$ substitution lines showed that 2M
produced greater insensitivity than 2U which in turn was
greater than $2R^m$. Since CS was also included in the
analysis, it was possible to rank all chromosomes against each
other in terms of insensitivity to daylength. Thus 2B was
more potent than 2A, followed by 2M, then by 2U and 2D, and
finally by $2R^m$ which was the least potent of all the chromosomes studied.

Considerable variation affecting the response of the wheat
plant to different daylengths was therefore revealed by this
experiment. In addition, the experiment showed that although
the results were such as to permit an unambiguous ranking of
the chromosomes, interactions between the chromosomes, in
which insensitivity was dominant to sensitivity, did occur.
This suggests that it was the activities of the genes on these
chromosomes which were responsible for insensitivity to daylength rather than the converse.

This conclusion was confirmed in two further experiments
using aneuploid lines of CS designed to test the consequence
of varying the dosage of the chromosomes of homoeologous group
2 on response to daylength (Scarth and Law, 1984). The lines
used were either tetrasomic (four doses of a particular chromosome) or were nullisomic-tetrasomic (lacking a chromosome
completely, but partially compensated for by increased dosage
of a related homoeologue), or were ditelosomic (lacking an arm
of a chromosome). If the activities of a gene are responsible
for producing daylength insensitivity, then a negative corre-
lation between increased gene dosage and ear-emergence time
under SD would be expected. This was found to be the case
(Table 2). Each of the ditelosomics was later, and each of
the tetrasomics earlier than CS euploid; ditelosomic 2BL being
the latest and tetrasomic 2B the earliest of the lines
studied.

These experiments also agreed with the previous experiment
in showing CS 2B as having the greatest effect on daylength
insensitivity followed by 2A and 2D. In addition, the delayed
emergence of the ditelosomics demonstrated that it was the
short arm of 2B and the long arms of 2A and 2D which were the
probable location of the genes controlling insensitivity.
Although the arms implicated differ in length, independent
evidence has established that the arms are nevertheless gene

TABLE 2. *Days to ear emergence under SD of group 2 aneuploids of Chinese Spring (CS). Significant differences from CS euploid are indicated.*

Lines	Experiment 1	Experiment 2
Chinese Spring euploid	96.0 ± 2.70	115.4 ± 0.60
CS tetrasomic 2A	–	113.8 ± 1.01
CS tetrasomic 2B	–	108.8 ± 1.01**
CS tetrasomic 2D	–	117.2 ± 1.74
CS nullisomic 2D tetrasomic 2A	102.4 ± 4.46	116.2 ± 1.32
CS nullisomic 2D tetrasomic 2B	93.2 ± 1.16	110.3 ± 1.17**
CS nullisomic 2B tetrasomic 2D	136.0 ± 2.00**	155.4 ± 1.03**
CS ditelosomic 2AS	119.8 ± 8.78**	–
CS ditelosomic 2BL	158.0 ± 7.00**	–
CS ditelosomic 2DS	111.8 ± 13.51	–

** P 0.01–0.001

tically similar. This suggests strongly that the genes for insensitivity on these three chromosomes are related and probably reflect allelic variants at identical loci. The nullisomic–tetrasomic lines also confirmed the rankings between the chromosomes, CS nullisomic 2B tetrasomic 2D was much later than Chinese Spring, but was not as late as CS ditelosomic 2BL, presumably because of the effects of chromosome 2D. Likewise CS nullisomic 2D tetrasomic 2B was earlier than CS, but not as early as CS tetrasomic 2B, again due to the activity of chromosome 2D.

THE IDENTIFICATION OF THE GENES FOR DAYLENGTH RESPONSE

Having located the chromosomal arms responsible for daylength control, the next stage is to identify the numbers of genes involved using homozygous recombinant lines derived from the hybrid between an appropriate inter–varietal chromosome substitution line and its recipient variety. It is evident that CS carries a gene or genes having a major effect on insensitivity to daylength on chromosome 2B. Because of this, substitutions for this chromosome in CS from other varieties are often delayed, one of the most marked being the line having 2B of the variety Marquis replacing 2B of CS. This line was therefore hybridized with CS and homozygous recombinant lines produced (Scarth and Law, 1983).

Nearly 100 lines were obtained and these were grown under SD conditions. At ear-emergence time, the lines fell into two distinct classes of equal size, indicating that a single gene was responsible for the different parental responses to day-length. Within each of the classes, however, a second factor of much smaller effect could also be recognized. This was associated with genes for disease resistance which segregated between the lines and were known from previous studies to be located on the long arm of 2B. Two genetic factors were therefore located on 2B. The first, having a large effect, was found on the short arm and was evidently responsible for the major effects observed in the earlier experiments. This gene has now been designated *Ppd2* to denote its sensitivity to daylength or photoperiod. The second, having a much smaller effect, was located on the long arm. Subsequent tests have shown that this gene is not responsive to daylength.

Using similar procedures, a second gene of major effect on daylength response was identified on chromosome 2D and designated *Ppd1* (Welsh *et al.*, 1973; Scarth and Law, 1984). A single gene has yet to be localized on chromosome 2A, but the significant effects of varying this chromosome upon response to daylength indicate that it is likely that a single gene will also be found on this chromosome. This has provisionally been designated *Ppd3*.

It is now known that variation amongst these chromosomes, particularly at the *Ppd1* and *Ppd2* loci are responsible for the close adaptation of major groups of wheat to different regions of the world. The *Green Revolution* wheats bred in Mexico owe their wide adaptability to an allele of *Ppd1* conferring extreme insensitivity to daylength. This enabled such wheats to be grown under the SD winter conditions of India and Pakistan. It also seems likely that Australian wheats owed their adaptability to winter-growing conditions from the introduction of Indian wheats carrying an insensitive allele of *Ppd2*. Italian and Mediterranean wheats also avoid the high temperatures of their summers because of an insensitive *Ppd1* allele derived initially from the introduction of a Japanese variety in the early part of this century. There is thus considerable interest by breeders in understanding more about the extent of the variation controlled by these genes and also the nature of the processes that are controlled by them.

THE EFFECT OF THE GENE *Ppd2* ON DEVELOPMENT

The homozygous recombinant lines obtained from the cross of CS with its substitution line carrying Marquis 2B can now be used to study the effect of *Ppd2* on development. Eight lines were chosen, four carrying *Ppd2* and four carrying the more sensi-

tive allele, *ppd2*. All the lines were grown under SD and
plants from each of the lines were sampled at intervals, the
number of primordia counted and the length of the apex from
the collar primordium determined (Scarth, Kirby and Law,
unpublished results).

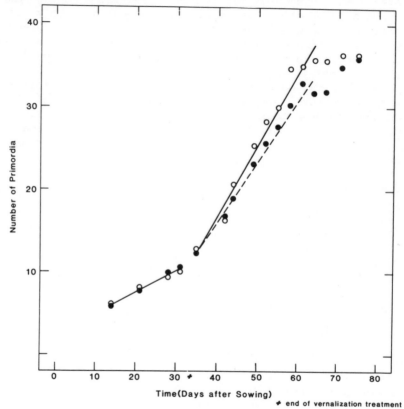

Fig. 2. *The total number of primordia plotted against time
for the period of leaf and spikelet initiation of lines
carrying either* Ppd2 *(O) or* ppd2 *(●) grown under SD vernalized
conditions. For most of the period the rate of initiation was
identical between the lines (Scarth 1981).*

In both the *Ppd2* and *ppd2* lines, the time of initiation of
spikelet primordia as well as the number of spikelet primordia
produced were identical. The rates at which these primordia
were produced were also the same throughout most of the period
of spikelet formation, although for the last three spikelets,
the rate was much lower in the *ppd2* lines and the terminal
spikelet was formed some 20 days later than in the *Ppd2* lines
(see Fig. 2). The most striking effect between the two sets

of lines, however, was in the rate of growth of the spike as a whole. The growth of the apex in the *ppd2* lines lagged behind that of the *Ppd2* lines and this was reflected in their different relative growth rates (Fig. 3)

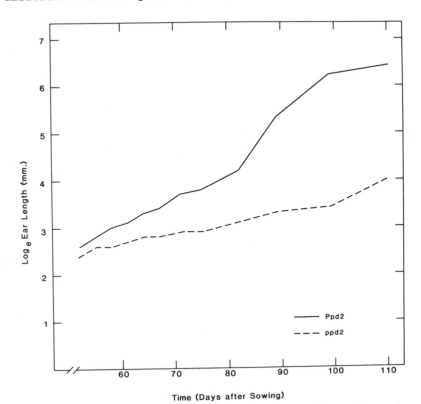

Fig. 3. *Log$_e$ floral apex length plotted against time, for lines carrying either Ppd2 or ppd2 grown under SD vernalized conditions (Scarth, 1981).*

A similar pattern of behaviour was also observed for the effects of the *Ppd1* locus on chromosome 2D (Scarth, Kirby and Law, unpublished results). Amongst lines of CS carrying the extremely potent *Ppd1* allele from Mexican wheats, spikelet initiation commenced at the same time as in CS and the rates of primordia formation were identical. However, spikelet production ended much earlier than in CS and this was followed by a phase of rapid growth and differentiation. The only difference between the *Ppd1* and *Ppd2* lines was thus the earlier cessation of spikelet formation. This is probably due to the greater responsiveness of the *Ppd1* allele to SD than the *Ppd2* allele.

The major effect of the *Ppd* loci is, therefore, not on the timing of the change from vegetative to reproductive development, but on the duration of the growth and development of the reproductive phase. In the presence of the most active *Ppd* alleles the number of spikelets produced is reduced but the most general effect of substituting a more active allele is to increase the rate of growth and differentiation once the formation of spikelet primordia has been completed.

OTHER GENES AFFECTING FLOWERING IN WHEAT

The influence of the group 2 chromosomes and their *Ppd* genes are not the only effects on flowering that have been identified and described in wheat. A number of other genes have been located, some of which have major effects on this

TABLE 3. *Summary of chromosomal and genetical effects on ear emergence in wheat.*

	GENOME			
	A	B	D	
1	1A	1B	1D	Carry genes inhibiting ear emergence and sensitive to both daylength and vernalization.
2	2A	2B	2D	Major genes sensitive to daylength but also carry additional factors
	Ppd3?	Ppd2	Ppd1	acting independently of daylength and vernalization.
3	3A	3B	3D	Some effects on vernalization response identified.
4	4A	4B	4D	
5	5A	5B	5D	Major genes sensitive to vernalization, mainly responsible for
	Vrn1	Vrn2	Vrn3	spring—winter wheat differences.
6	6A	6B	6D	
7	7A	7B	7D	Probably carry major genes for vernalization on each of their short arms;
	Vrn4?	Vrn5		additional factors also sensitive to vernalization have also been identified.

character. Although the picture is still by no means complete, a summary of the known genes and chromosomes controlling various aspects of flowering is presented in Table 3.

Perhaps the most important, certainly so far as adaptation
in wheat is concerned, are the vernalization genes, $Vrn1$, $Vrn2$
and $Vrn3$, located on each of the group 5 chromosomes. Almost
certainly these genes are identical since they are located at
similar positions on the three chromosomes. Variation amongst
these genes is mainly responsible for the differences between
spring and winter cereals in their reaction to temperatures.
Plants carrying alleles for a reduced vernalization
requirement, such as spring wheat, initiate spikelet primordia
earlier and also give increased rates of primordia formation
at normal growing temperatures compared with winter wheats.
In the U.K. this ensures that autumn-sown winter wheats are
maintained at the vegetative or early reproductive state until
the low temperatures of winter are over. Chromosome dosage
experiments have shown that the presence of the gene reduces
the vernalization requirement (Halloran, 1966) suggesting that
it promotes the level of a substance responsible for the
change from vegetative to reproductive development and that it
is increased levels of this substance which accelerate this
process. Vernalization presumably acts by mirroring this
effect, perhaps because low temperature reduces the breakdown
of the substance. The differential effect of these Vrn genes
on vernalization requirement can be removed by subjecting
wheat plants to continuous SD.

Recently, the consequences of changing the chromosome
dosage of the group 1 chromosomes have been studied (Suarez,
Worland and Law, unpublished results). These studies have
provided genetical evidence for an inhibitor of flowering in
wheat (Table 4). Removal of chromosome 1A of CS or its
short-arm, in particular, brings about a reduction in days to
ear-emergence whereas increased dosage of this chromosome has
the opposite effect. At the moment, it is not clear how many
genes are responsible, since interactions with both daylength

TABLE 4. *Days to ear-emergence of Chinese Spring, Chinese
Spring tetrasomic 1A and Chinese Spring ditelosomic 1AL grown
in the field following a Spring sowing.*

	Dosage of 1AS	Ear emergence
Chinese Spring tetrasomic 1A	4	84.33 ± 0.95
Chinese Spring euploid	2	80.00 ± 0.56
Chinese Spring ditelosomic 1AL	0	75.80 ± 0.31

and vernalization have been observed and at least two genes
may consequently be involved. However, this evidence could
provide support for the idea that flowering is due to a shift
in the balance between promoting and inhibiting substances.

Finally, a major gene, $Vrn5$, responsive to vernalization,
has been located on the short arm of chromosome 7B and a
similar effect, but as yet not analysed in terms of genes, ha
been associated with chromosome 7A. A factor having a smalle
effect on ear emergence but also sensitive to vernalization
has also been detected on the long arm of 7B. The consequenc
of removing these genes is not known at the moment, so that i
is not possible to ascertain whether the genes are acting as
promoters or inhibitors. Although the magnitude of the
effects of these genes is not as great as those located on th
group 5 chromosomes, they are nevertheless of major effect an
are important sources of variation in breeding.

THE EFFECT OF THE CYTOPLASM

A number of cytoplasmic substitution lines have been produced
in wheat in which wheat chromosomes have been transferred by
recurrent backcrossing into the cytoplasm of a wild relative.
A well-known example of this is the substitution into the
cytoplasm of the tetraploid $Triticum$ $timopheevi$ to produce
male-sterility which may have a potential use in the production of hybrid wheat. A range of different $Aegilops$ cytoplasms has also been transferred and some of these have marke
effects on the duration of flowering. One of the most
striking effects is produced by the cytoplasm of $Ae. ovata$
which consistently delays the time to ear-emergence, irrespective of the varietal chromosomes that are substituted into
it (Tsunewaki and Endo, 1973).

The nature of this effect has been studied in greater
detail using a number of CS inter-varietal chromosome substitution lines, carrying different alleles at the $Vrn1$ and $Vrn3$
loci, which have been backcrossed on to $Ae. ovata$ cytoplasm.
These lines were vernalized and, along with unvernalized
controls, were grown in a controlled-environment chamber unde
LD conditions and the days to ear emergence scored (Table 5).
Analysis indicated that under vernalized conditions differences between the lines disappeared but a constant difference
was maintained between the two cytoplasmic sources. The
unvernalized controls, on the other hand, showed the
differences expected from the action of their different Vrn
genes, although the delaying effect of the $ovata$ cytoplasm
became less the greater the vernalization requirement of the
Vrn gene. This interaction with cytoplasm under unvernalized
conditions and its absence following vernalization, suggests

that vernalization has no direct effect on the cytoplasmic differences, but the cytoplasm does influence the response of the *Vrn* genes to vernalization.

A striking feature of the results is the behaviour of the

TABLE 5. *Days to ear emergence, from an arbitrary date, for lines of wheat carrying different alleles at the* Vrn1 *and* Vrn3 *loci on chromosomes 5A and 5D respectively, substituted on to two different cytoplasms,* Aegilops ovata *and* Triticum aestivum, *and grown under vernalized (V) and unvernalized (UV) conditions.*

Nuclear genotype		*aestivum* cytoplasm	*ovata* cytoplasm	Difference
Chinese Spring (CS)	V	5.00	25.50	20.50
Vrn1a Vrn3	UV	39.50	64.00	24.50
CS (*Triticum spelta* 5A)	V	2.75	23.75	21.00
Vrn1 Vrn3	UV	5.75	36.25	30.50
CS (Cappelle—Desprez 5A)	V	4.50	29.00	24.50
vrn1b Vrn3	UV	51.00	74.50	23.50
CS (Cappelle—Desprez 5D)	V	10.75	31.00	20.25
Vrn1a vrn3	UV	68.75	70.50	1.75

line CS (Cappelle—Desprez 5D) which has the greatest verna- lization requirement. Under unvernalized conditions this line showed very little difference in ear—emergence in *ovata* and *aestivum* cytoplasms. This could reflect the operation of an upper limit to ear emergence which, when approached, causes the activation of other genes to bring about ear development. A similar kind of operation may be advanced to explain the action of 5D, which apparently can substitute for vernali- zation by removing the differences in ear—emergence time between lines and varieties whilst at the same time delaying ear emergence. This concept of an upper limit, and also a lower limit to ear emergence may explain many of the inter- actions which have been observed with different environmental treatments. It deserves to be considered much more closely than has been the case up to now.

The major feature of these results, however, is the relative insensitivity of the cytoplasmic substitution to vernalization. Experiments were therefore continued to deter-

mine the influence that daylength may have on the timing of
this character. These showed that under LD the differences
between the two cytoplasms were maintained but under SD the
difference increased (Table 6). There is thus a positive
interaction between daylength and the *ovata-aestivum* cytoplasmic difference. This differs, however, from the positive
interactions produced by the *Ppd* genes where the differences
disappear under long days. This suggests that there is a
fundamental difference between the processes involved, as well
as implicating the activities of organellar genes in the
regulation of the flowering process.

TABLE 6. *Days to ear emergence for Chinese Spring and Chinese
Spring (ovata) grown under SD (8 h) and LD (8 h + 16 h low
light intensity) conditions. (Scarth, 1981).*

	SD	LD
Chinese Spring	54	40
Chinese Spring (ovata)	130	84
difference	76	44

MOLECULAR STUDIES

At the present time, no account of genetics should avoid
mentioning the revolution that is currently taking place in
molecular biology. This is having a major impact upon genetics and it is likely that it will have important consequences
in many other areas of biology including the study of the
flowering process of plants. In the application of recombinant DNA techniques to the study of eukaryotic organisms, it
has been difficult to see how such techniques might be used in
investigating the molecular biology of genes affecting complex
characters. In the main this has been due to lack of knowledge about such genes, about the products they produce and
about the time at which they act, so that it has been impossible to isolate the appropriate mRNA and produce a copy of
the gene for cloning.

However, given some knowledge of genetics, a method is
beginning to emerge which may allow the isolation and cloning
of genes for complex characters such as flowering. This
depends upon the observation made some years ago in maize by
McClintock (1956) that mutations at unstable loci result from
the integration of small pieces of DNA from one part of the
nuclear genome into genes to give mutant phenotypes. These
mobile elements transpose either spontaneously or can be

induced genetically to do so with a higher frequency. A similar phenomenon referred to as hybrid dysgenesis has also been observed in *Drosophila* (Kidwell *et al.*, 1977). The presence of these mobile elements within a gene provides the solution to the problem of gene isolation. Because, if it is possible to clone a mobile element, then it should also be possible to use this as a probe to isolate the mutant gene carrying the element as an insert. This procedure has in fact been applied successfully already to *Drosophila* and at least two genes have been isolated and cloned (Bingham *et al.*, 1981; Searles *et al.*, 1982). In plants, the methodology has not advanced as far, but in maize and in *Antirrhinum majus*, mobile elements have been isolated so that it cannot be long before genes from these plants are obtained. The attractiveness of this technique is that it is not necessary to know anything about the details of the processes that a gene controls, all that is required is an ability to recognize a mutant of the gene that needs to be isolated.

A strategy for isolating the *Ppd* gene affecting daylength insensitivity in wheat is described in Fig. 4. This of course assumes the presence of a mobile element in wheat, that it has been cloned and that it can be activated or induced to trans-pose. Given these possibilities then selection would be prac-tised for a daylength sensitive mutant, since inactivation of *Ppd* by the element will produce such a phenotype. By growing the wheat in the field on a large scale following a winter sowing, daylength sensitive plants could readily be identified in the U.K. since they would be late in flowering. The DNA of these late flowering mutants would then be restricted and cloned. Such clones could then be screened for the presence of the mobile element and the clones carrying the element isolated. Confirmation that the pieces of DNA carrying the element were in fact taken from the *Ppd* locus could be made by using the selected cloned DNA as a probe on to lines of wheat lacking the chromosome arms known to be the location of the active *Ppd* gene. Homozygous recombinant lines could also be used with the probe to establish a much closer association with the *Ppd* locus. Once this had been established then it would be relatively easy to obtain the normal *Ppd* gene by using the already cloned inactive gene to probe for the normal gene amongst the DNA from insensitive plants.

Having isolated the gene, the next step would be to sequence its DNA and then to predict the structure of the protein produced by the gene. A further use of the cloned DNA would be to use it as a probe to study the action of the gene throughout development and under different daylengths in order to determine the precise moment at which the gene is activated and the particular cell or tissue in which this activation

takes place. Ultimately, it would be possible to introduce
the gene into bacteria or indeed into other plants and attempt
to get expression.

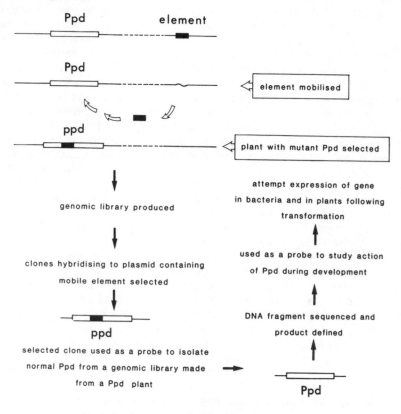

Strategy for isolating a gene for day–length insensitivity from a plant
using a mobile element

Fig. 4. A proposed strategy for isolating a Ppd *gene from a
plant.*

Admittedly the strategy outlined requires a great deal of
perfecting. Certainly in wheat the consequences of a mobile
element on variation have yet to be identified let alone
isolated. In maize and in *Antirrhinum*, however, mobile
elements are known and have been isolated, and almost certainly the steps outlined above or something very similar, are
being actively pursued at the present. The prospects for
isolating genes for flowering are therefore good, provided of

course there is sufficient will to make the attempt. Most molecular biologists are probably not even aware that plants flower, let alone that there are such things as flowering genes! It will, therefore, be up to the physiologist or the geneticist interested in flowering to provide the will and the direction. The isolation of genes for flowering, the description of their products, and their position within the scheme of events leading to flowering are surely objectives well worth the effort.

REFERENCES

Bernier, G., Kinet, J.M. and Sachs, R.M. (1981). *In* "The Physiology of Flowering" Vol. 1. CRC Press, Florida

Bingham, P.M., Levis, R. and Rubin, R. (1981). *Cell* 25, 693–704

Halloran, G.M. (1966). *J. Aust. Inst. Agric. Sci.* 52, 228–229

Kidwell, M.G., Kidwell, J.F. and Sved, J.A. (1977). *Genetics* 86, 813–833

Law, C.N., Sutka, J. and Worland, A.J. (1978). *Heredity* 41, 185–191

McClintock, B. (1956). *Carnegie Inst. Wash. Year Book* 55, 323–332

Scarth, R. (1981). Ph.D. Thesis, Cambridge, England

Scarth, R. and Law, C.N. (1983). *Heredity* 51, 607–619

Scarth, R. and Law, C.N. (1984). *Z. Pflanzenzuecht.* 92, 140–150

Searles, L.L., Scott Jokerst, R., Bingham, P.M., Voelker, R.A. and Greenleaf, A.L. (1982). *Cell* 31, 585–592

Sears, E.R. (1954). *Mo. Agric. Exp. Stn. Res. Bull.* 572, 59

Tsunewaki, K. and Endo, T. (1973). *Proc. 4th Int. Wheat Gen. Symp. Mo.* 391–397

Welsh, J.R., Keim, D.L., Pirasteh, B. and Richards, R.D. (1973). *Proc. 4th Int. Wheat Gen. Symp. Mo.* 879–884

FLOWER DEVELOPMENT AND LIGHT

Chapter 15

LIGHT AND FLOWER DEVELOPMENT

JEAN—MARIE KINET[1] AND ROY M. SACHS[2]

[1]Centre de Physiologie Vegetale Appliquee (I.R.S.I.A.),
Departement de Botanique, Universite de Liege, B-4000,
Sart Tilman, Liege, Belgium
[2]Department of Environmental Horticulture,
University of California, Davis, CA 95616, U.S.A.

INTRODUCTION

In numerous fundamental studies the term, "flowering", is used interchangeably with flower initiation; hence, post—initiation stages of flower development through anthesis are often neglected because they are viewed as the inescapable consequence of initiation. There is little question that flowering is a continuous and, from an evolutionary viewpoint, unitary process. Yet much research shows that it consists of numerous sequential steps, each of which may have its own specific requirements (control points) and be affected differently by environmental and chemical parameters. Light appears to have a central role in development as it does in initiation. Daylength and irradiance affect development of the reproductive structures either independently or in combination since they both contribute to total photosynthetically active radiation, an important parameter for many species.

Daylength and Flower Development

The role of daylength in controlling flower development was recognized in early work by Garner and Allard (1920, 1923) who found that in some species, including soybean (*Glycine max*), tobacco (*Nicotiana tabacum*) and aster (*Callistephus chinensis*), flower initiation occurs after a minimal number of inductive cycles but, when plants are returned to non—inductive conditions, flower buds abort prematurely.

Depending on the species or cultivar, flower development may
have absolute (qualitative) or facultative (quantitative)
photoperiodic requirements. Plants with an absolute photoperiodic requirement for flower development never develop any
flowers to anthesis when grown, after flower initiation, under
an inappropriate daylength, as is the case for *Sinapis alba*
(Table 1) and *Chrysanthemum morifolium*. In facultative photoperiodic species, the rate of flower development is decreased
and anthesis is delayed in unfavourable photoperiods, as is
found in many cereals.

TABLE 1. *Development of the terminal inflorescence of* Sinapis
alba *(LDP) as a function of increasing number of 16 h LD given
to 2-month old vegetative plants. One 16 h LD was sufficient
to induce flowering in all plants. After the LD treatment,
the plants were returned to 8 h SD. The observations were
discontinued 30 days after the start of the different LD
treatments.*

Number of LD	Per cent plants developing at least one flower to anthesis	Number of flowers reaching anthesis per terminal inflorescence	Days from start of the LD treatment to the first anthesis
1	0	0	–
4	7	8	23
7	33	7	19
10	80	12	18
13	93	16	17
16	100	29	17

   Photoperiod not only affects the rate of development and
the abortion of the reproductive structures, it has various
morphogenetic effects as well. It is a potent factor determining sex expression and fertility in various monoecious,
dioecious and hermaphroditic species; it controls the production of cleistogamous or chasmogamous flowers in some
plants and affects the onset of flower bud dormancy in several
woody species (Vince–Prue, 1975; Kinet et al., 1984). Non-
inductive photoperiodic conditions also induce varied reproductive abnormalities indicating that a given primordium in a
reproductive structure is not fully committed at initiation
and that developmental paths remain optional for some time
(Kinet et al., 1984).

In a number of species the optimal daylength may change with the stage of development of the reproductive organs and even differ for initiation and further development of the flower. As a consequence, classifications based upon photoperiodic requirements for the complete flowering process have been proposed (Vince-Prue, 1975).

Irradiance and Flower Development

Rose, many bulbous species, tomato, and grapevine are dayneutral for flower development, although precise investigations sometimes reveal a slight quantitative photoperiodic requirement (Kinet, 1977a). Most often flower development in these species is strongly influenced by irradiance and the irradiance-daylength integral (and also temperature). The light integral affects the rate of development of the reproductive structure, and frequently is decisive for normal development of the flower to anthesis or its premature abortion, as shown for tomato (Kinet, 1977a).

Strong interactions between daylength and light intensity have been observed in several photoperiodic species; this is particularly well illustrated in a series of papers by Hughes and Cockshull (see review by Cockshull, 1972) for *Chrysanthemum*. In *Bougainvillea* cv San Diego Red, which is usually considered as a SDP for flower development, high light not only promotes inflorescence development, but overrides the photoperiodic signal so that this plant flowers rapidly in LD (Sachs and Hackett, 1969).

TIME DEPENDENCE OF LIGHT EFFECTS

Appropriate light conditions are usually not required for the entire process of flower development but they do appear essential for a limited time interval, through to completion of some precise stage, suggesting that only some developmental sequences involved in the ontogeny of flowers and inflorescences are light-limited. For example, in late cultivars of *Chrysanthemum*, which in some conditions have an absolute requirement of SD for capitulum development, the appropriate daylength is essential only around the time of macroscopic appearance of the inflorescence bud (Fig. 1).

In tomato, one critical stage in inflorescence development is between the 5-6th and 10-12th days after macroscopic appearance of the truss (Kinet and Leonard, 1983). Unfavourable light conditions (8 h SD, 12 W m^{-2} at the top of the canopy) during this period induce the complete failure of numerous inflorescences. At the time of the transfer the meiotic processes in the anther are in progress at the tetrad

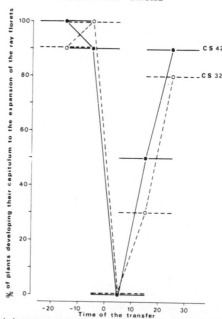

Fig. 1. Capitulum development as a function of the time of insertion of a 20-day, 16 h-LD treatment in Chrysanthemum morifolium *(cvs Blanche Poitevine Angora BB CS 32 and CS 42) grown under 12 h SD.*

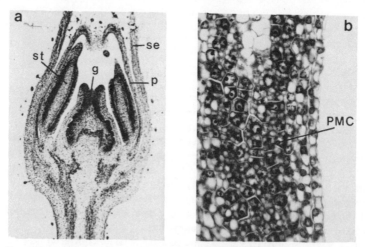

Fig. 2. The stage of development of the first flower of a tomato inflorescence cv King Plus undergoing abortion in continuous unfavourable light conditions. The first flower is complete (a) but its development is halted at the pollen mother-cell stage (b) (Haematoxylin stain). se = sepal; p = petal; st = stamen; g = gynoecium; PMC = pollen mother cell.

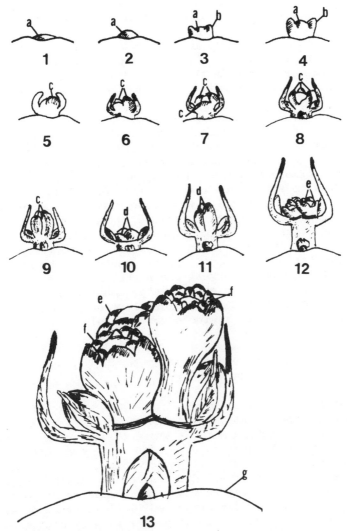

Fig. 3. Stages of development of the inflorescence of **Bougain-**
villea *cv San Diego Red. 1: Slab-shaped meristem. 2: Dome-*
shaped meristem. 3: Meristem subtended by 2 bracts. 4: Meri-
stem is a raised dome. Stages 5,6,7: Initiation of 3 bracte-
oles (showy bracts). Note indeterminate vegetative bud sub-
tending inflorescence. 8: Bracteole ring, dome still visible.
9: Bracteoles cover dome. 10: Tripartitioning of apical meri-
stem; bracteoles pulled away. 11: Three floret initials. 12:
Five perianth lobes on each floret. 13: Stamens and pistils.
a. meristem, b. bract, c. bracteole, d. floret primordium, e.
perianth, f. stamens and pistils, g. leaf scar. (From
Gallaher, 1983).

and free-spore stages. Low light results in degenerated
pollen grains.

When plants are continuously grown under unfavourable light
conditions, abortion occurs at an earlier stage. All floral
organs are initiated in the first flower of the inflorescence
(Fig. 2a) but development stops at the pollen mother-cell
stage (Fig. 2b).

As noted, inflorescence primordia progress only to the
bracteole initiation stage (Fig. 3, stage 5) in *Bougainvillea*
plants grown at 4,500 lx for 8 h. Floret primordia are initiated at higher light inputs, in excess of 10,000 lx for 8 h,
but the inflorescence bud usually aborts before functional
reproductive structures are initiated (Stage 10). Reproductive axes cannot catch-up when given later exposure to high
irradiance. Development to anthesis (after stage 13) requires
continuous periods (up to 3 weeks) of irradiance to the mature
leaves of 25,000 lx for 8 h, and more rapid development occurs
with greater production of inflorescences as the irradiance
integral increases (Hackett and Sachs, unpublished results).

Since, depending on experimental conditions, flower development ceases at different developmental stages it is clear
that there cannot be a single control point for the entire
process.

THE MECHANISMS INVOLVED IN THE CONTROL OF FLOWER DEVELOPMENT
BY DAYLENGTH AND LIGHT QUALITY

Some studies, particularly with the SDP *Caryopteris x clandon-
ensis* (Piringer et al., 1963), LD lines of *Pisum sativum*
(Reid, 1979), the LDP Marquis wheat (Friend et al., 1963) and
Wintex barley (Deitzer et al., 1979, 1982 and this volume,
Chapter 4), have shown that phytochrome is the photoreceptor
involved in the photoperiodic control of flower development,
acting in some species in the high irradiance response mode.
In *Bougainvillea* cv San Diego Red, inflorescence development
to anthesis requires that the plants receive high irradiance
in the FR region for most of an 8 h photoperiod; the ratio of
730/660 nm must be about 0.79 (Sachs and Hackett, 1977).
Beginning or end-of-day exposures to high FR do not replace
continuous 8 h exposure; if this is a phytochrome mediated
response it is clearly of the HIR type. There is one finding
with *Bougainvillea* that may warrant further attention. When
the 6 most recently unfolded leaves are removed, the requirement for high FR is essentially eliminated (Sachs and Hackett,
1977). As discussed later we believe that some inhibitor of
inflorescence development is removed with the young leaves;
according to this hypothesis, the role of high FR irradiance
could be to suppress release of the inhibitor from the young

leaves.

Addition of FR to R promotes flower bud development in roses (Mor and Halevy, 1980; Mor et al., 1980); this appears to be the result of direct activation in the bud (see discussion below) with consequent changes in assimilate partitioning in the shoot. Also in Chrysanthemum cv Bright Golden Anne inflorescence development is faster in high FR conditions although leaf number to initiation is not reduced (Sachs and Hackett, unpublished results). For both Bougainvillea and Chrysanthemum, overall plant growth (shoot dry weight gain and leaf initiation) is promoted in the high FR irradiance conditions (Sachs and Hackett, unpublished results); hence the promotion of inflorescence development in these species may result in part from greater net assimilation rates and more favourable assimilate partitioning in the shoot system. A clear indication that dry matter partitioning may change as a function of daylength is found in Raper and Thomas (1978) study with soybeans exposed to SD during the pod-filling period only; unfortunately, similar studies on inflorescence development tracing back to the earliest post-initiation stages are not common in the literature.

THE MECHANISMS INVOLVED IN HIGH-LIGHT-INDUCED PROMOTION OF FLOWER DEVELOPMENT

Sink Activation by Light

In a few species including rose (Mor and Halevy, 1980; Mor et al., 1980), grapevine (May, 1965) and probably bulbous iris (Mae and Vonk, 1974), the high light requirement cannot be explained by increased photosynthesis only. A direct action of light on the developing rose bud with a consequent promotion of sink activity has been described by Halevy and co-workers (Zieslin and Halevy, 1975; Mor and Halevy, 1980). In Bougainvillea and tomato we found no evidence for irradiance-induced sink activation. Inflorescence buds of tomato plants, darkened from the time of their macroscopic appearance with a black plastic cap, all developed to anthesis at the same rate as buds covered with transparent plastic caps (Table 2a). When Bougainvillea (Table 2b) shoot tips, containing developing inflorescences, were shaded, there was no reduction in development if the leaves were maintained in high light. Greatly reduced rates of inflorescence development and/or abortion before floret initiation (Fig. 3, stage 10) occurs in Bougainvillea if irradiance to the leaves falls below 25,000 lx with an 8 h photoperiod even if the shoot tips receive 40,000 lx. Hence, the high light requirement for flower development does not function as a sink activator in all species.

Source Activation by Light

Shading experiments show clearly that higher photosynthetic
activity in the source leaves is a major contributing factor
to high-light induced promotion of flower development (even in

TABLE 2a. *Effect of darkening the inflorescence of tomato
plants cv King Plus growing under favourable light conditions
(16 h LD, 20 W m^{-2} at the top of the canopy) on the development of this inflorescence. The dark treatment is applied
from the macroscopic appearance of the inflorescence to anthesis.*

Treatment	Per cent inflorescences which develop at least one flower to anthesis	Days from macroscopic appearance to anthesis
Inflorescence darkened with a black plastic cap	100	14.7
Inflorescence covered with a transparent plastic cap	100	14.7

TABLE 2b. *Inflorescence development in Bougainvillea cv San
Diego Red as a function of shading of shoot tips with aluminium caps. Plants in greenhouse, with 8 h SD for 21 days.*

Treatment	First node to anthesis
not shaded	5 ± 2.3
shaded	5 ± 0.8[a]

[a] Bracteoles remain green

those species where sink activation by light has been found).
Further support comes from the observations that mature leaf
removal is detrimental to inflorescence development in tomato
and that inflorescence development in *Bougainvillea* is a
direct function of leaf area (Ramina *et al.*, 1979).

In tomato, CO_2 fixation is markedly reduced under unfavourable as compared to favourable light conditions (Fig. 4).
Since, in both light conditions, the proportion of assimilates
exported out of the leaf is the same, it is clear that the
plant is strongly source-limited under unfavourable light
conditions.

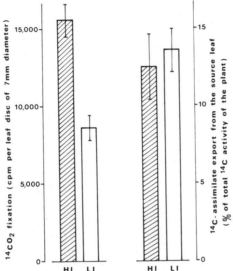

*Fig. 4. $^{14}CO_2$ fixation by a source leaf of tomato cv King
Plus and ^{14}C-assimilate export from the same leaf in favourable light (HI = 16 h LD, 20 W m^{-2}) and unfavourable light (LI
= 8 h SD, 12 W m^{-2}) conditions. (Adapted from Leonard et al.,
1983).*

*Assimilate Distribution - Competing Sinks - The Involvement of
Growth Regulators*

Strong competition between the apical shoot tissues and the
inflorescence in tomato plants grown under unfavourable light
conditions has been revealed by defoliation experiments.
Removal of young leaves promotes reproductive development (de
Zeeuw, 1954; Kinet, 1977b). Also, abortion in unfavourable
light conditions is prevented by applying cytokinins and GAs
to the inflorescence (Kinet, 1977b). These compounds have a
sequential effect. The action of the cytokinin is exerted
first and that of the GA only subsequent to the cytokinin
action (Kinet et al., 1978; Kinet and Leonard, 1983). Thus,
under constant unfavourable light conditions, 1) GA alone does
not promote inflorescence development, 2) BA alone has some
promotive action, 3) GA followed by BA is not better than BA
alone, but 4) when BA is followed by GA all treated inflor-

escences develop to flower opening (Fig. 5). The involvement
of these plant growth regulators in the control of inflorescence development in tomato is further supported by the finding that the light regime strongly influences their endogenous levels in the reproductive structure. Under unfavourable light conditions, trusses which abort early suffer a

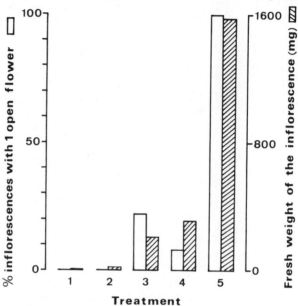

*Fig. 5. The effect of BA and GA, applied alone or in sequence
on the development of the first inflorescence of tomato plants
cv King Plus continuously kept under unfavourable light conditions. Treatments: 1. control; 2. 5 applications of GA;
3. 5 applications of BA; 4. 5 applications of GA followed by 5
applications of BA; 5. 5 applications of BA followed by 5
applications of GA. (From Kinet, J.M. and Leonard, M., 1983).*

severe cytokinin deficiency while their content of GAs is high
in comparison with levels in inflorescences that develop normally in favourable light conditions (Leonard and Kinet,
1982). The ^{14}C-assimilate supply to the inflorescence treated
with a mixture of a cytokinin and a GA under unfavourable
light conditions has been shown to increase concomitantly with
a decrease in the ^{14}C import into the apical shoot (Fig. 6).
Dry matter partitioning between the various parts of the plant
30 days after the start of the treatment, also indicates that
the treated inflorescence is favoured at the expense of the
young leaves located above it (Kinet *et al.*, 1978).
    Similar results were obtained with *Bougainvillea* cv San

Diego Red where removal of young leaves and apical cytokinin
applications promoted inflorescence development and assimilate
accumulation in the terminal bud and the inflorescence primordia (Tse *et al*, 1974). The role of GAs in *Bougainvillea*
appears more complex; GA-induced inhibition of development is

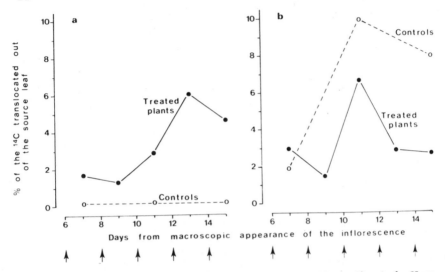

*Fig. 6. Effect of treating tomato cv King Plus first inflor-
escences with a BA + GA mixture on the accumulation of ^{14}C-
assimilates (a) into these inflorescences and (b) into the
apical shoot. The plants were continuously grown under unfavourable light conditions (8 h SD, 12 W m^{-2}). The growth
regulator treatment began 6 days after the macroscopic appearance of the inflorescence; it consisted of 5 applications, at
2-day intervals (arrows) directly to the inflorescence. (From
Leonard et al., 1983).*

observed at all stages between bracteole and floret initiation
(Fig. 3, stages 5 to 10) whereas GA-induced promotion occurs
only after perianth initiation (Fig. 3, stage 12). The GA-
induced inhibition is accompanied by a reduced rate of growth
of the potential reproductive (apical meristematic) tissue
distal to the peduncle (Gallaher and Sachs, unpublished
results). GA-induced inhibition of reproductive development
in the early stages of inflorescence differentiation was also
found in tomato (Abdul and Harris, 1978; Kinet *et al.*, 1984).
These studies, together with those of Kinet and Leonard
(1983), reveal a dual role for GAs in tomato inflorescence
development similar to that found in *Bougainvillea*.

Promotion of inflorescence development in both tomato (Abdul and Harris, 1978) and *Bougainvillea* by removing young leaves may be related in part to a reduction in GA-like substances that inhibit the early stages of reproductive development. Since, in *Bougainvillea*, leaf, bract, stem and peduncular tissue growth is promoted by GA applications, GA-induced inhibition of floret development may be the result of reduced competition for assimilates by the apical meristematic region of the inflorescence relative to surrounding tissues.

Important corollaries to these studies with growth substances, organ removal, and ^{14}C-transport are that any factors that increase sink strength of the flower relative to that of vegetative tissues appear as promoters and conversely factors that decrease sink strength of flowers relative to vegetative tissues appear as inhibitors of flower development (Sachs and Hackett, 1983).

ASSIMILATE SUPPLY - SUBSTRATE LEVELS - QUANTITATIVE AND QUALITATIVE DIFFERENCES

The hypothesis implied in several sections of this paper, and stated explicitly elsewhere (Sachs and Hackett, 1983), is that substrate (or energy) supply must be greater to programme for flower than vegetative development. Possibly there are qualitative differences, too, in assimilates translocated from the leaves to the flowers as a function of irradiance (or as a consequence of growth substance treatment of the flower bud), but this cannot be deduced from studies where dry weight gain is the only variable measured. Unfortunately, there are relatively few publications on quantitative and qualitative analyses of substrates in developing inflorescences. Mohapatra *et al.* (1982) found that sucrose concentrations in the apices of spring wheat (LDP) are generally higher in SD than LD, even though the inflorescences are growing more rapidly in the latter conditions. The authors assumed that supply is the same in the two treatments because they established equal irradiance integrals in LD and SD. Thus, they reasoned that the lower sucrose levels in LD reflect substrate depletion due to demand exceeding supply in the rapidly growing inflorescences. They computed a nearly 20-fold greater demand for substrates in LD than in SD. In reproductive axes of *Bougainvillea*, oligo- and monosaccharide analyses (by HPLC) revealed primarily sucrose (0.1 to 2% w/w), very low glucose and fructose and an unidentified compound at a concentration roughly equal to that of sucrose. Treatments that accelerated inflorescence development (cytokinin, high light, SD, young leaf removal) did not increase concentrations of any of the above, yet soluble solids (80% ethanol extractable) did increase as a function of inflorescence-promoting treatments (Ramina *et al.*, 1979) and ^{14}C accumulation was much greater (Tse *et al.*, 1974). These data indicate that there is much to learn, qualitatively and quantitatively, about substrate turnover and presumed substrate-limitations for growth of reproductive axes. This is confirmed by *in vitro* culture of excised *Bougainvillea* axes. The carbon source requirements for growth and development of these axes are not simple (Steffen, Cimato, Hacket and Sachs, unpublished results). Floret initiation was greatest in cultures supplied with fructose or glucose, and very low when supplied with sucrose (Table 3). Regardless of the success of the qualitative analyses, the increased supply of compounds to the repro—

TABLE 3. *Floret initiation and development in* Bougainvillea *cv San Diego Red axes cultured in vitro as a function of C source. Axes were excised at the bracteole initiation stage and placed in modified Murashige and Skoog medium containing 3% of the indicated sugar, 1 mg/litre benzyladenine, and 0.1 mg/litre naphthylacetic acid. Sugars were autoclaved with the entire medium (After Steffen, Cimato, Hackett and Sachs, unpublished results).*

Sugar	Per cent axes with florets mean ± S.D.	Average number of florets mean ± S.D.
Fructose	79.2 ± 11.8	1.00 ± 0.06
Glucose	64.2 ± 10.8	0.65 ± 0.11
Sucrose	25.0 ± 2.7	0.27 ± 0.01

ductive axes induced by SD, cytokinin or high-light may also involve rapid changes in the capacity of these axes to meta-bolize sucrose, which appears to be the first labelled sugar formed in *Bougainvillea* leaves fed with $^{14}CO_2$ (Ripperda and Sachs, unpublished results). If sucrose is the major trans-locatable sugar, and since there is rapid ^{14}C accumulation with no increase in sucrose concentration in the axes, then there must be an equally rapid increase in sucrose metabolism. At best one would expect to find a transient increase in sucrose levels, but inadequate tissue synchrony, or the sampling and analytical techniques used have so far prevented the detection of short-term changes.

CONCLUSIONS

Reproductive development is strongly dependent on daylength,
irradiance and light quality. Although there are a few cases
where high irradiances appear to be required for sink activation in developing flowers, it is clear that in all species
increased photosynthesis in the source leaves is the major
system promoting flower development. The distribution of the
assimilates between the different plant parts is also a major
factor controlling reproductive development. Under source-
limited conditions, sink competition may account for developmental failure of the reproductive structures. Growth regulators, which are able to divert assimilate flow to treated
tissues, probably play an essential role in assimilate partitioning. Their level and metabolism are undoubtedly
strongly affected by light quality, daylength, and total
irradiance. Qualitative changes in assimilate supply or in
the metabolic capacity of developing inflorescences, as a
function of light and assimilate supply, cannot be excluded.
    Further progress in the elucidation of the mechanisms
involved in the control of flower development is strongly
dependent on identifying, localising and ordering the sequence
of events that are integral parts of reproductive development.
This work, however, is feasible only with well-synchronized
systems which also permit detection of short-term events.
Unfortunately there are very few such systems.

ACKNOWLEDGEMENTS

Financial support from the Belgian Government through the
programme of "Action de Recherche Concertee" (No. 80/85 - 18)
is gratefully acknowledged.

REFERENCES
Abdul, K.S. and Harris, G.P. (1978). Ann. Bot. (Lond.) 42,
    1361-1367
Cockshull, K.E. (1972). In "Crop Processes in Controlled
    Environments" (eds. A.R. Rees, K.E. Cockshull, D.W. Hand
    and R.G. Hurd). pp. 235-250. Academic Press, London
de Zeeuw, D. (1954). Meded. Landbouwhogesch. Wageningen 54,
    1-44
Deitzer, G.F., Hayes, R. and Jabben, M. (1979). Plant
    Physiol. 64, 1015-1021
Deitzer, G.F., Hayes, R. and Jabben, M. (1982). Plant
    Physiol. 69, 597-601
Friend, D.J.C., Fisher, J.E. and Helson, V.A. (1963). Can. J.
    Bot. 41, 1663-1674

Gallaher, C.M. (1983). M.S thesis. University of California, Davis, California

Garner, W.W. and Allard, H.A. (1920). *J. Agric. Res.* 18, 553–606

Garner, W.W. and Allard, H.A. (1923). *J. Agric. Res.* 23, 871–920

Kinet, J.–M. (1977a). *Sci. Hortic. (Amst.)* 6, 15–26

Kinet, J.–M. (1977b). *Sci. Hortic. (Amst.)* 6, 27–35

Kinet, J.–M. and Leonard, M. (1983). *Acta Hortic.* 134, 117–124

Kinet, J.–M., Hurdebise, D., Parmentier, A. and Stainier, R. (1978). *J. Am. Soc. Hortic. Sci.* 103, 724–729

Kinet, J.–M., Sachs, R.M. and Bernier, G. (1984). "The Physiology of Flowering. Vol. III. Development of Flowers" CRC Press, Boca Raton, Florida (In press)

Leonard, M. and Kinet, J.–M. (1982). *Ann. Bot. (Lond.)* 50, 127–130

Leonard, M., Kinet, J.M., Bodson, M. and Bernier, G. (1983). *Physiol. Plant.* 57, 85–89

Mae, T. and Vonk, C.R. (1974). *Acta Bot. Neerl.* 23, 321–331

May, P. (1965). *Aust. J. Biol. Sci.* 18, 463–473

Mohapatra, P.K., Aspinall, D. and Jenner, C.F. (1982). *Ann. Bot. (Lond.)* 49, 619–626

Mor, Y. and Halevy, A.H. (1980). *Plant Physiol.* 66, 990–995

Mor, Y., Halevy, A.H. and Porath, D. (1980). *Plant Physiol.* 66, 996–1000

Piringer, A.A., Downs, R.J. and Borthwick, H.A. (1963). *Am. J. Bot.* 50, 86–90

Ramina, A., Hackett, W.P. and Sachs, R.M. (1979). *Plant Physiol.* 64, 810–813

Raper, C.D. and Thomas, G.F. (1978). *Crop Sci.* 18, 654–656

Reid, J.B. (1979). *Z. Pflanzenphysiol.* 93, 297–301

Sachs, R.M. and Hackett, W.P. (1969). *Hortscience*, 4, 103–107

Sachs, R.M. and Hackett, W.P. (1977). *Acta Hortic.* 68, 29–49

Sachs, R.M. and Hackett, W.P. (1983). *In* "Strategies of Plant Reproduction, BARC Symposium 6" (ed. W.J. Meudt). pp. 263–272. Allenheld–Osmun, Totowa, New Jersey

Tse, A.T.Y., Ramina, A., Hackett, W.P. and Sachs, R.M. (1974). *Plant Physiol.* 54, 404–407

Vince–Prue, D. (1975). "Photoperiodism in Plants" McGraw–Hill, London

Zieslin, N. and Halevy, A.H. (1975), *Sci. Hortic. (Amst.)* 3, 383–391

Chapter 16

PHOTOPERIOD AND THE ABSCISSION OF FLOWER BUDS IN
PHASEOLUS VULGARIS

D. G. MORGAN and CLARE B. MORGAN

*Department of Applied Biology, University of Cambridge,
Cambridge, CB2 3DX, U.K.*

INTRODUCTION

Most cultivars of *Phaseolus vulgaris* flower readily and produce pods within the growing season in Britain. However,
under our conditions it has been found that certain cultivars
native to Columbia and Peru produce few fruits, largely because most of the flower buds formed in mid summer drop before
anthesis; it is not until late summer and autumn that bud
abscission decreases and some fruits are produced. A series
of experiments in which plants were grown in a range of daylengths indicated that it is the long photoperiod of the
British summers that is largely responsible for the abscission
of flower buds in the sensitive South American cultivars
(Ojehomon *et al.*, 1968, 1973; Zehni and Morgan, 1976). There
is a sharp contrast in floral development of plants grown in
SD and LD, i.e. shorter or longer than a certain critical
length which depends on the cultivar (Fig. 1).

RESPONSES TO PHOTOPERIOD

With plants grown in SD, flowers and fruits develop on the
main axis and secondary branches while most flowers on the
tertiary and quaternary branches do not develop. In LD, on
the other hand, not only do the flowers on the main axis and
secondary branches drop, but tertiary and quaternary branches
develop and bear flower buds, all or most of which also abscise. In SD the terminal inflorescence of the plant is well
formed, with robust buds, while under LD it is very short and

scarcely distinguishable from the leaves growing around it;
this reduction in size is associated with poor development of
the internodes between the triad units.

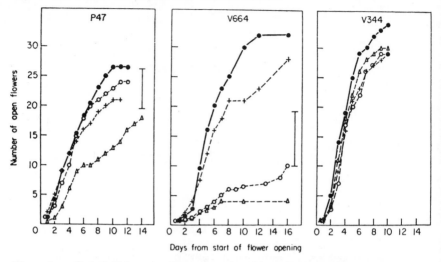

Days from start of flower opening

*Fig. 1. Cumulative totals of flowers that opened from an-
thesis in cvs P 47 and V 664 (daylength-sensitive) and V 344
(insensitive) grown in different photoperiods.*
●—●, *11 h;* +—+, *12 h;* O——O, *13 h;* △——△, *14 h. Plants
grown in a greenhouse for 11 h each day and then transferred
to photoperiod rooms to receive 0, 1, 2, or 3 h low-intensity
incandescent light. Means of 5 plants. Bars: LSD, 5%.*

The initiation of the first formed flower bud in the axil
of the uppermost trifoliate leaf takes place simultaneously in
LD and SD. Subsequently, development in the two daylengths
proceeds at the same rate until approximately 20 days after
sowing, after which differences become apparent. This is
shown for one cultivar, designated P 47, in Fig. 2. In SD the
flower bud continues to increase in size until it opens, but
in LD its development slows down and the bud never reaches
more than 4 mm in length. An abscission layer develops at the
base of the pedicel and abscission takes place a few days
later.

The flower buds on the terminal inflorescence, secondary
and other branches also become inhibited and eventually
abscise in LD. Any flower buds that do eventually open and
form fruits are mostly those that develop on the tertiary
branches. Quantitative differences in the extent of the
abscission of flower buds in LD have been observed in
different experiments and the following factors have been
shown to be involved.

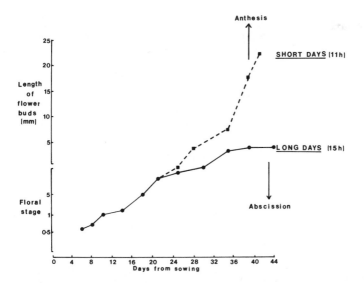

Fig. 2. Rate of development of the first-initiated flower bud of cv P 47 grown in SD (11 h) and LD (15 h). Plants grown in a greenhouse before transfer to darkness in photoperiod rooms. Means of 5 plants.

Light Quality and Intensity

In greenhouse experiments where the photoperiod was extended by low-intensity incandescent light some buds, and especially the later developed ones, were retarded even though they did not abscise, while in other experiments, when the daylength was extended by natural daylight, all the buds dropped (Ojehomon *et al.*, 1973).

Cultivar

In a 14 h photoperiod more flower buds abscised in a photo-period-sensitive Columbian cultivar (V 664) than in a Peruvian cultivar (P 47) (Fig. 1), and flower development in cv V 664, was more affected by a 6-min light break imposed two-thirds of the way through a 13-h dark period (Fig. 4).

Number of Long Days

In an experiment in which 0, 5, 10 and 15 LD were imposed before subjecting plants of cv P 47 to SD, increasing the time in LD increased the inhibition and abscission (Fig. 3).

The truly photoperiodic nature of the daylength effects has been established in experiments where a dark period which was

adequate for normal development of flower buds if given continuously was interrupted with light breaks at different time

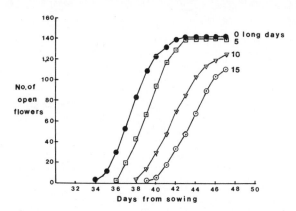

*Fig. 3. Cumulative totals of flowers that opened on plants o
cv P 47 grown in controlled environment cabinets from seedlin*
*emergence in LD (16 h) for 0, 5, 10 or 15 days before trans-
ference to SD (11 h). Photoperiod extended with 5 h low-
intensity incandescent light for LD treatment.*

(Morgan and Zehni, 1980). In one of these, a 6-min light
break imposed in the middle or, more effectively, two-thirds
of the way through a 13-h dark period inhibited the development of the flowers and induced abscission, as assessed by it
effects on the rate of development of the first-initiated

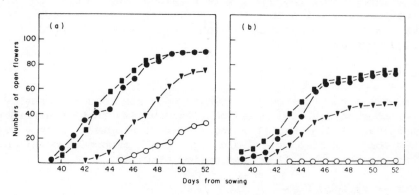

*Fig. 4. Effect of a 6-min light break on the numbers of open
flowers produced by the sensitive cvs (a) P 47 and (b) V 664.
Light break imposed one-third (●), one-half (▼) and two-thirds
(O) of the way through the 13-h dark period; control plants
kept in continuous darkness for 13 h (■). Cumulative totals
for 5 plants.*

flower and the rate of production of open flowers in the two
sensitive cvs P 47 and V 664 (Fig. 4). These effects were
similar to those of long photoperiods applied continuously and
provide clear evidence of the importance of the dark period in
mediating the effects of daylength on flower development in
these two cultivars.

PHYSIOLOGY OF THE PHOTOPERIODIC EFFECTS ON FLOWER BUD
DEVELOPMENT

Physiological evidence for the mechanisms involved in the
photoperiodic effects on flower bud development was obtained
in experiments in which a leaf or leaflet of plants of cv P 47
was exposed to a photoperiod different from that given to the
remainder of the plant. In one of these, exposure of the
lowermost trifoliate leaf to LD on an intact plant otherwise
kept in SD led to inhibition and abscission of flower buds on
the terminal and axillary inflorescences (Fig. 5). On the
other hand, keeping the lowermost trifoliate leaf in SD when
the rest of the plant was given LD led to the development and
retention of some flower buds. The first trifoliate leaf was
therefore shown to respond to either long or short photoperiods and thereafter evoke inhibitory or promotory effects,
respectively, on developing flower buds all over the plant
(Zehni *et al.*, 1970).

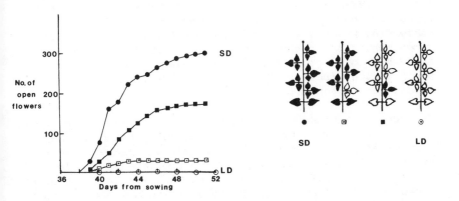

*Fig. 5. Effect on production of open flowers on intact plants
of cv P 47 of exposing the oldest trifoliate leaf to a
daylength different from the remainder. Photoperiods: SD
(11 h in greenhouse), LD (16 h: 11 h in greenhouse and 5 h in
low-intensity incandescent light in photoperiod room).
Cumulative totals for 5 plants.*

Corroboration of the role of the first trifoliate leaf in mediating the effects of LD in inhibiting flower development, and of SD in promoting it, was obtained in an experiment using a two-branch system in which a donor branch, consisting of a decapitated shoot subtended by a primary leaf and carrying only the first trifoliate leaf, was given a daylength treatment different from that given to a receptor branch subtended by a primary leaf, and on which there was only the first trifoliate leaf but on which flower buds were developing (Fig. 6). Exposing a donor branch to LD led to inhibition and abscission of some of the flower buds on a receptor branch kept in SD. On the other hand, keeping a donor branch in SD led to promotion and the development and retention of flower buds on the receptor branch (Saad, 1972).

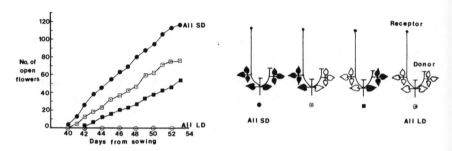

Fig. 6. Effect on production of open flowers on a receptor branch in cv P 47 of exposing a donor branch and its subtending primary leaf to a daylength different from the remainder of the plant. Photoperiods: SD (8 h in greenhouse), LD (8 h in greenhouse and 2 h low-intensity incandescent light break in the middle of the 16-h dark period). Cumulative totals for 6 plants.

Further evidence of the participation of leaves in the LD and SD effects was obtained in experiments using another simplified plant system. In this case the leaves were restricted to a single primary and the two lateral leaflets of the lowermost trifoliate leaf (Fig. 7). The contrast between flower bud development in LD and SD which had been found in intact plants (Fig. 5) was observed once more, with all the buds abscissing when leaflets were kept continuously in LD (d) but many developing normally when leaflets were given SD continuously (a). Exposing one leaflet continuously to SD while the other was given LD (b) led to a pattern of flower development broadly comparable to that produced by giving both leaflets SD (a). However, if one leaflet was given a single SD alternating with a single LD, while at the same time the

other one was given a single LD alternating with a single SD
(c), then all the buds abscissed; thus the SD did not counteract the abscission-inducing effect of the LD. In another
experiment it was found that when the alternating periods were
increased to 3 SD followed by 3 LD, or 6 SD followed by 6 LD,

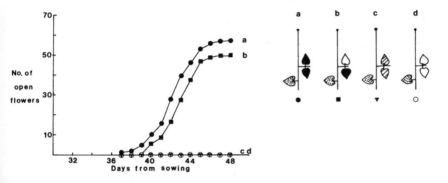

*Fig. 7. Production of open flowers in cv P 47 when leaves
were restricted to a primary leaf and two lateral leaflets of
the first trifoliate leaf. The leaflets were given the
following treatments for 24 days: (a) both SD, (b) one SD and
the other LD, (c) one leaflet 1 SD alternating daily with 1 LD
while the other leaflet had 1 LD alternating daily with 1 SD
and (d) both LD. All plants were transferred to LD after 24
days; the primary leaf was kept in 13 h (the critical
daylength) until this transfer. Photoperiods: SD (11 h in
greenhouse), LD (11 h in greenhouse and 5 h incandescent light
in photoperiod room). Cumulative totals for 5 plants.*

then the SD did have a counter effect, resulting in promotion:
many of the flower buds opened, but even then only about half
the number that opened when both leaflets were given SD (Saad,
1972).
      Thus it is clear that single leaflets are capable of per-
ceiving the LD and SD stimuli and of transmitting either inhibitory or promotory effects to the flower buds. It is also
evident that there is a quantitative interaction between the
two effects of different photoperiods where the duration of a
particular photoperiod, and the order in which LD and SD are
given, play important roles in determining the degree of
inhibition and abscission.
      In many such experiments indications were obtained that
under the influence of photoperiod both inhibitory and promotory factors were probably being produced, these exerting
their maximum effect above or below the critical daylength

respectively. They pointed clearly to the involvement of at least the first trifoliate leaf, and probably others, in the photoperiodic effects and it seemed likely that these effects could be mediated via growth substances which were inhibitory or promotory to development of the flower buds. It then became important to investigate the chemical nature of these substances and their production in different organs of the plant in different photoperiods.

CHEMICAL EVIDENCE FOR INHIBITORY AND ABSCISSION-INDUCING FACTORS IN LD

Exogenous application of either IAA or GA_3 to the leaves or flower buds of cv P 47 plants kept in SD failed to induce the bud abscission experienced in LD. However, it was found that application of synthetic ABA to the differentiating flower buds of plants in SD resulted in inhibition and eventual abscission of many of the buds at a later stage of development. The effect was dependent on the amount applied and was greatest on the buds of the terminal inflorescence and at the uppermost node (Fig. 8).

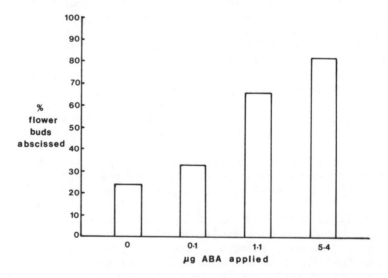

Fig. 8. Effect of ABA on flower buds of cv P 47 in SD. A 10 μl droplet containing 0, 0.1, 1.1 or 5.4 μg ABA was applied daily for 21 days to the differentiating buds of intact plant. in a 12 h photoperiod in a controlled environment cabinet. The number of flower buds which had abscissed 38 days after the start of the treatment is expressed as a percentage of the total number produced on the plant. Means of 4 plants.

In view of the above results, indicating the possible participation of ABA in the regulation of flower bud development in cv P 47, numerous experiments were carried out over three summers to study the effects of photoperiod on the endogenous concentrations of ABA (Bentley, 1974; Bentley *et al.*, 1975). ABA was extracted (Milborrow, 1970) from different organs and the concentrations estimated, mostly by wheat coleoptile bioassay, with some confirmed by gas liquid chromatography which gave results of the same order. Table 1 shows the results of one of these experiments. The concentrations of ABA in the flower buds and leaves of plants on which the buds were inhibited or had abscissed (18-h photoperiod and natural long days) were higher than in plants where flower development was normal (8- and 13-h photoperiods).

TABLE 1. *Concentrations of ABA (µg/kg fresh tissue) in flower buds and leaves of plants of cv P 47 in different photoperiods .*

Organ	Photoperiod			
	8 h	13 h	18 h	15-17 h
	Natural daylight	8 h natural daylight + 5 h low-intensity incandescent	8 h natural daylight + 10 h low-intensity incandescent	Natural daylight
Terminal flower buds	121	123	729	848
5th trifoliate leaf (unfolding)	20	36	305	308
4th trifoliate leaf	30	—	91	31
3rd trifoliate leaf	39	22	55	60
2nd trifoliate leaf	21	53	37	86
1st trifoliate leaf	42	35	51	130
	SD		LD	
	Normal flower buds		Flower buds inhibited	

These differences were large in the buds and youngest leaves but smaller in the mature leaves. Very high concentrations o ABA were found in the inhibited buds, the highest values bein found when the daylength was extended beyond 8 h by natural daylight; these buds also contained considerable amounts of bound ABA. All other experiments confirmed that the ABA content of the buds and leaves of plants grown in LD was greater than that of those grown in SD; this was also true for ABA found in the stems and petioles.

The fraction of plant extract analysed in these experiment was obtained after solvent extractions and TLC, and the fact that it contained (+)-cis-ABA was established by ORD, GLC, conversion to closely related derivatives and bioassay. This fraction was isolated on a large scale from plants grown in LD, purified by extensive solvent extractions and chromatography and then re-applied daily for 7 days to the differentiating buds of plants growing in SD. This evoked the effect of LD: flower bud development was drastically inhibited and abscission was induced at a later stage, particularly on the terminal inflorescence and at the uppermost node; this was also the case when the same amount of (+)-ABA in a synthetic (racemic) sample was applied.

The results of the exogenous application and extraction experiments provide strong evidence that ABA plays an important role in mediating the effects of LD on flower bud development in cv P 47. It would seem that under the influence of long photoperiods there is an increased production of ABA in the leaves and a greater accumulation of the substance in the buds; in all probability this eventually leads to their inhibition and abscission. This was corroborated by a single experiment in which abscissing buds were found to contain more ABA (331 µg/100 g dry wt.) than they did 6 days previously (105 µg/100 g dry wt.) Further support for the involvement of ABA was obtained by comparing the concentrations of ABA in leaves of different cultivars grown in LD. The highest concentration (66 µg/kg fresh wt.) was found in cv V 664 which is the most sensitive to LD, and the lowest (13 µg/kg) in V 334, a daylength-insensitive cultivar; the concentration in cv P 4 was 46 µg/kg.

ABA may not be the only inhibitor involved in the LD effect on flower bud development. It is interesting to note that the closely related inhibitor xanthoxin was also found to be present in the leaves of cv P 47. However, it did not possess the abscission-provoking properties of ABA when applied to plants in SD.

CHEMICAL EVIDENCE FOR PROMOTORY AND ABSCISSION-PREVENTING FACTORS IN SD

Exogenous applications of cytokinins to the developing apices of cv P 47 plants grown in LD has been found to promote flower bud development and reduce abscission. Using a simplified unbranched plant system in which the leaves were restricted to a single primary leaf and the terminal leaflet of the first trifoliate leaf, application of kinetin or BA to the differentiating flower buds of plants in LD resulted in the development of flower buds that would otherwise have abscissed (Fig. 9(a)) (Saad, 1972). In another experiment, using intact plants, the naturally occurring cytokinin, zeatin, was similarly applied to plants in LD but under conditions producing less extensive abscission; it increased the number of flowers produced (Fig. 9(b)) and led to an earlier appearance of the first open flower, a faster rate of open flower production and a delay and reduction of abscission of flower buds on the terminal inflorescence (Lynas, 1981).

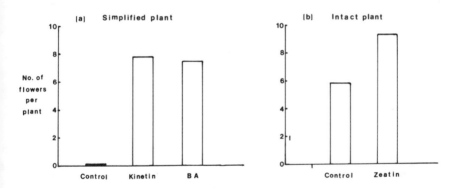

Fig. 9. Effect of cytokinins on the number of open flowers produced in cv P 47 in LD. Plants were grown in a greenhouse for 8 h and the photoperiod extended by incandescent light in a photoperiod room. Cytokinin (0.1 μg) was applied in a 10 μl droplet to the differentiating buds daily. (a) Simplified plant system (see text) in 16-h photoperiod. Kinetin or BA applied for 10 days. Mean totals for 5 plants 33 days after start of treatment. Control remained at zero. (b) Intact plants in 14-h photoperiod. Zeatin applied for 20 days. Mean totals for 12 plants 42 days after start of treatment.

Although the exact nature of the cytokinins in cv P 47 is unknown, the ability of zeatin to counteract the effects of LD and to promote flower development suggested that the endogenous cytokinins might be influenced by photoperiod and exert

a positive effect in promoting normal development in SD.
Attempts were therefore made to estimate the cytokinins in
plants growing in different photoperiods; however, some
difficulties were experienced due to the very low concentrations present in the plants, as has also been reported for
another cultivar of *Phaseolus vulgaris* (Palmer *et al.*, 1981;
Scott and Horgan, 1984). The concentration in the leaves was
found to be so low that no clear evidence of differences in LD
and SD could be obtained, and it was not possible to obtain
enough bud material for satisfactory analysis. However, xylem
sap proved to be a source of suitable extract and this was
collected at intervals during the later stages of development
of plants in SD and LD and the cytokinin content determined
(Lynas, 1981). In two experiments, one of which is illus-

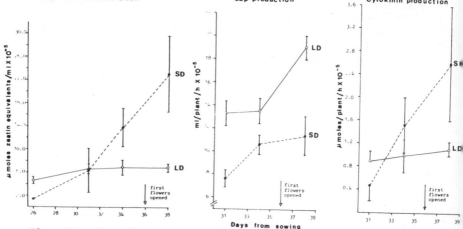

*Fig. 10. Cytokinin production in the xylem sap of cv P 47 in
SD and LD. Plants were grown in a greenhouse in photoperiods
of 8 h and 16 h (extended with incandescent light in a
photoperiod room). Plants were decapitated below the primary
leaves just after the end of the dark period; the sap was
collected from 3 replicate groups of 5 plants, frozen and
stored at -15°C before analysis 2-10 days later. After cellu-
lose phosphate chromatography the total cytokinin eluted by
1 M ammonia was estimated by the soybean hypocotyl bioassay
(Newton et al., 1980).*

trated in Fig. 10, the cytokinin concentration in sap from the
plants in SD increased with time while that in sap from plants
in LD remained approximately the same. The volume of sap
exuded from plants was always found to be greater in LD but,
notwithstanding this, the rate of cytokinin production per
plant became significantly higher in SD. No information was
obtained regarding any qualitative difference in the cytokinin

content in the different photoperiods, which might also be a
relevant factor, or regarding the contribution of any nucleo-
tide present. Even so, this evidence, taken in conjunction
with the effects obtained with exogenously applied cytokinins,
suggests that cytokinins could perhaps play a part in mediating the promotory effects of SD on flower bud development in
cv P 47.

CONCLUSIONS

The research described here provides clear evidence of the
influence of photoperiod on the control of flower bud development in the daylength-sensitive South American cultivars of
Phaseolus vulgaris and the involvement of leaves in perceiving
the stimuli and transmitting their effects to the developing
buds. The mechanisms by which the inhibitory effects of LD
and the promotory ones of SD are evoked are less clear,
although it is apparent that under LD there is a greater production of ABA in the leaves and an accumulation in the buds,
which could be responsible for inhibition and eventual
abscission of the buds. This effect may perhaps be accen-
tuated during the later stages of bud development by an unfavourable ABA/cytokinin ratio in the buds, since in LD the
production of cytokinins in the xylem sap remained constant
whereas in SD it started to increase just before anthesis.
The results lend support to a hypothesis that the balance
between ABA and cytokinins plays an important part in regu-
lating flower bud development in these bean cultivars. It is
possible that in SD there is a preponderance of cytokinins,
produced in the roots, which results in normal development of
the flower buds, whereas in long days there is a preponderance
of ABA, produced in the leaves, which leads to inhibition and
abscission of the buds.

The promotory effects of exposing leaves to SD could be
explained by an increased production of promoters (cytokinins)
and the results of the leaf participation, cytokinin application and sap experiments are consistent with this explanation. At the same time, lower levels of ABA produced in
leaves in SD could also favour flower bud development and
further work is needed to assess the relative contributions of
these factors. With the more sensitive analytical methods now
available it would be informative to study the production of
both ABA and cytokinins in different photoperiods and determine the ABA/cytokinin ratio in different organs at various
stages of flower bud development.

Other workers have obtained evidence of the influence of
photoperiod on the production of ABA (Zeevaart, 1971) and
cytokinins (Beever and Woolhouse, 1973; Henson and Wareing,

1977) in other plant systems in relation to their involvement in the initiation of flowers. There have been relatively few such studies on the development of flowers after initiation and this is a deficiency from both fundamental and applied standpoints. The present work goes a little way towards remedying this and the daylength–sensitive cultivars of *Phaseolus vulgaris* provide a useful tool for the studies.

ACKNOWLEDGEMENTS

We wish to acknowledge with thanks the financial support received from the Agricultural Research Council, Perry Foundation and Leverhulme Trust in support of the above research. In addition we are indebted to Mr Roger Day for his technical assistance and interest throughout the course of the work.

REFERENCES

Beever, J.E. and Woolhouse, H.W. (1973). *Nature, New Biol.* 246, 31–32

Bentley, B. (1974). Ph.D. Thesis. University of Cambridge

Bentley, B., Morgan, C.B., Morgan, D.G. and Saad, F.A. (1975). *Nature (Lond.)* 256, 121–122

Henson, I.E. and Wareing, P.F. (1977). *New Phytol.* 78, 35–42

Lynas, C. (1981). Ph.D. Thesis. University of Cambridge

Milborrow, B.W. (1970). *J. Exp. Bot.* 21, 17–29

Morgan, D.G. and Zehni, M.S. (1980). *Ann. Bot. (Lond.)* 46, 37–42

Newton, C., Morgan, C.B. and Morgan, D.G. (1980). *J. Exp. Bot.* 31, 721–729

Ojehomon, O.O., Rathjen, A.S. and Morgan, D.G. (1968). *J. Agric. Sci.* 71, 209–214

Ojehomon, O.O., Zehni, M.S. and Morgan, D.G. (1973). *Ann. Bot. (Lond.)* 37, 871–884

Palmer, M.V., Horgan, R. and Wareing, P.F. (1981). *Planta* 153, 297–302

Saad, F.A. (1972). Ph.D. Thesis. University of Cambridge

Scott, I.M. and Horgan, R. (1984). *Plant Sci. Lett.* (In press)

Zeevaart, J.A.D., (1971). *Plant Physiol.* 48, 86–90

Zehni, M.S. and Morgan, D.G. (1976). *Ann. Bot. (Lond.)* 40, 17–22

Zehni, M.S., Morgan, D.G. and Saad, F.A. (1970). *Nature (Lond.)* 227, 628–629

Chapter 17

PHOTOCONTROL OF FLOWER-OPENING IN PHARBITIS NIL

ATSUSHI TAKIMOTO and SUMIKO KAIHARA

Laboratory of Applied Botany, Faculty of Agriculture,
Kyoto University, Kyoto 606, Japan.

INTRODUCTION

Pharbitis nil blooms around dawn in summer in Kyoto, as its
name Morning Glory implies, but in autumn it blooms much
earlier. Although the time of flower-opening varies considerably with the weather, the average time of flower-opening
of cv Usuzakura, at various times of year in Kyoto is shown in
Fig. 1, together with the times of dawn and dusk.

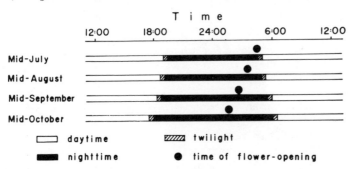

Fig. 1. Average time of flower-opening of Pharbitis nil, cv
Usuzakura, under natural conditions at various times of year
in Kyoto (35°N).

The dusk signal rather than the dawn signal seems to play the
decisive role in determining the time of flower-opening, but
the length of darkness before flower-opening is shortened in
autumn.

A series of experiments was conducted to elucidate the
factors controlling the time of flower-opening in *Pharbitis*.
The cultivar Violet was used in the following experiments
because most of the work on flowering has been done with this
plant. When experiments were to be continued for longer than
24 h, potted plants bearing many flower buds were used, but
flower buds were cut from plants growing in the field for use
in experiments lasting less than 24 h. Mature buds cut in the
afternoon and placed in water, opened the next morning just as
did those on intact plants. The process of flower-opening was
observed at intervals during the experiment, using a green
safe light during the dark period, and the degree of opening
was assessed by comparison with the stage numbers shown in
Fig. 2.

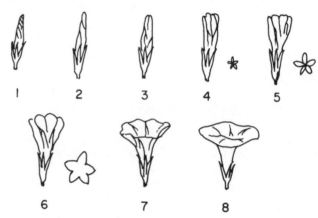

*Fig. 2. Stage number of flower-opening. Side view at all
stages and the shape of the tip viewed from above for stages
4-6.*

FLOWER-OPENING UNDER DIFFERENT PHOTOPERIODIC SCHEDULES

Pharbitis plants in pots bearing many flower buds were
transferred to a room kept at $24 \pm 1°C$, and subjected to the
various photoperiodic schedules shown in Fig. 3. Light from
daylight fluorescent lamps only was used (about 5,000 lx at
plant level). The time of flower-opening was observed on the
5th day in order to avoid any transient effects. Under a
photoperiod of 10 h or longer, the buds opened about 10 h
after the onset of darkness irrespective of the length of the
photoperiod, but if the photoperiod was shorter, the buds
opened about 20 h after the onset of the photoperiod under all
photoperiodic schedules used. The simplest explanation for
this phenomenon is that the time of flower-opening is deter-

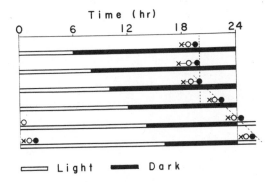

Fig. 3. Time of flower-opening under various photoperiodic
schedules. Temperature: ± 1°C, X : stage 4, O : stage 6,
● : stage 8 (fully opened). (After Kaihara and Takimoto,
1979).

mined by one or more circadian oscillators which are reset by
light–on and light–off signals. There are two main possibilities. One is that a single oscillator which is initiated
by a light–on signal controls flower–opening. When the photoperiod is shorter than 10 h, the phase of the oscillation is
not affected by the light–off signal, but in light that has
lasted for more than 10 h, the oscillation is held in a fixed
or nearly fixed state, and the light–off signal phases the
oscillation (see Pittendrigh, 1966). The second possibility
is that flower–opening is controlled by two oscillators which
are initiated independently by the light–on and light–off
signals (see Takimoto and Hamner, 1964). The former plays the
crucial role when the photoperiod is shorter than 10 h, and
the latter when it is longer than that.

Under natural conditions, Pharbitis does not grow when the
daylength is shorter than 10 h. So, in its natural environment, the time Pharbitis blooms is assumed to be determined by
the dusk signal of the previous day.

PARTICIPATION OF A CIRCADIAN RHYTHM

Potted plants bearing many flower buds were transferred at
18.00 to dark rooms kept at 20, 24 and 28°C and were observed
at intervals for four consecutive days (Fig. 4).

Buds opened at about the same time every day at all temperatures tested, although at a high temperature, flower-
opening on the 1st and 2nd day was somewhat delayed. Thus, a
circadian rhythm with a cycle length of about 24 h is considered to control the flower–opening of Pharbitis. In this
experiment, the buds often failed to open completely after the

first few nights, especially at a high temperature. This may
be because the plants had been deprived of light for a long
period.

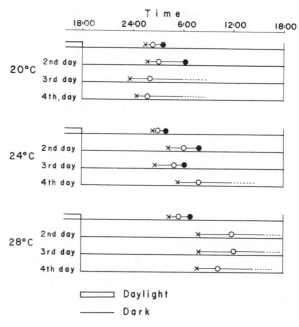

Fig. 4. Time of flower-opening in continuous darkness.
----: Buds withered without opening fully. (After Kaihara and
Takimoto, 1979).

PHASE-SHIFT OF THE CIRCADIAN RHYTHM CONTROLLING FLOWER-OPENING
BY A LIGHT PULSE

Potted plants with many flower buds were placed in continuous
darkness (23 ± 1°C) and exposed to fluorescent light (about
6,000 lx) for 10 min at different times. Flower-opening on
the 1st day was not influenced greatly, but on the 2nd day it
was hastened by some 10 h by the light pulse given 10-16 h
after the onset of darkness (Kaihara and Takimoto, 1979). A
similar hastening of the flowering was observed on the 3rd day
when the light pulse had been given 28-36 h after the onset of
darkness (on the 2nd day). Probably, the phase of the circadian rhythm which controls the blooming of Pharbitis was
shifted by a light pulse, although none of the light pulses
retarded flower-opening, i.e., the phase delay usually observed in circadian rhythms was absent. Fig. 5 shows the
phase response curve for the rhythm of flower-opening in
Pharbitis nil.

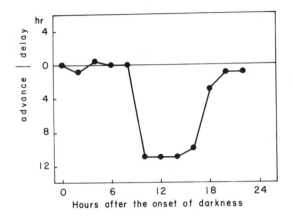

Fig. 5. *Phase response curve for a 10 min light pulse (6,000 lx white light) of the rhythm of flower-opening in* Pharbitis nil. *A 10 min light pulse was given at different times during the first 24 h of the dark period, and the time of flower-opening on the 2nd day (the time fully opened) was compared with that in control plants. (Data from Kaihara and Takimoto, 1979).*

EFFECT OF LIGHT ON THE FLOWER-OPENING DURING THE 1ST NIGHT

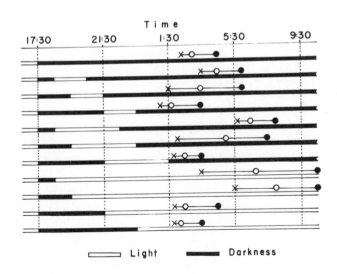

Fig. 6. *Effect of light given at various times during the dark period at 23 ± 1°C on the time of flower-opening. (After Kaihara and Takimoto, 1980).*

Light given for various hours at different times during the
first part of the dark period (23°C) was examined for its
effect on flower-opening during the 1st night (Fig. 6). If
any part of the first 4 h period was illuminated, the flower
buds opened significantly later than those of the control. In
other words, if the first 4 h period was kept dark, the buds
opened as rapidly as, or more rapidly than the control. Light
given only during the 4th to 8th hour or after the 6th hour
was rather promotive.

PARTICIPATION OF PHYTOCHROME

Because R given after dusk was very effective in delaying
flower-opening (Yamaki et al., 1966), the possibility of the
participation of phytochrome in mediating this reaction was
examined. Five-minute R pulses given every 30 min for 4 h
delayed flower-opening nearly as much as 4 h of continuous R,
but intermittent FR pulses given every 30 min had little
effect (Fig. 7). If every 5-min R pulse was immediately

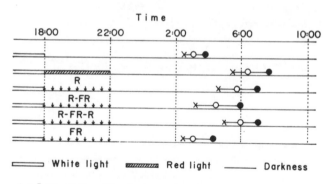

⇒ White light   ▨▨ Red light   ── Darkness

✦ : 5 min of R or FR, singly or alternately

*Fig. 7. Effects of intermittent light on the time of flower-
opening and red/far-red reversibility. Temperature, 23 ± 1°C,
R: 3 W m^{-2}, FR: 15 W m^{-2}. (After Kaihara and Takimoto, 1980).*

followed by a 5-min FR light pulse, the delay was less and
subsequent exposure to 5 min of R again produced a delay equal
to that produced by the 5-min light pulse alone. Thus, a
partial red/far-red reversible reaction is seen in this
experimental system. Presumably, the absence of Pfr during
the first 4 h of the dark period is necessary to start the
timing mechanism controlling flower-opening.

As mentioned above (see Fig. 5), a brief exposure to light
at the 10th hour of the dark period greatly advances the time
of flower-opening occurring on the following day. That is, the

light pulse causes a phase shift of the circadian rhythm controlling the time of flower-opening. The possibility of the
participation of phytochrome in this phase shift was next
examined by exposing the buds to R and FR pulses singly or
alternately at the 10th hour of the dark period (Fig. 8). In
this experiment, 5 min of R given at the 10th hour advanced

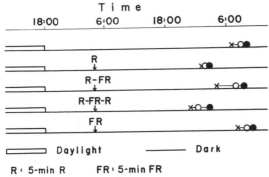

Fig. 8. *Red/far-red reversible photoreaction at the 10th hour
of the dark period. Effects of R and FR pulses on the time of
flower-opening the next day were observed.
Temperature: 23 ± 1°C; R: 3 W m⁻²; FR: 15 W m⁻². (After
Kaihara and Takimoto, 1980).*

the time of flower-opening by some 7 h. This effect was
almost totally reversed by a 5-min FR pulse given immediately
after the R pulse, and the effect of the FR pulse was again
nullified by subsequent exposure to R. Thus, phytochrome is
presumed to be the photoreceptor in this response.

EFFECT OF TEMPERATURE ON FLOWER-OPENING

The length of the dark period necessary to cause normal
flower-opening (10-12 h after the onset of darkness) was about
4 h in the experiment shown in Fig. 6. Later, however, the
length was found to be greatly influenced by temperature
(Table 1). At 25°C, 4 h of darkness was not enough to cause
normal flower-opening but 8 h was. The lower the temperature,
the shorter was the dark period necessary to cause rapid
flower-opening. At 20°C, even the buds kept under continuous
light opened just as did those kept in darkness at 23 or 25°C.
At 30°C, the buds opened very slowly even when an 8 h dark
period was given, and the stage number was only 4.4 at the

TABLE 1.   *Effect of temperature on flower-opening*

Dark period	Temperature (^{o}C)			
(h)	20	23	25	30
0	8.0	2.3	2.0	2.0
4	8.0	8.0	5.2	2.0
8	8.0	8.0	8.0	4.4

Flower buds cut at 17.15 were placed in darkness for 0, 4 or 8 h followed by continuous light at 20, 23, 25 or 30°C. Numerals in the table show the average stage of flower-opening at 04.30 the next morning.

time of observation. The buds kept at 30°C often failed to open fully even in darkness.

High temperature (28°C) during the first 6 h of darkness slightly delayed the time of flower-opening but when given after that the time of blooming was greatly delayed (Fig. 9).

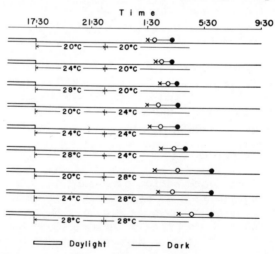

Fig. 9.   Effect of night temperature on the time of flower-opening (After Kaihara and Takimoto 1979).

Therefore, the later part of the flower-opening process seems to be suppressed at high temperatures. This may be why

flower-opening during the summer under natural conditions
required a longer period of darkness than in autumn (see
Fig. 1).

COMPARISON OF THE EFFECTS OF DARKNESS AND LOW TEMPERATURE

The experiment shown in Table 1 suggests that lowering the
temperature to 20°C under continuous light has the same effect
on flower-opening as darkness at 23–25°C. To examine this
possibility, buds expected to open the following morning were
exposed to either darkness at 25°C or continuous light at
20°C, starting at 13.30, 17.30 and 21.30. Only the times when
all the buds in each experimental group were fully opened
(average stage number 8.0) are given in Fig. 10. The buds

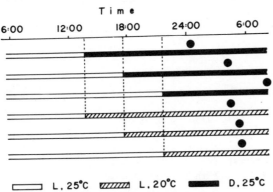

$\boxed{}$ L. 25°C   ▨▨▨ L. 20°C   ▬▬▬ D. 25°C

*Fig. 10. Flower-opening of Pharbitis nil kept in continuous
darkness at 25°C or continuous light at 20°C from 13.30, 17.30
and 21.30. The buds for the treatments starting at 13.30 and
17.30 were cut from plants in the field just before the treatment, and those for the treatments starting at 21.30 were cut
at 17.30, and exposed to artificial light (5,000 lx) at 25°C
until the treatment was started. (After Kaihara and Takimoto,
1981a).*

placed in continuous darkness at 25°C opened about 10 h after
the onset of darkness irrespective of the time of light-off.
In contrast, the buds placed under continuous light at a low
temperature (20°C) opened at about the same time regardless of
when the low-temperature treatment was begun. Thus, the onset
of darkness resets the timing mechanism which controls flower-
opening, but the onset of low temperature cannot. The time of
flower-opening at a low temperature is probably determined by
the time of the sunset on the day before or the time of the
preceding sunrise.

PHYSICAL BASIS OF FLOWER-OPENING

One may assume that flower-opening is the result of the expansion of petals due to water absorption. If this were true,
the buds placed under conditions favourable for flower-opening
would enlarge more quickly than those kept under unfavourable
conditions. To examine this possibility, flower buds were cut
at 17.30, then placed in darkness at 25°C, in light at 20°C,
in darkness at 29°C, or in light at 25°C. The length of the
flower buds (from the base of the sepal to the tip of the
petal) was measured as an indicator of petal enlargement
(Fig. 11). Buds placed in the dark at 29°C enlarged rapidly,

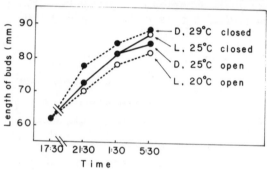

*Fig. 11. Increase in length of flower buds kept in darkness
for 8 h at 29°C, darkness for 8 h at 25°C, continuous light at
25°C, and continuous light at 20°C. The experiment was begun
at 17.30. (After Kaihara and Takimoto, 1981b).*

but could not open, whereas those exposed to light at 20°C
enlarged slowly, but opened rapidly. The buds exposed to
light and those kept in darkness at 25°C enlarged at similar
rates, but only the latter opened. Thus, the enlargement of
the bud (expansion of the petal) is not the only cause of
flower-opening.

Next, the parts of the petals other than the midribs were
removed from the buds expected to open the following morning.
These buds having only sepals and petal midribs, and intact
buds as the control were placed in water at 17.30, and kept in
continuous darkness or in continuous light at 25°C. Fig. 12
shows the buds at 08.00 the next morning. Intact buds kept in
the dark opened completely, but those kept in light remained
at stage 2-3. The petal midribs separated from the other
parts of the petals showed epinasty in the dark but no
epinasty under light at 25°C (Fig. 12). The epinasty of the
petal midribs was observed under continuous light at 20°C as
well as in darkness at 25°C, and this is considered to be the

primary force of flower-opening either in darkness or at a low
temperature.

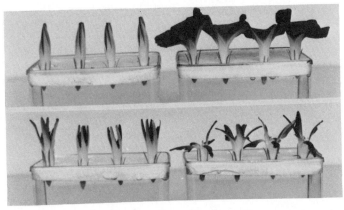

*Fig. 12. Opening of intact flower buds (top) and buds having
only petal midribs and sepals (bottom) which had been kept in
continuous darkness (right) or under continuous light (left)
at 25°C. Treatment was started at 17.30, and the photograph
was taken at 08.00 the next morning. (After Kaihara and
Takimoto, 1981b).*

EFFECT OF ABA AND IAA ON FLOWER-OPENING

Various plant hormones were added to the water in which the
cut ends of flower buds were immersed (Kaihara and Takimoto,
1983). GA_3, BA and "ethephon" (an ethylene-releasing compound) had no effect on flower-opening either in darkness at
25°C or in continuous light at 20°C. ABA treatment, however,
caused flower-opening even under continuous light at 25°C
under which control buds never opened fully. IAA completely
suppressed flower-opening both in darkness and in continuous
light at 20°C. An interesting phenomenon is that the buds fed
ABA under continuous light at 25°C starting at 16.00 and 20.00
opened about 11 h after the start of ABA treatment, which is
about the same as required for flower-opening in darkness
(Fig. 13). This means that the effect of darkness is mimicked
by ABA treatment. When the ABA treatment was given at 12.00,
however, the buds did not open as rapidly as did those in the
dark, which implies that ABA cannot totally mimic the action
of darkness.

In the other experiment, buds cut at 16.00 were placed in
100 μM ABA solution or water, and immediately exposed to
darkness at 25°C or continuous light at 20°C (Fig. 14). Buds
placed in water opened at about the same time in both groups

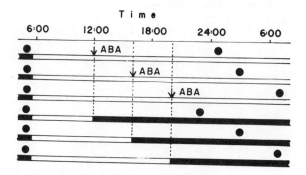

Fig. 13. Effect of ABA (100 µM) on the flower-opening of
Pharbitis under continuous light at 25°C. Buds due to open
the next morning were placed in 100 µM ABA solution at 12.00,
16.00 or 20.00, and exposed to continuous light at 25°C. For
comparison, some buds were placed in water and exposed to
continuous darkness at 25°C starting at these times. All buds
were cut from plants in the field just before treatment, but
the buds for the treatment starting at 20.00 were cut at
16.00, placed in water, and exposed to continuous light at
25°C until the treatment was started. (After Kaihara and
Takimoto, 1983).

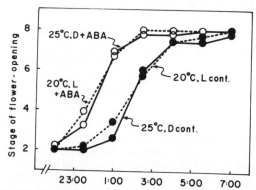

Fig. 14. Effect of ABA on the flower-opening of buds placed
in darkness at 25°C, or in continuous light at 20°C. Buds cut
at 16.00 were placed in water or 100 µM ABA solution, and
exposed to darkness at 25°C or continuous light at 20°C.
(After Kaihara and Takimoto, 1983).

subjected to darkness at 25°C and to continuous light at 20°C
in this experiment, and the addition of ABA promoted flower-
opening by some 2 h in both conditions (Fig. 14). Thus ABA
not only mimics the action of darkness but also promotes

flower-opening in darkness.

IAA at 100 μM inhibits flower-opening completely both in darkness at 25°C and continuous light at 20°C. The promoting effect of ABA is also completely nullified by simultaneous application of IAA (Kaihara and Takimoto, 1983). ABA is presumed to inhibit the growth (or expansion) of the inside and outside of the petal midribs differently, causing flower-opening, and IAA counteracts the effect of ABA.

There is another possibility that ABA promotes flower-opening by resetting the circadian rhythm which determines the time of flower-opening, because ABA has been reported to affect the circadian clock in *Oxalis regnelli* (Skrove *et al.*, 1982). If we accept this idea, however, we must assume that ABA not only resets the oscillator, but also advances the phase of the rhythm that has been reset by a light-off signal, because ABA promotes flower-opening by some 2 h even in darkness.

The change in endogenous IAA and ABA of the petal midribs in relation to various light-dark treatments and temperature conditions, and the effect of these plant hormones on the growth of the inside and outside of the petal midribs must be examined in detail to elucidate the mechanism of flower-opening more clearly.

REFERENCES

Kaihara, S. and Takimoto, A. (1979). *Plant Cell Physiol.* 20, 1659-1666

Kaihara, S. and Takimoto, A. (1980). *Plant Cell Physiol.* 21, 21-26

Kaihara, S. and Takimoto, A, (1981a). *Plant Cell Physiol.* 22, 215-221

Kaihara, S. and Takimoto, A. (1981b). *Plant Cell Physiol.* 22, 307-310.

Kaihara, S. and Takimoto, A. (1983). *Plant Cell Physiol.* 24, 309-316

Pittendrigh, C.S. (1966). *Z. Pflanzenphysiol.* 54, 275-307

Skrove, D., Rinnan, T. and Johnsson, A. (1982). *Physiol. Plant.* 55, 221-225

Takimoto, A. and Hamner, K.C. (1964). *Plant Physiol.* 39, 1024-1030

Yamaki, T., Gordon, S.A. and Chorney, W. (1966). *Annu. Rev. Argonne Natl. Lab., Biol. Med. Res. Div.* ANL-7278, 290-292

CONCLUSIONS

Chapter 18

THE INTERACTION OF PHOTOSYNTHESIS AND PHOTOPERIODISM
IN INDUCTION

D. J. C. FRIEND

Dept. of Botany, University of Hawaii,
3190 Maile Way, Honolulu, Hawaii 96822, U.S.A.

INTRODUCTION

One can make a distinction between the process of induction
"those events that take place in the leaves which commit a
plant to flowering" (Moshkov, 1937) and the process of evocation, "events at the apex which commit the plant to
flowering" (Evans, 1969), but it is not so easy to separate
the two in practice.

One approach is to give minimal photoperiodic treatments
that result in histochemical changes in the apex (the beginning of induction), further photoperiodic treatments being
required for evocation, as in the LDP *Spinacia oleracea*. In
the absence of any chemical test for the presence of substances in the leaf that lead to the evocation of flowering at
the apex (for convenience I shall call these substances the
floral stimulus), we can only determine induction by a bioassay, the formation of floral primordia at the apex. Such a
bioassay also includes possible effects of leaf treatments on
the delivery of materials to the apex, modifying the process
of evocation. As Bernier *et al.*, (1981) have stressed, many
factors are involved in changing the vegetative apex to the
flowering state and different factors may limit the transition
at different times and under different environmental conditions. The transition to flowering may be blocked not only
by the absence of induction but also by a break in the causal
chain between induction and evocation, or even later during
floral morphogenesis. Treatments given to leaves that promote
or prevent flower development may, however, influence evo-

LIGHT AND THE FLOWERING PROCESS
ISBN 0.12.721960.9

cation as well as induction. In view of these difficulties,
which will only be solved when the substances formed and
transmitted from the leaves have been chemically identified,
this survey of the effects of photosynthesis will seldom
separate effects on induction from possible effects on evocation, the topic of the following chapter in this volume.

PHOTOSYNTHESIS

To summarize briefly the main effects of photosynthesis on the
physiology of the plant (Stumpf and Conn, 1981), the first
direct effect of light is the excitation of chlorophylls and
other light-harvesting pigments, including carotenoids. In
falling back to the ground state, energy is channelled to the
chlorophyll in the reaction centres of PSI and PSII which in
turn become excited. The transfer of electrons from these
reaction centres puts the chlorophyll back in the ground state
but in an oxidized condition. Donation of electrons back to
chlorophyll from water (PSII) or plastocyanin (PSI) allows the
cycle to repeat. The passage of electrons through a chain of
carriers results in the oxidation of water, production of
oxygen, reduction of nicotinamide adenine dinucleotide phosphate (NADP) and establishment of an electrical potential and
proton gradient. Through a chemi—osmotic mechanism, discharge
of these gradients causes the formation of ATP. Some of the
captured energy may be re—radiated as fluorescence at longer
wavelengths, especially at high photosynthetic photon flux
densities (PPFD) when the photosynthetic system becomes over-
loaded. Less direct effects of light on photosynthesis include the light activation of a number of Calvin cycle enzymes, probably through the reduction of thioredoxin by
reduced ferrodoxin produced during the light reactions of
photosynthesis, changes in the distribution of photons between
PSI and PSII, and the activation of the xanthoxin—violaxanthin
epoxidation cycle. Enzymatic reactions activated by reduced
NADP (NADPH) and ATP include CO_2 reduction by ribulose—1,
5—bisphosphate carboxylase oxygenase (RUBISCO), the regeneration of ribulose—1, 5—bisphosphate (RBP) in the Calvin cycle,
nitrate and sulphate reduction, lipid and protein synthesis
and the active transport of substances through different cell
organelles and compartments. These effects of light in photosynthesis are summarized in Table 1.

The rate of photosynthesis is governed by a number of
external factors such as PPFD, temperature, CO_2 and O_2 supply,
as well as internal factors such as chlorophyll content, leaf
morphology and anatomy, water content, degree of stomatal
opening, mineral content and whether the plant has a C_3 or C_4
pattern of CO_2 assimilation. These factors may also interact

TABLE 1. *Effects of Light in Photosynthesis*

Excitation of light harvesting pigments
Fluorescence of chlorophyll
Excitation of PSI and PSII reaction centres
Electron transfer from reaction centres to cytochromes,
    plastoquinone, plastocyanin, ferredoxin, etc.
Formation of proton and potential gradient in grana
ATP formation, altered energy charge of cell
NADP reduction
Oxidation of water, release of oxygen
Changes in Mg, P and other ion concentrations
Decrease in CO_2 concentration in leaf
Reduction of CO_2, nitrate, sulphate and their further
    metabolism
Increase in carbohydrate and other metabolite levels, decrease
    in osmotic potential
Promotion of cytoplasmic streaming
Activation of phloem loading, export of carbohydrates from
    leaf
Thioredoxin reduction, activation of some Calvin Cycle enzymes
De-activation of respiratory enzymes in Krebs Cycle and
    Pentose Phosphate Pathway
Promotion of photorespiration
PEP formation in C_4 plants
Reduction of oxaloacetic acid in C_4 and CAM plants
Promotion of de-acidification in CAM plants
Violaxanthin de-epoxidation
Promotion of stomatal opening
Changes in leaf anatomy

---

with photoperiodic responses. Chlorophyll, for example
absorbs red wavelengths to a greater extent than far-red
wavelengths so that, depending on the distribution of phytochrome in the leaf, the ratio of Pr to Pfr will vary with
chlorophyll content. These are parallel effects on photoperiodic responses rather than a direct consequence of photosynthesis and will not be considered here.

INTERACTIONS BETWEEN PHOTOSYNTHESIS AND PHOTOPERIODIC
INDUCTION

In the following section I shall list the processes that are
known to participate in both photoperiodic responses and
photosynthesis, and consider the evidence for an interaction
between the two (Table 2).

TABLE 2. *Possible interactions between photosynthesis and photoperiodic induction.*

Processes affecting photoperiodic induction	Effect of photosynthesis
1. Metabolite concentration	a. carbohydrates providing energy for leaf metabolism b. carbohydrates providing energy for translocation of substances in the phloem out of the leaf c. synthesis of substances involved in flower induction, hormones, florigen, benzoic acid derivatives etc.
2. Phytochrome activation	a. membrane potential changes, proton fluxes b. altered availability of substrates for phytochrome action through membrane permeability changes, ATP and NADPH concentration changes, formation of other metabolites c. enzyme activation altering phytochrome action
3. HIR activation	(as HIR processes probably involve phytochrome the list is the same as (2) above)
4. Blue-absorbing reactions	a. presence of reductants and electron transport systems b. energy transfer from light harvesting systems such as carotenoids
5. Enzyme activation	a. activation of enzymes through thioredoxin
6. Sink activity (nutrient diversion)	a. diversion of photosynthates to roots or other organs changing pattern of hormone or other metabolite flux from sink organs to meristem
7. Endogenous rhythms	a. initiation and phase may depend on timing of energy inputs from photosynthesis

Metabolite Concentration

Carbohydrates The simplest method for preventing accumulation of metabolites in photosynthesis is to keep the plant in continuous darkness. Transfer to darkness may still allow growth to continue if the plant has an adequate store of carbohydrates, either in large seeds or in a storage organ, and in some plants such as vernalized biennial sugar beet (LDP) and radish (LDP) both leaves and flower primordia are initiated (Fife and Price, 1953; Lang, 1965).

In small plants, sugar must be supplied, either by leaf injection or by growing the plant in sterile culture on sucrose-containing media (Scorza, 1982). A number of both SDP and LDP will flower in complete darkness under these conditions, (Lang, 1965) and any dependance of induction on photosynthesis is presumably limited to the supply of a carbohydrate energy source. The process of induction is not necessarily involved in these texperiments; for this the evidence would be that leaf removal prevents flowering in darkness. This is not the case in *Hyoscyamus niger*, where plants in continuous darkness flower only when leaves are removed (Lang, 1965).

A second way to prevent accumulation of carbohydrates through photosynthesis is to deprive the plant of CO_2 (Fig. 1) although it should be remembered that withdrawal of CO_2 will have several other effects that may also interact with induction (Sachs, 1979; Hinklenton and Jollife, 1980). Experi-

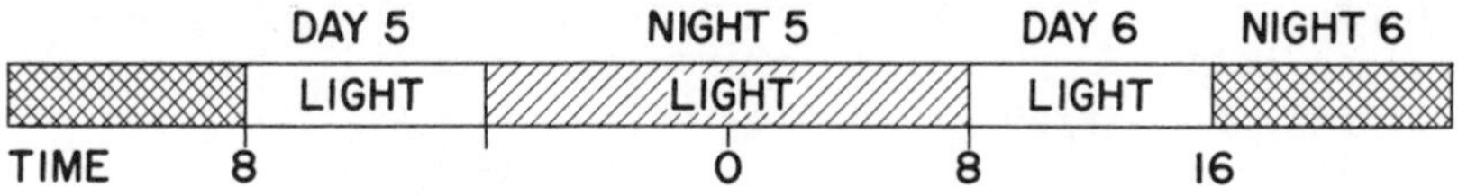

MAIN LIGHT	SUPPLEMENTARY LIGHT	% FLOWER INITIATION
$+CO_2$	$+CO_2$	69
$+CO_2$	$-CO_2$	11
$-CO_2$	$+CO_2$	26
$-CO_2$	$-CO_2$	3
SHORT DAY CONTROL		0

Fig. 1. *Effect of removal of CO_2 during a single main light period or a 16-h supplementary light period (high intensity) or both, on flowering of* Brassica campestris *cv Ceres (After Friend* et al., *1984).*

ments of this type have been summarized by Chailakhyan
(Table 3). In general, both SDP and LDP require CO_2 during
the light period, but feeding sucrose or some other energy-
providing metabolites substitutes for the absence of CO_2.

TABLE 3. *Effect of inhibition of photosynthesis by CO2 withdrawal or DCMU application on flowering of LDP and SDP (After
Chailakhyan* et al., *1978).*

Treatment during light period of inductive day	Flowering response	
	LDP	SDP
+ CO_2	Fl	Fl
− CO_2	Veg	Veg
− CO_2 + sucrose	Fl	Fl
DCMU	Veg	Veg
DCMU + sucrose	Veg or Fl*	Fl

*Imhoff, 1973

    Prevention of chlorophyll accumulation has been used to
determine the dependence of flower initiation on current
photosynthesis. Three general methods for this are the use of
genetic albino mutants, low temperatures, or chemical inhibitors such as the pyridazinone herbicides. Chlorophyll-less
mutants of the LDP barley and Norflurazon-bleached plants both
have an active phytochrome system and flowering has a normal
photoperiodic response (Borthwich *et al.*, 1951; Deitzer *et
al.*, 1979; Jabben and Deitzer, 1978; see Chapter 4 this
volume). *Brassica campestris* bleached with Norflurazon also
initiates flowers (Friend *et al.*, 1984) as does *Pharbitis nil*
bleached at low temperature (King *et al.*, 1978) or given a
short R photoperiod that does not induce net photosynthesis
(Friend, 1975; King *et al.*, 1982).
    Blocking photosynthesis by use of 3-(3, 4-dichlorophenyl)-
1, 1-dimethyl urea (DCMU) prevents flowering in a number of
both LDP and SDP (Table 3) and in some cases the effect can be
overcome by sugar feeding (Imhoff, 1973). Other chemical inhibitors of photosynthesis such as ammonium and cadmium ions,
salicaldoxime, metronidazole, antimycin A, sodium nitrate,
2,5-dibromo-3-methyl-6-isopropyl-p-benzoquinone (DBMIB) and
disalicylidenepropanediamine (DSPD) have been used to inhibit
photosynthesis, as shown by reduced CO_2 uptake or O_2 evo-
lution, but as the effect of these inhibitors is not in
general reversed by sucrose feeding it is not clear that their
only action is to prevent CO_2 assimilation (Friend *et al.*,

1979; Ireland and Schwabe, 1982a, b). Inhibitory effects of DCMU on flower induction by long periods of illumination with light of low R/FR ratio in the SDP *Chenopodium rubrum* were overcome by sugar feeding. This photosynthetic effect of light, however, was on floral evocation rather than on induction, as shown by negating the effect of DCMU by applications of 2,6 dichlorophenolindophenol (DCPIP) immediately after the inductive light treatment (Sawhney and Cumming, 1971).

In certain types of *in vitro* organ or tissue culture, leaves are not present during a photoperiodic treatment that results in flowering (Scorza, 1982). In such cases the floral stimulus normally provided by leaves is presumably supplied by

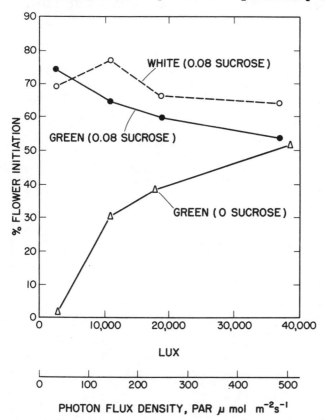

Fig. 2. *Effect of photon flux density (fluorescent light) on flowering of* Brassica campestris *cv* Ceres *grown under a 16-h daylength on vermuculite or in sterile culture provided with 0.08 M sucrose. White plants treated with Norflurazon to prevent chlorophyll accumulation (After Friend et al., 1984).*

the medium. Alternatively, the tissue normally contains the
floral stimulus and lack of flowering under non-inductive
photoperiods is caused by the action of inhibitors formed
directly by the tissue. In either case the role of photosynthesis is replaced by the culture medium.

Another approach is to increase photosynthesis and determine whether flowering is promoted. Increasing the irradiance
promotes flowering in a number of LDP and SDP plants, and at
least part of this effect is probably through the increased
supply of energy substrates (Fig. 2). Feeding green plants of
Brassica with sugar in sterile culture promoted flowering and
reduced the final leaf number even under short daylengths.
The same effect was found with plants bleached with Norflurazon (Fig. 3). The need for accumulation of carbohydrates in

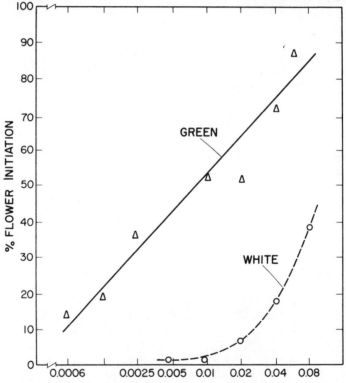

SUCROSE CONCENTRATION M

Fig. 3. *Effect of concentration of sucrose in the culture
medium of* Brassica campestris *cv Ceres grown on an 8 h daylength in fluorescent light. White plants treated with Norflurazon to prevent chlorophyll accumulation (After Friend et
al ., 1984).*

photosynthesis is, however, not the only reason for the high PPFD required to saturate the flowering response in *Anagallis arvensis*. Here, the uptake of CO_2 was saturated at a lower PPFD than the flowering response (Quedado and Friend, 1978).

Increasing the CO_2 content to about 1000 ppm, as in greenhouse CO_2 fertilization, promotes flowering of a number of LD and day-neutral crop plants (Daunicht and Lenz, 1973), but delays flowering in others (Hesketh and Hellmers, 1973). In the LDP *Silene armeria* flowering was promoted in SD when the CO_2 concentration was increased to 0.15% (Purohit and Tregunna, 1974). The effects of CO_2 are complicated, however, as increasing the level above atmospheric for an extended period retards flowering of several SDP maintained under normally inductive SD conditions (*Xanthium strumarium* and *Pharbitis*, Purohit and Tregunna, 1974; and *Lemna paucicostata*, Posner, 1971). Under LD conditions, high CO_2 leads again to a negation of the effects of light in some SDP, and in this case flowering is induced (*Pharbitis*, Hinklenton and Jollife, 1980). High CO_2 levels are probably not operating through carbohydrate accumulation in photosynthesis however, as the inhibition brought about by increasing the CO_2 level from 0.1 to 0.5% was not related to any increased growth (Table 4). The level of photosynthesis in C_3 plants can also be increased through repressing photorespiration with low levels of oxygen but this technique has not received much attention in photoperiodic studies.

TABLE 4. *Effect of CO_2 on* Pharbitis *under long days. (From Hinklenton and Jollife, 1980).*

	CO_2%			
	0.03	0.1	1.0	5.0
Relative growth rate (g g^{-1} day^{-1})	0.18	0.19	0.18	0.16
% flowering	0	0	33	16

A further complication in studying the effect of withholding or adding CO_2 or adding carbohydrate is that the timing of the treatment may influence the flowering response. This probably represents an interaction with an endogenous rhythm and will be considered later.

Translocation The concentration gradient between the soluble carbohydrates in the leaf and in the sink organs probably

determines the rate and direction of loading and translocation
in the phloem (Moorby, 1977). As there is considerable evidence that the floral stimulus moves in the translocation
stream (Bernier *et al.*, 1981; see Chapter 10 in this volume),
one would expect the rate of photosynthesis to increase the
rate of translocation of flower-inducing substances.
Carbohydrates may be a necessary component of a complex floral
stimulus in addition to acting as an energy source for phloem
loading and unloading and as an osmoticum for bulk flow.

Synthesis of substances other than carbohydrates These essential components may not always be synthesized from carbohydrate reserves already in the leaf, but require instead some
early product of photosynthesis or photorespiration. The
qualitative SDP *Impatiens balsamina* probably holds a record
for the number of metabolites that induce flowering under
normally non-inductive conditions. Although it has not been
shown that current photosynthesis is needed for the formation
of these compounds, it at least indicates the wide range of
metabolites that may be involved in induction (Sawhney, 1978).
In the SDP *Pharbitis*, the role of photosynthesis is probably
the provision of metabolites other than carbohydrates. High
light intensity given before a period of 6 days at low temperature was needed for floral induction in LD (Shinozaki *et
al.*, 1982). This need for high intensity light was probably
photosynthetic, as it was inhibited by DCMU. The effect of
DCMU was not reversible by applications of sucrose, ATP or
NADPH. It was suggested that possible metabolites formed in
photosynthesis included 5-chlorosalicyclic acid, 4, 4-dich-
lorobenzoic acid and some other benzoic acid derivatives.
These substances were also effective in the induction of
flowering of the SDP *L. paucicostata* under long-day conditions
(Watanabe *et al.*, 1981). Salicylic acid induces flowering of
the LDP *Lemna gibba* under non-inductive conditions (Cleland
and Ajami, 1974; see Chapter 9 in this volume).

Gibberellins promote flowering in a number of species and
inhibit flowering in others (Bernier *et al.*, 1981) but are not
generally regarded as a flowering hormone, as discussed in
Chapter 10 in this volume.

Phytochrome Activation

Membrane potential changes Phytochrome is present in plant
membranes, including the plastids (Marme, 1977). It is,
therefore, possible that membrane potential changes and proton
fluxes produced in these membranes during photosynthesis could
interact with phytochrome. Phytochrome phototransformation

results in a pH change in the medium (Tokutomi et al., 1982) and it is possible that similar proton movements brought about during photosynthesis could facilitate the action of phytochrome.

Membrane permeability changes are involved in phytochrome action, as well demonstrated by work with leaflet movement in *Samanea saman* (Satter and Galston, 1981), and Cleland (Chapter 9 in this volume) has referred to the photomimetic effects of the membrane-active substance valinomycin in relation to membrane effects of phytochrome in *L. gibba*.

Altered availability of substrates for phytochrome action

Phytochrome activates a number of enzymes that require ATP or NAD, including ATP-ase and NAD kinase, (Marmé, 1977; Schopfer, 1977). The increased supply of these compounds during electron and proton transport in photosynthesis could affect phytochrome action. Attempts to replace effects of high intensity light by adding ATP or NADPH to plants have seldom been effective, but it is often doubtful whether the material was taken up by the plant and reached the effective site within the cell (Friend et al., 1979; Ireland and Schwabe, 1982a, b; Shinozaki et al., 1982). In the LDP *L. gibba*, the flower-promoting effect of adding ADP was attributed to formation of a higher ATP level in the plant. DCMU had a similar effect to ADP and it was suggested that the promotion of flowering was again brought about by an increased concentration of ATP within the plant through photophosphorylation (Kandeler, 1969a). Repression of flowering in *L. gibba* by ammonium ions, probably through the inhibition of photophosphorylation, could also be overcome by addition of ATP (Kandeler, 1969b).

In *Xanthium* there is a requirement for CO_2 during a short interruption of the dark period in order to prevent flowering. It is doubtful that this effect is brought about by the need for the very small amount of carbohydrate that would be formed during this 5 min period, and it was suggested that the CO_2 requirement may be related to some action of phytochrome (Bassi et al., 1976).

HIR Activation

As at least part of the HIR, particularly prominent in the photoperiodic responses of LDP, involves the action of phytochrome (Mancinelli, 1980), possible interactions with photosynthesis would include the factors of electron transport and proton gradients already mentioned. It is clear however that any interaction of photosynthesis with the HIR in *Brassica* does not require CO_2 uptake for the flower promoting effects

of high intensity FR radiation. Flowering was significantly
promoted by a 16-h irradiation that had no effect on the rate
of CO_2 exchange as compared with plants kept in the dark
(Friend et al., unpublished results).

Blue-absorbing-pigment Reactions

The flower promoting effects of high irradiances of blue light
may represent the activity of a flavonoid pigment involved in
several photomorphogenetic effects such as phototropism and
stem elongation (Senger, 1982; Senger and Briggs, 1981). As
these wavelengths are very active in photosynthesis, separ-
ation of the effects of blue light on photoperiodic induction
in the leaf from carbohydrate accumulation in photosynthesis
would entail the use of CO_2-free conditions, chemical inhibitors etc., and this does not seem to be reported in the literature. Reduction of cytochrome b by flavonoid compounds
activated by blue light could affect phytochrome activity,
although no experimental evidence for this has been reported.

Other possible effects of photosynthesis on the blue-
absorbing-pigment system include changes in membrane permea-
bilities, and excitation of the pigment by light harvested by
photosystems I and II.

Enzyme Activation

Plant enzymes known to be light-activated include some which
are activated by reduced thioredoxin. This is produced from
reduced ferredoxin during electron transport in photosynthesis
(Table 5). Light-activation of particular enzymes could
provide substrates for phytochrome, HIR or blue-absorbing-
pigment action or for the formation of flower-inducing substances. DCMU inhibits the reduction of ferredoxin and thus

TABLE 5. *Enzymes activated by thioredoxin in photosynthesis*
(from Buchanan, 1980).

Fructose 1, 6-bisphosphatase
Sedoheptulose 1, 7-bisphosphatase
*NADP-glyceraldehyde 3-phosphate dehydrogenase
Phosphoribulokinase
*NADP-malate dehydrogenase
*Phenylalanine ammonialyase

* Also reported controlled by phytochrome (Schopfer, 1977)

---

the activation of some enzymes, and this action may account
for some of the effects of DCMU that are not reversed by the
application of sugar.

Sink Activity (Nutrient Diversion)

Changed patterns of assimilate production under different
photoperiods may alter cytokinin and other hormone syntheses
in the roots and other organs, which in turn could alter the
supply of nutrients to the apex, changing the pattern of
morphogenesis, as outlined in the nutrient diversion hypothesis of Sachs and Hackett (1977) and Kinet and Sachs (1984).
    In the LDP *Sinapis alba*, sink effectiveness for both assi-
milates and floral stimulus may be increased by application of
cytokinins to the apical meristem, resulting in increased
flowering under inductive daylengths (Bernier *et al.*, 1981;
Bodson, 1984). Reduced export of assimilates from cotyledons
of the SDP *Pharbitis* can be obtained by applications of cytokinin, also reducing transmission of the flowering stimulus
(Ogawa and King, 1979). Chailakhyan and co-workers have
documented cases where cytokinins in the roots may alter the
sex expression of developing flowers (Chailakhyan, 1979).
Cutting off roots of the SDP *Chenopodium* maintained under
marginal conditions of induction promoted flowering but
flowering was reduced when BA was applied to the plumule of
de-rooted plants (Krekule, 1979).

Endogenous Rhythms

The importance of endogenous rhythms in the control of
flowering is stressed in several chapters in this volume.

TABLE 6. *Effect of time of glucose feeding (0.6M) for 6 h
during a 72-h dark period, on flowering of* Chenopodium rubrum
(After Cumming, 1967).

Time of glucose feeding	Difference in % flowering from control
1st skotophile phase	− 9.5
1st photophile phase	+ 38
2nd skotophile phase	− 16
2nd photophile phase	+ 56
3rd skotophile phase	+ 66
3rd photophile phase	+ 12

Photosynthesis or its products can initiate or set the phase
of a rhythm as shown by experiments in which the timing of
sugar feeding altered the flowering response of *Chenopodium*
(Frosch *et al.*, 1973; Table 6). Wagner has suggested that
rhythms and photosynthesis intermesh to optimize the energy
input into the plant apex during the vegetative stage before
switching to reproduction (Sachs, 1979). In *Sinapis* the
effect of witholding CO_2 during the supplementary light period
depends strongly on the time. Absence of CO_2 during the first
8 h of a 16-h light period reduced flowering, but when given
during the last 8 h flowering was accelerated. These effects
could be duplicated by sugar feeding in darkness (Bodson *et
al.*, 1979).

EFFECTS OF PHOTOPERIOD ON PHOTOSYNTHESIS

While photosynthesis may affect photoperiodic induction, the
process of CO_2 uptake may itself be affected by photoperiod.
A given photoperiodic treatment may alter leaf morphology. In
wheat, the thickness of the lamina was dependent on the total
daily irradiation independently of photoperiod, but leaf
length was greater under long photoperiods than short (Friend
et al., 1962).

   Short daylengths increase leaf thickness and induce the CAM
pattern of CO_2 uptake in the SDP *Kalanchoe blossfeldiana*
(Queiroz, 1974) but these changes are probably not causally
related to floral induction.

SUMMARY

There is good evidence that some plants, including *Pharbitis*
(Friend, 1975; King *et al.*, 1978), *L. gibba* (see Chapter 9 in
this volume), *Brassica* (Friend *et al.*, 1984) and barley
(Jabben and Deitzer, 1978; see Chapter 4 in this volume), do
not require the input of energy from immediate photosynthesis
for floral induction. Immediate products of photosynthesis
are apparently required by some plants however, as shown by
the inability of sucrose to substitute for photosynthesis
inhibited by DCMU (Ireland and Schwabe, 1982a, b).

   The role of photosynthesis in photoperiodic induction is
therefore mainly to provide an energy source for the synthesis
or control of promotors and inhibitors and their translocation
from the leaf, or to provide some more immediate products of
the intermediary steps in photosynthesis that are essential
for these processes. In addition, photosynthates, especially
sucrose, may be regarded as having a controlling or hormone-
like action themselves (Pontis, 1977) and this role may be
especially important in controlling cell divisions in the

apex (Van't Hof and Kovacs, 1972). Stimulation of mitosis is a well-documented early event in evocation (e.g. Lyndon and

TABLE 7. *Possible substances in leaves affecting floral evocation at meristem in SDP.*

	Short Days (Flowering)	Long Days (Vegetative)
1 Flowering hormone DNA	a normally de-repressed* b de-repressed by SD	l normally de-repressed m normally repressed n repressed by LD inhibitor
2 Mobilizing hormone	c absent d normally de-repressed e de-repressed by SD	o absent p normally repressed q repressed by LD
3 Inhibitor that re-presses flowering hormone DNA	f absent	r absent s formed in LD
4 Inhibitor that re-presses mobilizing hormone DNA	g absent h normally repressed i repressed by SD	t absent u normally de-repressed v de-repressed in LD
5 Inhibitor that re-presses meristem floral organogenesis DNA	j absent	w absent x formed in LD
6 Photosynthates	k low daily photosynthate	y high daily total photosynthate

*The expression of DNA activity could be controlled at levels other than through repression and de-repression, e.g. through inhibition of translation.

Francis, Chapter 13 in this volume). Considering some of the
multiple possibilities that are involved in flower induction
(Table 7) photosynthates would take their place among the
promotors of flowering, mobilizing hormones, inhibitors of
these substances and inhibitors of floral organogenesis at the
apex (see Chapter 11 in this volume). It is proposed, in this
elaboration of Wellensiek's (1977) scheme, that photosynthates
are an important component of the floral stimulus in both LDP
and SDP (see Chapter 12 in this volume). De-repression of
floral organogenesis DNA in the apex may require not only the
activity of a flowering hormone but also stimulation of DNA
replication by an increase in the carbohydrate level (Van't
Hof and Kovacs 1972). Such an increase could result from
increased photosynthesis brought about by increased photon
flux density or by longer daylengths (in LDP) or from the
action of a carbohydrate-mobilizing hormone (such as cytokinin) arriving in the translocation stream from an induced
leaf or indirectly from some other organ, (Table 8). In
Brassica grown under short daylengths, photosynthate supply

TABLE 8. *Requirements for floral evocation at the meristem of
SDP and LDP.*

Sufficient carbohydrates to induce mitosis*	a	Carbohydrate supply non-limiting even in non-inductive daylengths.
	or b	Carbohydrate supply only sufficient in long days (LDP).
	or c	Mobilizing hormone from leaf increases carbohydrate supply.
Floral organogenesis DNA de-repressed	a	Normally de-repressed, no inhibitors translocated from leaf.
	or b	de-repressed by arrival of flowering hormone.

*Control of the early stages of evocation may not necessarily
involve major qualitative changes in gene expression (See
Lyndon and Frances, Chapter 13 in this volume).

may be a limiting factor in flower initiation, as shown by sugar feeding experiments (Friend et al., 1984).

Under natural conditions the induction of flowering by photoperiod occurs at daylengths just past the critical. In LDP this will be at a time of increasing photosynthetic input from the slowly increasing daylengths, and the importance of mobilizing hormones may be less than in SDP where the critical daylength is reached at a time of diminishing photosynthesis.

REFERENCES

Bassi, P.K., Tregunna, E.B. and Joliffe, P.A. (1976). *Can. J. Bot.* 54, 2881–2887

Bernier, G., Kinet, J.-M. and Sachs, R. (1981). *In* "The Physiology of Flowering" Vol. I. CRC Press, Boca Raton, Florida

Bodson, M. (1984). *In* "Handbook on Flowering" (ed A.H. Halevy). CRC Press, Boca Raton, Florida. (In press)

Bodson, M., Bernier, G., Kinet, J.-M., Jacqmard, A. and Havelange, A. (1979). *In* "Photosynthesis and plant development" (eds R. Marcelle, H. Clijsters and M. Van Poucke). pp. 73–94. W. Junk, The Hague

Borthwick, H.A., Hendricks, S.B. and Parker, M.W. (1951). *Bot. Gaz.* 113, 95–105

Buchanan, B.B. (1980). *Annu. Rev. Plant Physiol.* 31, 341–374

Chailakhyan, M.Kh. (1979). *Am. J. Bot.* 66, 717–736

Chailakhyan, M.Kh., Aksenova, N.P., Konstantivova, T.N. and Bavrina, T.V. (1978). *In* "Views on Physiology of Flowering" (eds A.N. Purohit and K. Gurumarti). pp. 47–68. Bishen Singh Mahendra Pal Singh Dehra Dun, India

Cleland, C.F. and Ajami, A. (1974). *Plant Physiol.* 54, 904–906

Cumming, B.G. (1967). *Can. J. Bot.* 45, 2173–2193

Daunicht, H.J. and Lenz, F. (1973). *Gartenbauwissenschaft* 38, 533–546

Deitzer, G.F., Hayes, R. and Jabben, M. (1979). *Plant Physiol.* 64, 1015–1021

Evans, L.T. (1969). *In* "The Induction of Flowering" (ed L.T. Evans). pp. 328–349. Cornell University Press, Ithaca, New York

Fife, J.M. and Price, C. (1953). *Plant Physiol.* 28, 475–480

Friend, D.J.C. (1975). *Physiol. Plant.* 35, 286–296

Friend, D.J.C., Bodson, M. and Bernier, G. (1984). *Plant Physiol.* (In press)

Friend, D.J.C., Helson, V.A. and Fisher, J.E. (1962). *Can. J. Bot.* 40, 1299–1311

Friend, D.J.C., Deputy, J. and Quedado, R. (1979). *In* "Photosynthesis and Plant Development" (eds R. Marcelle, H. Clijsters and M. Van Poucke). pp. 59–72. W. Junk, The Hague

Frosch, S., Wagner, E. and Cumming, B.G. (1973). *Can. J. Bot.* 51, 1355–1367

Hesketh, J.D. and Hellmers, H. (1973). *Environ. Control Biol.* 11, 51–53

Hincklenton, P.R. and Jolliffe, P.A. (1980). *Plant Physiol.* 66, 13–17

Imhoff, C. (1973). *C.R. Hebd. Seances Acad. Sci.* 276, 3303–3306

Ireland, C.R. and Schwabe, W.W. (1982a). *J. Exp. Bot.* 33, 738–747

Ireland, C.R. and Schwabe, W.W. (1982b). *J. Exp. Bot.* 33, 748–760

Jabben, M. and Deitzer, G.F. (1978). *Photochem. Photobiol.* 27, 127–131

Kandeler, R. (1969a). *Z. Pflanzenphysiol.* 61, 20–28

Kandeler, R. (1969b). *Planta* 84, 279–291

King, R.W., Vince-Prue, D. and Quail, P.H. (1978). *Planta* 141, 15–22

King, R.W., Schäfer, E., Thomas, B. and Vince-Prue, D. (1982) *Plant Cell Environ.* 5, 395–404

Krekule, J. (1979). *In* "La Physiologie de la Floraison" (eds P Champagnat and R Jacques). pp. 19–57. CNRS, Paris

Lang, A. (1965). *In* "Encyclopedia of Plant Physiology" (ed W Ruhland). Vol. 15-1, pp. 1380–1536. Springer-Verlag, Berlin

Mancinelli, A.L. (1980). *Photochem. Photobiol.* 32, 853–857

Marme, D. (1977). *Annu. Rev. Plant Physiol.* 28, 173–198

Moorby, J. (1977). *In* "Integration of Activity in the Higher Plant" (ed D. H.L Jennings). pp. 425–454. *Symp. Soc. Exp Biol.* Cambridge University Press, Cambridge.

Moshkov, B.S. (1937). *Dokl. Acad. Nauk. SSSR.* 15, 211

Ogawa, Y. and King, R.W. (1979). *Plant Physiol.* 63, 643–649

Pontis, H.G. (1977). *Int. Rev. Biochem.* 13, 79–117

Posner, H.B. (1971). *Plant Physiol.* 48, 361–365

Purohit, A.N. and Tregunna, E.B. (1974). *Can. J. Bot.* 52, 1283–1291

Quedado, R. and Friend, D.J. (1978). *Plant Physiol.* 62, 802–806

Queiroz, O. (1974). *Annu. Rev. Plant Physiol.* 25, 115–134

Sachs, R. (1979). *In* "La Physiologie de la Floraison" (eds P Champagnat and R. Jacques). pp. 169–208. CNRS, Paris

Sachs, R.M. and Hackett, W.P. (1977). *Acta Hortic. (The Hague)* 68, 29–49

Satter, R.L. and Galston, A.W. (1981). *Annu. Rev. Plant Physiol.* 32, 83–110

Sawhney, S. (1978). *In* "Views on Physiology of Flowering" (eds A.N. Purohit and K. Gurumarti). pp. 189. Bishen Singh Mahendra Pal Singh, Dehra Dan, India

Sawhney, R. and Cumming, B.J. (1971). *Can. J. Bot.* 49, 2233–2237

Schopfer, P. (1977). *Annu. Rev. Plant Physiol.* 28, 223–252

Scorza, R. (1982). *Hortic. Rev.* 4, 106–127

Senger, H. (1982). *Photochem. Photobiol.* 35, 911–920

Senger, H. and Briggs, W.R. (1981). *Photochem. Photobiol. Rev.* 6, 1–38

Shinozaki, M., Hikichi, M., Yoshida, K., Watanabe, K. and Takimoto, A. (1982). *Plant Cell Physiol.* 23, 473–477

Stumpf, R.K. and Conn, E.E. (1981). *In* "The Biochemistry of Plants Vol. 8. Photosynthesis" Academic Press, New York

Tokutomi, S., Yamamoto, K.T., Miyoshi, Y. and Furuya, M. (1982). *Photochem. Photobiol.* 35, 431–433

Van't Hof, J. and Kovacs, C.J. (1972). *Adv. Exp. Med. Biol.* 18, 15–32

Watanabe, K., Fujita, T. and Takimoto, A. (1981). *Plant Cell Physiol.* 22, 1469–1479

Wellensiek, S.J. (1977). *Acta Hortic. (The Hague)* 68, 17–27

Chapter 19

THE FACTORS CONTROLLING FLORAL EVOCATION: AN OVERVIEW

GEORGES BERNIER

Centre de Physiologie Vegetale Appliquee (I.R.S.I.A.),
Departement de Botanique, Universite de Liege, Sart Tilman,
B-4000 Liege, Belgium.

THE CONTROL OF DEVELOPMENTAL PROCESSES IN PLANTS AND ANIMALS

All growth and developmental processes in higher plants are
affected by more than one class of exogenous regulators and it
is generally believed that these processes are internally
controlled by two or more substances acting synergistically,
antagonistically and/or sequentially (Letham et al., 1978).
These endogenous regulators, although they may be produced
preferentially in particular regions of the entire organism,
are always manufactured by unspecialized tissues and may be
produced under appropriate conditions by tissues not normally
synthesizing them, e.g., after injury or organ amputation or
during tissue and organ senescence (Sheldrake, 1973; Letham et
al., 1978). The phenomenon of habituation of cultured tissues
illustrates this unique property of plants: some tissues which
when first isolated and cultured *in vitro* require an exogenous
supply of growth regulators, e.g., auxin or cytokinin, may
acquire in time the ability to produce their own supply of
these compounds. Meins and Binns (1978) have shown that this
is a gradual and reversible process, involving epigenetic
changes rather than stable genetic transformations or stable
changes in phenotypes. Habituation is a property exhibited so
far by cultured tissues only and we do not know if similar
processes occur in intact plants.

   This situation contrasts sharply to that found in animals
where developmental processes are, as a rule, strictly dependent on the presence or absence of highly specific mole-

LIGHT AND THE FLOWERING PROCESS
ISBN 0.12.721960.9

cules, the hormones, produced in specialized organs or glands (Graham and Wareing, 1976). Amphibia metamorphose only when the level of thyroxine released by the thyroid gland is above some threshold. Pupation and moulting in insects are similarly controlled by the ecdysone hormone produced by the prothoracic gland. In mammals, the development of the reproductive tract and secondary sex differences are essentially under the influence of steroid hormones synthesized in the gonads. Regeneration of amputated parts may occur in higher animals but this is a phenomenon restricted to very special cases, like the tail of lizards or a limb of salamanders and Crustacea. Amputation of the hormone–synthesizing organs leads usually to the suppression of the corresponding developmental processes, if not to death of the organism. Processes similar to the habituation of plant tissues have never been reported for cultured animal tissues or cells.

The way chemical messengers are produced and act within the entire organism appears so different in plants and animals that it has been suggested that the name hormone is totally inappropriate for plant regulators which should rather be called growth substances.

The concept of a universal specific hormone – florigen – controlling the transition to reproductive development in plants was elaborated in the 1930s just after the discovery early in this century of circulating steroid sex hormones in animals, at a time when the modes of production and action of plant growth substances were still largely unknown. However, despite extensive investigations in many laboratories, no specific organ–forming hormones have yet been identified in higher plants and there is no a priori reason to suppose that the situation for flowers is different from that for other organs.

Support for the florigen concept is of a purely physiological nature, i.e., it comes from experiments showing (a) transmission of the floral stimulus through a graft union, and (b) movement of this stimulus in photoperiod–sensitive plants from the induced leaves to the receptor meristem(s) (Fig. 1a). The results of grafting experiments, frequently negative or anomalous, will not be discussed here since they were critically reviewed by Zeevaart (1976) and Bernier et al. (1981a, b). The significance of the so–called translocation curves for the floral stimulus, obtained after sequential defoliations of induced leaves in species induced to flower by a single photoinductive–cycle (Fig. 1a), can be questioned first on the basis that the defoliation technique grossly interferes with the normal balance of leaf tissues and causes considerable wounding which may lead to important physiological disturbances within the plant. Also, it is puzzling that, in

plants like *Xanthium strumarium, Pharbitis nil, Sinapis alba*
and *Anagallis arvensis,* dramatic changes in the meristem can
be observed many hours before the time of arrival of the
purported floral stimulus as determined by defoliation experiments (Bonner and Zeevaart, 1962; Bernier 1979).

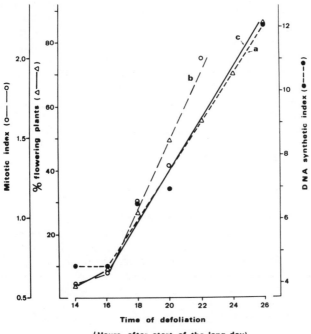

Time of defoliation

(Hours after start of the long day)

*Fig. 1. Effect of timing of defoliation on export of the
stimuli for (a) flowering, (b) early mitoses and (c) DNA
synthesis in the apical meristem, from induced leaves of
plants of* Sinapis alba *exposed to a single 22 h LD. Only the
8 youngest mature leaves were left on the plants; only the 6
upper leaves were exposed to the LD and removed at various
times while the 2 lower leaves were continuously in SD. The
mitotic and DNA synthetic indices were determined 26 and 38 h
respectively after start of LD. The percentage of plants
flowering was determined 2 weeks after the start of the LD
(Bernier, unpublished).*

Finally, it must be stressed that this kind of curve may be
misleading as far as the nature of the floral stimulus is
concerned. Consider the case for *Sinapis* plants exposed to
one LD, in which the technique of sequential defoliation was
used to determine for the same experimental batches the timing
of export out of the leaves of (a) the stimulus for flower

initiation, (b) the stimulus for the early mitotic wave, and
(c) the stimulus for nuclear DNA synthesis. The stimulation
of mitoses and DNA synthesis in the meristem are two processes
believed to be essential for evocation in this species
(Bernier et al., 1981b). As seen in Fig. 1, the timing of
transport is identical for the three stimuli, a result that
could be taken as indicating that there is a single stimulus
for the entire evocation process. However, as discussed
elsewhere (Bernier et al., 1981b), there is evidence that the
mitotic stimulus in Sinapis is a cytokinin whereas the stimulus for DNA synthesis is not, and thus that identical timings
of export do not imply chemical identity.

Because of these shortcomings I feel it is necessary and
urgent to explore new approaches to the problem of the nature
of the factors controlling evocation.

HOW IS EVOCATION CONTROLLED?

The Lessons from Work on Woody Perennials.

Besides a few species which exhibit photoperiodic or cold
requirements similar to those of monocarpic herbaceous plants,
the majority of woody perennials seems to be influenced by a
variety of factors, such as low and high temperatures, light
conditions, water stress, ringing, top or root pruning, trans-
planting, etc. None of these factors seems to act in a specific way: they may partly substitute for each other or may be
combined in various ways. In addition, flower formation in
trees is influenced by the plant history. Metabolites and
growth substances, as well as tissues and other anatomical
details, produced in response to past conditions may still be
present and are parts of the biochemical and morphological
microenvironment of the present meristems, influencing their
responses to today's conditions. This situation in woody
perennials was taken by Romberger and Gregory (1974) to suggest that numerous biochemical or physiological systems are
involved in the control of flower formation in every bud on
these plants and that all these systems should be permissive
if evocation is to proceed.

The Lessons from Work on Cultured Plant Fragments.

Plant fragments totally devoid of organized primary meristems
at the time they are brought into culture are ideally suited
for a study of the effect of the chemical environment on the
production of flower primordia. In all such cases the
flowering process is found to be under the influence of a
variety of chemicals, including carbohydrates, nitrates,

growth substances, phenolics, nucleic acid constituents etc.
(Bernier et al., 1981b; Scorza, 1982). These compounds may
promote or inhibit flower formation in explants depending on
their concentrations in the medium, the plant species, the
type and size of explant and other conditions. Provided the
culture medium for root explants of the biennial chichory
contains carbohydrates and the root explants are exposed to
LD, regenerated meristems initiate an inflorescence even in
the total absence of a vernalization treatment (Margara,
1982). This is in complete contrast to the behaviour of the
entire plant which requires first low temperatures and then LD
if flower initiation is to occur. Root explants not subjected
to LD during the first 2 weeks of culture lose their capacity
to respond to LD induction and regenerate meristems that
remain inexorably vegetative whatever the further daylength
conditions. Absence of carbohydrates, excessive water availability or presence of auxin during the first week of culture
also results in permanent loss of photoinducibility by LD.
The factors required for preserving photoinducibility during
this early period of culture are varied and may substitute for
one another. Thus, carbohydrates are necessary only if the
mother-root is not vernalized before explant excision. The
inhibitory effect of excess water is reversed by the addition
of GA_3 or proline to the medium. By combining unfavourable
and favourable factors in various ways, Margara obtained 0 to
100% flowering of explants. Finally, it is of interest that,
once it has been lost, the only way to restore photoinducibility is to submit the explants to a low-temperature treatment. The root explant in vitro now behaves like the intact
plant. Thus, in the intact plant, the vernalizing treatment
in chicory seems to be required to overcome a loss of meristem
sensitivity to the LD stimulus. This loss is supposed to be
due to complex correlative influences operating during the
early stages of vegetative growth, such as low carbohydrate
supply due to insufficient mature leaf area, high auxin levels
due to a disproportionately high ratio of immature to mature
leaves and/or excessive water supply from the rains of the
early spring.
    The lessons arising from the in vitro work are very similar
to those derived from studies on woody perennials: the fate of
any shoot meristem is controlled by a variety of trophic and
regulatory chemicals that are presumably produced in various
plant parts in response not only to present conditions but
also to conditions that prevailed during the previous stages
of development. There seems to be no basic difference in the
way flower initiation is controlled in perennials and other
plants; they differ only in a quantitative way, in the sense
that the correlative influences are obviously much more

complex in perennials.

*Partial Evocation in Photoperiodic annuals: A Clue to the
Controlling Factors of Evocation.*

Because the photoperiod is primarily perceived by the leaves,
evocation in photoperiodic annuals was classically believed to
be controlled by a stimulus produced in the induced leaves and
translocated to the shoot meristems in the phloem, together
with assimilates (Lang, 1965). Leaf photoinduction was

TABLE 1. *Selected cases of partial evocation.*

Partial evocation treatment	Plant species	Evocational event produced	Reference
Subminimal photo-induction	*Silene coeli-rosa*	Increase in RNA content	Miller and Lyndon, 1977
	Lolium temulentum	Increase in rate of leaf initiation	Evans, 1969
	Several species	Precocious initiation of axillary buds	Bernier *et al.*, 1981b
Auxin antagonist	*Epilobium hirsutum*	Increase in rate of leaf initiation	Meicenheimer 1981
		Changes in meristem shape	
		Altered phyllotaxis	
Gibberellin	*Silene coeli-rosa*	Increase in RNA content	Miller and Lyndon, 1977
	Xanthium strumarium	Increase in mitotic activity	
		Increase in meristem size	Maksymowych *et al.*, 1976
		Increase in rate of leaf initiation	
		Increase in internode growth	
		Altered phyllotaxis	
Cytokinin	Several species	Increase in mitotic activity	Bernier *et al.*, 1981b
	Several species	Increase in rate of leaf initiation	

thought to have a marked all-or-none character and from this
it was often inferred that evocation is also an all-or-none
process, going automatically to completion once initiated. A
number of studies during the last decade have indicated that,
on the contrary, some typical evocational events can be produced by two types of treatments that cause no flower primordium formation: firstly by a subminimal photoinduction, and
secondly by the application of certain chemicals, particularly
growth substances, to vegetative plants (Tables 1 and 2).
These observations have generally been disregarded in the past
because the individual evocational changes so produced occur
in plants that stay vegetative and can thus be considered as
unrelated to flowering. I suggest caution against this way of
thinking which overlooks two important physiological aspects
of the control of flower initiation.

Firstly, photoinduction (as well as thermoinduction) is not
an all-or-none process but is clearly progressive and has thus
a quantitative nature, as shown in several experiments in
which two sub-threshold inductive treatments of similar or
different nature can be summated and thus cause flowering
(Zeevaart, 1976; Bernier et al., 1981a). Thus, some degree of
induction can exist even before a threshold permitting minimal
flowering is reached. Secondly, in the case of a floral
stimulus consisting of more than one component, as suggested
above from investigations on trees or cultured plant fragments, each individual component is responsible for only part
of the evocational changes, not the entire transition. Thus,
flowers will never be produced if only one of these components

TABLE 2. *Partial evocation in the LDP* Sinapis alba

Partial evocation treatment	Evocational event produced
One SD at high irradiance	Increase in respiratory substrates Increase in activity of acid invertase Ultrastructural changes in chondriome and nucleolus
One application of a cytokinin	Ultrastructural changes in vacuolar apparatus Early mitotic wave (cell population synchronization) Increase in rate of leaf initiation

*[This table is based on experimental results discussed in
Bernier et al. (1981b), Havelange and Bernier (1983) and
unpublished data].*

is applied to the plants. Disregarding the observations of partial evocation on the simple basis that they are made on plants that do not flower implies that these data are in fact interpreted in terms of a single specific stimulus, i.e., the florigen.

If the results of studies on partial evocation (Tables 1 and 2) are accepted as a guide in the search for the factors controlling the transition to flowering, we may conclude that: (a) the factors controlling the various evocational events are multiple including, among others, carbohydrates, auxins, gibberellins and/or cytokinins. This is true whether one considers various species or a single one. The factors are either of a positive or a negative nature (e.g. auxin antagonists), that is these events are caused either by increased concentrations of a promoter above, or reduced level of an

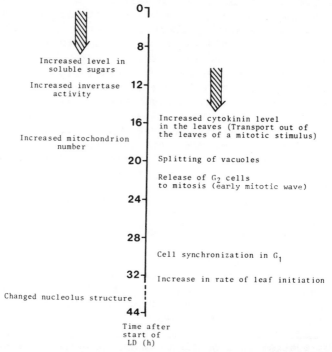

Fig. 2. Diagram showing the sequence of some evocational events in the apex of Sinapis alba plants induced to flower by one LD. The events on the left side of the time axis are caused by one SD at high irradiance and those on the right side by a single application of a cytokinin (see Table 2). The left sequence starts at least 6 h before the right sequence. This diagram is built from experimental results discussed in Bernier et al., (1981b) and unpublished data.

inhibitor below, a threshold value;
(b) each factor is an effective controlling agent of several
of the individual evocational events. The events controlled
by one and the same factor may occur at different levels of
organization (from the molecular to the macromorphological
level);
(c) a given evocational event, e.g., the increase in mitotic
activity or in rate of leaf initiation, may be controlled by a
different factor in different species;
(d) experimental evidence indicates that the different controlling factors act in sequence in *Sinapis* (Fig. 2), and that
their action may be short-lived. In *Xanthium* a single application of GA_3 to vegetative plants results in a number of
changes (Table 1) that are identical to those found in apices
of photoinduced plants (Erickson and Meicenheimer, 1977).
Some of these changes, e.g., the stimulation of apical internode growth and the alteration of phyllotaxis, are long-lived
in GA_3-treated apices whereas they are short-lived in evoked
apices. These observations are substantial in their implication of an early effect of GA during meristem evocation in
Xanthium; this effect is, however, rapidly blocked and factors
other than GA then come into play.

The entirety of these observations indicates that floral
evocation in photoperiodic annuals is controlled, as in woody
perennials or in cultured explants, by a complex system of
several interacting factors. One may speculate that, in a
given species, all factors required for evocation are not
necessarily absent in conditions not conducive to flowering.
The number and nature of the missing (or limiting) factors in
unfavourable conditions depend presumably on various environmental parameters and the past history of the plant. The
missing factor(s) may or may not be the same in different
species grown in conditions not conducive to flowering, and
this might explain the failures and anomalies frequently
encountered in attempts to transmit the floral stimulus across
a graft union (Bernier *et al.*, 1981b).

WHERE ARE THE EVOCATION FACTORS PRODUCED?

Using an induced or a non-induced *Perilla* leaf as the donor in
grafting experiments, Zeevaart (1958) elegantly demonstrated
that, in photoperiodic annuals, the floral stimuli (= evocation factors) are primarily produced in the photoinduced
leaves. Evidence for this comes also from the translocation
curves for the floral stimulus (Fig. 1a) discussed above.
Although these data give no clue about the immediate desti-
nation of the leaf-generated stimuli, it is believed classically that they are all directly transported to the meristems.

Based on their analyses of cytokinin levels in various
plant parts and root exudate of *Xanthium* plants induced by a
single SD-cycle, Wareing *et al.* (1977) were forced to postulate that part at least of the leaf-generated stimuli is
transmitted rapidly via the phloem to the roots where it
alters the course of cytokinin synthesis and/or release. As a
result there is a marked decline in the cytokinin levels in
the root exudate, leaves and buds. Interestingly both flower
initiation and the decrease in cytokinin levels are nullified
by interrupting the long night by a light break. Preliminary
results with *Sinapis* plants induced by a single LD also indicate that changes in cytokinin level occur very early in
roots, i.e., after 2 h into the supplemental light period of
the LD (Claes *et al.*,unpublished). The primary site of detection of the change in daylength in *Sinapis* being the leaves
(Bernier, 1969), it is necessary to postulate the formation in
the leaves of a stimulus which is rapidly translocated, as in
Xanthium, to the root system, affecting cytokinin metabolism
there. Transmission of a stimulus from leaves to the roots is
very plausible in *Sinapis* since all exporting leaves, even the
youngest, of a 2-month old plant have been found to transport
[^{14}C]-labelled assimilates not only to the apical bud but also
the root system (Bodson, unpublished).

After reception of the leaf-generated stimulus(i), the bud

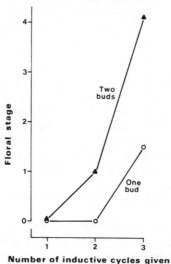

*Fig. 3. Influence of the number of active buds left on the
plants on flower initiation in the SDP* Xanthium *strumarium.
Plants bear only the primary leaves and one (O) or two (▲)
active cotyledonary buds (Adapted from the data of Lincoln et
al., 1958).*

itself may contribute to the production of one or several evocation factors. This was suggested by the observation of Lincoln et al., (1958) that the floral response is increased in Xanthium plants with two active buds compared to those having only one such bud (Fig. 3). Only the leaves received the inductive treatment in this experiment, eliminating a possible direct effect of the photoperiodic regime on the buds.

The multiple factors, essentially carbohydrates and growth substances, that I have proposed above to be involved in the control of evocation are known from the literature to have multiple sites of production in the intact vegetative plant. Most plant parts are thus expected to participate in the control of evocation and this is shown by the numerous observations that evocation is under the influence of a network of multiple organ interactions in both perennials and monocarpic plants (Zeevaart, 1976; Bernier et al., 1981b).

MERISTEM COMPETENCE TO RESPOND TO EVOCATION FACTORS

Trewavas (1982) has tentatively proposed that, during development in the intact plant, tissue sensitivity (that is, tissue competence to respond) to growth substances is far more important than growth substance levels and probably represents the limiting factor. Physiologists classically believe that, on the contrary, the shoot meristems in herbaceous species react well to the evocation factors at all developmental stages, i.e., their sensitivity is constant (Lang, 1965). Thus, the low (or lack of) sensitivity of young plants to conditions which later promote flower initiation is not due to meristem insensitivity but to the leaves having insufficient photosynthetic capacity (insufficient leaf area) and/or another metabolic limitation (insensitivity to daylength). This view is probably simplistic, however, since it is clear that, besides the fact that it is certainly possible to force the juvenile meristems of herbaceous species into the reproductive stage (Lang, 1965), the overall sensitivity of plants like Xanthium or Pharbitis to photoinduction is attributable to differences not only in the leaves but also in the meristems (Fig. 4).

Experimental evidence concerning changes in meristem sensitivity to carbohydrates and growth substances with age is unfortunately extremely limited. Studies by Besnard-Wibaut (1981) have shown that the stimulation of cell proliferation in the central zone of the meristem, and subsequent flower initiation, by exogenous GAs or cytokinin is possible in the LDP Arabidopsis only in plants having vegetative meristems with an intermediate configuration, i.e., plants grown in SD for at least 3 months. In young individuals, with typical zonate vegetative meristems, GAs or cytokinin increase the rate of leaf initiation and/or the growth of apical internodes but no flowering ensues (partial evocation): the peripheral zone and pith-rib meristem are activated but the central zone does not react. Preliminary results suggest that the sensitivity to exogenous cytokinin also increases with age in the meristem of *Sinapis* plants grown in SD: while the mitotic

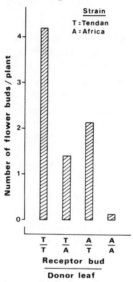

Fig. 4. Flowering response of plants of Pharbitis nil *synthesized from two different strains: one strain very sensitive to photoinduction, Tendan, and one poorly sensitive strain, Africa. The grafted composite was induced by 3 successive SD cycles (Adapted from data of Imamura et al., 1966). Similar results for* Xanthium strumarium *were published by Carpenter and Lincoln (1959).*

index increases by 200–300 percent after a single application of BA at 10 µg/ml in 2-month old plants, it rises by only 40–50 percent in 2-week old plants (Bernier, unpublished). Recall here that (a) 2-week old seedlings of *Sinapis* require 7 LD for full induction whereas 2-month old plants need only one LD, and (b) a cytokinin is an evocation factor in this species (Table 2). Thus, in *Arabidopsis* and *Sinapis* there is a clear suggestion that the florigenic effect of growth substances is related to the acquisition with age of sensitivity by meristematic cells.

There are also indications that the sensitivity of competent meristems changes during the course of the plastochron. In *Anagallis*, for example, Brulfert *et al.* (1976) have demon-

strated that the greatest sensitivity to the floral stimuli is
when the primordia of the last-initiated pair of leaves are
about 50 μm high. Generally, the batches of plants used in
experimental work on flower initiation are not selected on the
basis of their plastochron stages. They are presumably populations of individual plants randomly distributed among all
plastochron stages and thus having the same mean plastochron
stage. If this is the case, and if there is in all species
(as in *Anagallis*) a particular plastochron stage during which
the sensitivity to evocation factors is maximal, there is
reason to propose that evocation factors should be present at
the apex during a period extending at least over an entire
plastochron if evocation is to be completed in all individual
plants. Based on his work with the SDP *Perilla*, Jacobs (1972)
proposed that for full induction the number of 24 h inductive
cycles must equal the number of days in the plastochron at the
start of induction. Such a relationship does not seem to hold
true in all cases since in several species requiring a single
photoinductive cycle, e.g., *Xanthium*, *Lolium*, *Sinapis* and

TABLE 3. *Number of inductive cycles and plastochron duration.*

Species	Minimal number of photoinductive cycles required for full induction	Plastochron duration (days) at the start of induction	during evocation	Reference
SDP				
Perilla frutescens	9	8.3	3.4	Jacobs, 1972
Pharbitis nil	1	0.8	0.8	King and Evans 1969
Xanthium strumarium	1	2.1 – 1.9	1.2 – 0.4	Jacobs, 1972; Erickson and Meicenheimer, 1977
LDP				
Anagallis arvensis	1	6 – 5	unknown	Fontaine, 1972
Lolium temulentum	1	1.7	about 0.2	Evans, 1969
Silene coeli-rosa	7	3.9	2.6 – 0.5	Lyndon, 1977
Sinapis alba	1	2.0 – 1.7	1.1 – 0.7	Bernier, unpublished

Anagallis, the plastochron may be 2 days or longer (Table 3).
Recall, however, that the plastochron shortens in most, if not
all, species during evocation (Table 3). In *Sinapis*, for
example, the plastochron is about 2 days in 2-month old vegetative plants and is reduced to less than one day during the
period extending from 24 to 48 h after start of the inductive
LD. Thus, the number of inductive cycles required for full
induction does not match the plastochron duration at the start
of induction in this case but it equals the plastochron duration during evocation. Although a species like *Silene*, requiring many more inductive cycles than there are days in its
plastochron (either before or during evocation), does not fit
the hypothesis, there is possibly a relationship between the
rhythm of leaf initiation and the persistence of evocation
factors at the apex.

SUGGESTIONS FOR FURTHER WORK

Analyses of the content, metabolism and distribution of carbohydrates and other assimilates as well as of growth substances
in the apex and other plant parts during the floral transition
are urgently needed. Estimations of fluxes in assimilates and
growth substances (e.g., from analyses of leaf and root exudates) in experimental systems in which the timing of other
events of the transition is known are also required. The
results of such studies should be correlated with observations
on partial evocation in the same species.

Work on (a) partial evocation, and (b) on meristem competence to react to chemicals affecting evocation is still
insufficient and should be extended to a variety of plant
species and chemical factors.

In cases where the action of an evocation factor is short-
lived, e.g., GA in *Xanthium* (see above), one should try to
know whether this is due to a drop in its level, the action of
an inhibitor or a loss of meristem sensitivity to this factor.

ACKNOWLEDGEMENTS

This work was supported by grants from the F.R.F.C. (n[o]
2.4505.78) and from the Belgian Government through the
programme of "Action de Recherche Concertee" (n[o] 80/85-18).

REFERENCES

Bernier, G. (1969). *In* "The Induction of Flowering" (ed L. T.
     Evans). pp. 305-327. MacMillan, Melbourne
Bernier, G. (1979). *In* "La Physiologie de la Floraison" (eds
     P. Champagnat and R. Jacques). pp. 129-168. C.N.R.S.,
     Paris

Bernier, G., Kinet, J.M. and Sachs, R.M. (1981a). "The Physiology of Flowering" Vol. I. CRC Press, Boca Raton, Florida

Bernier, G., Kinet, J.M. and Sachs, R.M. (1981b). "The Physiology of Flowering" Vol. II. CRC Press, Boca Raton, Florida

Besnard-Wibaut, C. (1981). *Physiol Plant*. 53, 205–212

Bonner, J. and Zeevaart, J.A.D. (1962). *Plant Physiol*. 37, 43–49

Brulfert, J., Imhoff, C. and Fontaine, D. (1976). *In* "Etudes de Biologie Vegetale. Hommage au Professeur Pierre Chouard" (ed R. Jacques). pp. 443–455. CNRS, Paris

Carpenter, B.H. and Lincoln, R.G. (1959). *Science* 129, 780–781

Erickson, R.O. and Meicenheimer, R.D. (1977). *Am. J. Bot.* 64, 981–988

Evans, L.T. (1969). *In* "The Induction of Flowering" (ed L.T. Evans). pp. 328–349. MacMillan, Melbourne

Fontaine, D. (1972). *C.R. Hebd. Acad. Seances Sci.* 274, 58–61

Francis, D. and Lyndon, R.F. (1979). *Planta* 145, 151–157

Graham, C.F. and Wareing, P.F. (1976). "The Developmental Biology of Plants and Animals". Blackwell. Oxford

Havelange, A. and Bernier, G. (1983). *Physiol. Plant.* 59, 545–550

Imamura, S., Muramatsu, M., Kitajo, S.I. and Takimoto, A. (1966). *Bot. Mag. Tokyo* 79, 714–721

Jacobs, W.P. (1972). *Am. J. Bot.* 59, 437–441

King, R.W. and Evans, L.T. (1969). *Aust. J. Biol. Sci.* 22, 559–572

Lang, A. (1965). *In* "Encyclopedia of Plant Physiology" (ed W. Ruhland). Vol.XV-1. pp. 1380–1536. Springer Verlag, Berlin

Letham, D.S., Goodwin, P.B. and Higgins, T.J.V. eds. (1978). "Phytohormones and Related Compounds: A Comprehensive Treatise" Vols I and II. Elsevier/North-Holland Biomedical Press, Amsterdam

Lincoln, R.G., Raven, K.A. and Hamner, K.C. (1958). *Bot. Gaz.* 119, 179–185

Lyndon, R.F. (1977). *In* "Integration of Activity in the Higher Plant" (ed D.H. Jennings). pp. 221–250. *Symp. Soc. Exp. Biol.*, Cambridge Univ. Press

Maksymowych, R., Cordero, R.E. and Erickson, R.O. (1976). *Am. J. Bot.* 63, 1047–1053

Margara, J. (1982). "Bases de la Multiplication Vegetative. Les Meristemes et l'Organogenese" INRA, Paris

Meicenheimer, R.D. (1981). *Am. J. Bot.* 68, 1139–1154

Meins, F. Jr., and Binns, A.N. (1978). *In* "The Clonal Basis of Development" (eds S. Subtelny and I.M. Sussex). pp. 185–201, Academic Press, New York

Miller, M.B. and Lyndon, R.F. (1977). *Planta* 136, 167–172

Romberger, J.A. and Gregory, R.A. (1974). *In* "Proceedings of the Third North American Forest Biology Workshop" (eds C.P.P. Reid and G.H. Fechner). pp. 132–147

Scorza, R. (1982). *Hortic. Rev.* 4, 106–127

Sheldrake, A.R. (1973). *Biol. Rev. Camb. Philos. Soc.* 48, 509–559

Trewavas, A.J. (1982). *Physiol. Plant.* 55, 60–72

Wareing, P.F., Horgan, R., Henson, I.E. and Davis, W. (1977). *In* "Plant Growth Regulation" (ed P.-E. Pilet). pp. 147–153, Springer-Verlag, Berlin

Zeevaart, J.A.D. (1958). *Meded. Landbouwhogesch. Wageningen* 58, 1–88

Zeevaart, J.A.D. (1976). *Annu. Rev. Plant Physiol.* 27, 321–348

SUBJECT INDEX

SUBJECT INDEX

This is an index of Key Words and Plant Species